REASONS FOR HOPE

Reasons for Hope

The Faith and Future of the Friends Church

By John Punshon

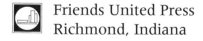 Friends United Press
Richmond, Indiana

Printed in the United States of America
Friends United Press, Richmond, Indiana.

Cover and book design: Shari Pickett Veach

Cover photo: Prayer altar, formerly part of the fabric of the
Friends Church, Newberg, Oregon.

Library of Congress Cataloging-in-Publication Data

Punshon, John, 1935–
    Reasons for hope : the faith and future of the Friends church /
    by John Punshon.
        p. cm.
    Includes bibliographical references (p.) and index.
    1. Society of Friends--Doctrines. 2. Evangelicalism--Society of
    Friends. 3. Public worship--Society of Friends. I. Title.

BX7731.3 .P86 2001
230'.96--dc21
                                                        2001033339

To the Friends of Indiana Yearly Meeting,
who gave me a home.

*"But in your hearts set apart Christ as Lord.
Always be prepared to give an answer
to everyone who asks you to give
the reason for the hope that you have...."*

1 Peter 3:14

Contents

Preface

When I first came to the United States, I had no intention of writing a book about evangelical Quakerism. I knew about worship services that had hymns and sermons, because I had visited Friends churches in Kenya, Honduras, and the United States. But I still preferred silent worship, and there was no sense in which I would have described myself as an evangelical. With the passage of time, however, that has changed. When the yearly meeting I came from relinquished its evangelical credentials a hundred years ago, it thereby gave up far more of the Quaker and Christian traditions than I now find myself willing to part with. I have discovered that in the Friends Church I do not have to make that sacrifice, and this book explains why.

The Friends Church is now a worldwide body, the outcome of a century of endeavor by missionaries from the United States. The yearly meetings that belong to it have a common faith and practice, but in matters of race, culture and nationality, they are very diverse. The contemporary Friends Church is actually the product of two formative influences. Much of its faith and most of its practice goes back to the beginnings of the Quaker movement in seventeenth-century England. Its doctrine and values, however, reflect the influence of the Wesleyan holiness revivals that swept the United States in the late nineteenth century and inspired the missions. Each of these traditions has great value, but there has never been a serious attempt to harmonize them.

A good opportunity to undertake this task now lies before us, since Friends are facing a number of important challenges. In North America, though there are some encouraging signs of growth, over-all membership is static or declining at a time of general evangelical prosperity, and we need to ask why. In Latin America and Africa, where indigenous cultures are very different, Friends churches are developing in divergent ways in response to local circumstances. Consequently, we can expect relationships between the different Friends communities in the world to change, perhaps quite radically. We may be called upon to give a constructive and corporate response to a number of new and quite unforeseen questions.

These questions arise out of two sets of relationships. First, there is our common loyalty to the Friends Church and the many ties of personal acquaintance, shared experience, and practical help that bind us together as one body. But then there is our membership of another, diverse, but immediately recognizable body known as the evangelical movement. Our own religious identity is a combination of both these sets of relationships. To understand ourselves, we need to know how they came about and what makes them work. So what do we make of ourselves? Who are we as a family?

When we look at our personal past, we see the family history that has made us what we are. Growing up in a family we gradually learn about our relatives, the shared experience of our kin, and the stories that shape our identity. If we were cut off from these things we would not truly understand ourselves because we would have no roots. In ordinary life, families give us values and emotional security. To see our relatives, like us yet different from us, gives us a sense of proportion. Indeed, to understand the history of our nation, what we read about needs to be grounded in the personal experiences of those we love or remember.

But we do not live in the past or within the confines of our family. We are people in our own right, and we have to make our own way in the world. Our lives are not determined by the influence of our family. We carry on our own conversation with the wider world and reach our conclusions without referring back to our upbringing all the time. On the other hand, if we are wise, we will realize that by temperament and training we are more suited for some things than others, and the influence and encouragement of our family is an invaluable asset in helping us to make the proper choices and decisions. If we are wise, we have a good idea about what we are and are not cut out to do and act accordingly.

To see who we are, then, requires us to look both backward and forward and to take note of both the influence of our family and the choices we have made on our own account. Part of growing up is to get these things together in the best possible way. We never entirely succeed, of course, but we are mature to the extent that we do and dysfunctional to the extent that we do not. What is important is that we recognize the benefits we have received and come to terms with those parts of our inheritance that for whatever reason we do not like. A normally reflective person will do this and thereby lead a successful and happy life. Someone who has not come to terms with the past is unlikely to deal successfully with the challenges of the future. It is the same thing with a church. I have called this book *Reasons for Hope* because I believe the Friends Church will have a very successful future if it grasps this truth and has the courage to act on it.

There are two main themes in this book that correspond to these two sets of personal relationships. They involve a look back into the past and a look forward to what the future might hold for Friends. At the heart of the book there is what might be called a primer of the evangelical Quaker faith. What I have tried to do in chapters 2 through 9 is to look at the origins and the history of the Friends Church in order to show that it rests on a clear, but misunderstood and sometimes forgotten, scriptural basis. Friends are a multi-cultural community. If their unique character is to be sustained, it will have to rest on an interpretation of biblical truth and not the cultural presuppositions of the Anglo-Saxon world.

Balancing the primer is the second main theme of the book. It is a polemic, or controversial argument, directed to the nature of Friends engagement with the wider evangelical world now and in the immediate future. The two themes intertwine, of course, but the polemic is located chiefly in the first, and last chapters. Its purpose is to substantiate the claim that the future of the Friends Church lies in a renewal of it devotion to its traditional faith and practice, the matters dealt with in the primer. The tradition is important for the Friends Church because it is biblical not because it is traditional; I therefore argue that it would be self-defeating to abandon the tradition on grounds of evangelical principle. The tradition has produced a distinctive discipleship and a vision of Christianity that has permanently enriched the world. This vision contains a set of doctrines that are flexible and authoritative and will show Friends that they relate to other churches as partners—not as clients or copies.

It also needs saying, if it is not clear already, that this is a personal statement. The emphasis of the book is on evangelical Quakerism as it might be, rather than as it is. Though I write as a member of Indiana Yearly Meeting, I have approached the Friends Church primarily as an observer, trying to make theological sense of it, rather than as a student, exercising a specific academic discipline to study present practice. It is necessary to emphasize this, so readers will know that my main concern in writing is to produce a model of what the Friends Church of the future might look like. Inevitably, that has to be an individual undertaking, and while I make arguments and quote sources, it needs to be borne in mind that this what I am trying to do. Sometimes I write in the first person, both singular and plural, sometimes the third person. This is a matter of convention, and I am writing about and for, a community to which I belong.

Some readers may also note that I do not begin as they might have expected: by offering a definition of either evangelicalism or Quakerism, the two main historical movements discussed in this book. The reason, which I explain in greater detail later, is that there are significant drawbacks in trying to be too specific. Hard-and-fast definitions can never capture the complexity, ambiguity, and internal arguments inseparable from both of these movements. It is precisely the complexity, ambiguity, and internal arguments that are my main concern. I hope the arguments, as I state them, will reveal the points at issue, and therefore show the similarities and differences between these two religious positions in practice rather than in theory.

The word "evangelical" is ambiguous in practice, and that is one of the reasons why I have resisted giving a definition of it. There are several Friends organizations that use "Evangelical Friends" as part of their name. Since the majority of Friends who regard themselves as evangelicals are not in fact associated with those bodies, I need to make it clear that I have in mind a rather wider readership than that. Friends are a diverse group, so I have tried to write for all Friends who call themselves evangelicals, regardless of where they live, what yearly meetings they belong to, or exactly what kind of evangelical they consider themselves to be. Other Christian Friends sympathetic to evangelical concerns may find this book interesting, but I have to say in advance that there is almost nothing about the liberal expression of Quakerism here. That is simply because liberal Friends do not share the presuppositions of evangelicalism, and it is precisely these presuppositions that the book is about.

I must conclude with the usual acknowledgments. I am very grateful to everybody who has helped me during the writing of this book. My wife, Veronica Punshon, was especially forgiving of my disruptions of household routine, and my sister and her husband, Lorraine and Peter Leighton, welcomed us into their home during the sabbatical when much of the actual writing was done. I am indebted to my colleagues at Earlham School of Religion for encouraging me in my writing and giving me relative freedom from committee assignments that enabled me to so. Among the many individuals with whom I discussed particular matters I would like to mention Paul Anderson, Gayle Beebe, Paul Buckley, Wilmer Cooper, Tom Hamm, Patrick Nugent, Steve Spyker, Arthur Roberts, and Carole Spencer, and the many Friends to whom I have talked generally in California, Indiana, Iowa, and North Carolina. Finally, my thanks are due to Elaine Nelson, Janet Wagner, and Patti Hartmannsgruber for helping me to track down the unusual or out-of-the-way books and publications.

John Punshon
Richmond, Indiana
18 May 2001

1

The Friends Church and Its Faith

1

The Friends Church and Its Faith

T his book is about the faith and practice of the Friends Church, the Quakers who call pastors to serve their meetings and leave only a limited place in their services for silent worship.[1] The Friends Church is an evangelical body, and this is frequently thought to be the reason for the programmed worship service and pastoral leadership. This is not the case, however, and to understand the nature of the Friends Church we must consider briefly how it came into existence in its present form. We are looking at an organized body, which has strong similarities to other evangelical churches, but possesses a vocabulary, a set of institutions, and a body of fundamental values that come down to it from the history it shares with other Quakers who are not evangelicals.

The body of evangelical Friends is not quite the same as the membership of the Friends Church, however. I shall be using the phrase "evangelical Friends" to include all those yearly meetings in North America that are affiliated solely to Friends United Meeting or the Evangelical Friends International, but to exclude the more liberal congregations that nevertheless belong to these yearly meetings. Also included within the definition are the evangelical monthly meetings that belong to the more liberal yearly meetings and all evangelical Friends in the rest of the world, whether yearly meetings like Honduras or individual meetings like the silent evangelical Friends meeting at Richhill, Northern Ireland.

Until the beginning of the nineteenth century, Friends were isolated from the world by a distinctive way of life and an interesting, if somewhat unusual, theology. By 1770 they had lost the predominance they once had in Pennsylvania, and their numbers were shrinking, both absolutely and relative to the population at large. These were times of great economic, political, and social change, and Friends proved unable to absorb new ideas without serious disruption. An argument over the compatibility of evangelical ideas with traditional Quakerism precipitated a major separation in Philadelphia Yearly Meeting in 1827 and spread throughout the Society in the following two decades. Evangelical principles profoundly influenced the beliefs of Friends, but made little mark on their silent meetings or their traditional way of life.

After 1865, however, radical changes occurred. The economy became much more diverse, and subsistence agriculture declined rapidly, bringing new and improved opportunities for both employment and recreation. The Second Great Awakening reached its climax as the old-style, frontier camp meeting gave way to the nationwide holiness revival. Many Quaker communities took part in the revival, and it was at this point that the pastoral meeting and the programmed worship service emerged. So did a renewed interest in missions, and Friends took the gospel to many parts of the world where they had hitherto been strangers. The contemporary evangelical branch of Friends is a complex phenomenon. It has strong affinity with the Quakerism of the past, but is also the outcome of two successive reinterpretations of that tradition.

A study of the Friends Church therefore has great intrinsic interest. Its pedigree includes Anabaptist, pietist, mainstream evangelical, holiness, and fundamentalist influences absorbed over a long enough period for Friends' particular history to be dovetailed fairly neatly into the development of Protestant Christianity as a whole.

These influences are fairly diverse, and if we were to regard them as chemical substances, we might have an explosive combination on our hands. But if we choose to look at them as genetic strains, each of which finds expression in our church, we might find that they are sources of strength and not disunity, for each of them is the outcome of historical circumstance, personal experience, and reflection on the truths of scripture.

This chapter will look at these diverse influences and think about how we might find a harmony in them. We begin with a consideration of the present state of the Friends Church, both in the United States and the rest of the world. Serious questions are being raised in some quarters about Friends distinctive doctrines and practices. It is necessary to ask why this is and then say why the maintenance of the distinctives is important. Much of it has to do with the fact that, historically, Friends have formulated their doctrine differently from the way it is done in other churches. We shall look at the influence of scripture, history, and personal experience on the formulation of belief, and conclude with the claim that our best course in pursuing this enquiry is to look at the continuing development of doctrine among evangelical Friends rather than trying to identify some essence of evangelical Quakerism that is valid for all times, places, and circumstances.

The Problem Stated

Several developments in recent years make this an appropriate time to ask what the Friends Church stands for. To begin with, there is the need for a common understanding of the gospel in a rapidly changing world. Until now, the unity of the Friends churches has come from their common origin in the United States. With the passing of time, as we have already suggested, the particular characteristics of each of our widespread cultural constituencies can be expected to assert themselves. In these circumstances we need to make sure that our status as an independent, self-governing church with its own doctrines and pattern of discipleship is not neglected, but properly understood and practiced. This makes it imperative to ensure that a common theological base unites all the branches of the family.

Consequently, we need to find new ways of maintaining the relationships between our yearly meetings. Connections between indigenous churches and mission bodies are never simple. The provision of personal service and material aid can sometimes mislead donor bodies into thinking that they cannot exercise these functions without giving leadership as well. But times are changing, and North American Friends have to learn how to relate in a different way to independent yearly meetings that were once their mission fields. Changing relationships will inevitably mean challenges to accepted ways of doing things and perhaps challenges on matters of faith and practice, too. The clearer the self-understanding of all parts of the Friends Church, the easier it will be to deal with these things constructively.

In the United States itself, there has been a radical change in the pattern of religious affiliation in the last few decades. The mainstream, liberal churches have suffered a catastrophic drop in membership, while evangelical churches have been growing rapidly. It is therefore a matter of serious concern that evangelical Friends have not benefited from these trends, manifesting, as they do, an evangelical theology but a liberal growth pattern. So the question arises as to why this should be. It can be argued that the main reason for this, apart from demographic and sociological factors, is that the identity of the Friends Church is far too fuzzy to have widespread appeal. Beyond the initial commitment to Christ, it is often unclear exactly what kind of body a new convert is joining.

Lastly, there is the question of realignment. Some years ago, four North American Yearly Meetings set aside the separations of the nineteenth century and reunited.[2] Each comprised a pastoral, evangelical element and an unprogrammed, liberal element. Though they still contain a number of programmed meetings and evangelical Friends, these yearly meetings are now largely liberal and remain affiliated to Friends United Meeting, an otherwise evangelical body. A number of Friends believe that this inhibits the mission of FUM and compromises its long-term future as an evangelical organization. A few years ago the suggestion was put forward that Friends United Meeting be dissolved and its non-liberal yearly meetings join the Evangelical Friends International, North American Section.

The subsequent controversy did not produce any major change. Some of the issues it raised, however, have not gone away, illustrating that, while church life is normally quite uneventful, there are times when we have to face fundamental questions about who we are or what we believe. We worship together, raise money, hire pastors, and run programs of all kinds, but seldom bother about the theological principles that underlie these things. But those principles are there, shaping and forming what is said and ultimately what is decided. Certain activities are within the basic principles by which the church is run. Others are not. There is an unavoidable dimension of theory to all of our practice, and we neglect it at our peril.

Behind each of these developments, in one way or another, lies the question of the distinctives. This word is customarily used to mean the language, institutions, historical perspective, practices, and particular doctrines that are unique to Friends. The distinctives include such matters as our egalitarian mode of running the church, the role of ministry and oversight committees, and the office of clerk. They cover matters of doctrine, like our belief that we can have direct communication with God without intermediary and the conviction that creeds are the enemies of true faith. They also explain why Friends differ from other churches in not ordaining ministers or observing the ordinances, and they indicate something of the Friends manner of discipleship—for example, that we reject war as incompatible with the will of Christ and embrace the values of simplicity, equality, and truthfulness.

These principles originated in the Quaker tradition and have continued in the Friends Church. However, with the passage of time, there have been changes in the way Friends understand them. Many Friends have lost the sense that the distinctives form a unified vision of the nature of Christian discipleship and the vocation of the church. The distinctives come to be seen as a list rather than an integral whole. This is due to the tendency to justify them by proof texts rather than the use of a theological rationale derived from the meaning of scripture as a whole. As a result, the possibility arises that the separate distinctives can be ordered into more and less important items, and, indeed, that some of them can be dispensed with entirely.

Perhaps the clearest example of discomfort with the distinctives is the pressure exerted in some quarters for Friends to permit the ordinances. In 1994, Southwest Yearly Meeting amended its discipline specifically to accommodate this demand. But the consequences of this step may lead to a fundamental change in Friends self-understanding. If pastors acquire the right to baptize and preside at the Lord's Supper, as well as enjoy the right to perform marriages, which they already have, it is easy to envision the emergence of ordination among us. This would obviously be a significant change in our understanding of the nature of the church. The possibility needs to be faced without delay, lest neglect encourages its development by default.

The transaction of business by voting, although the example might appear to be trivial, also goes to the root of Friends' distinctive understanding of the nature of the Christian community. Very often, voting is concealed by the practice of making minutes and then recording the names of those standing aside, instead of postponing decisions in order to wait for unity. Although we are under a duty to transact business expeditiously and efficiently, these are not the most important criteria to be applied when the church comes together to make decisions. The body of Christ is supposed to act in a harmonious way because its members belong to one another. Waiting for unity is a sign of obedience to the Holy Spirit, and trying to anticipate its guidance is a fundamental departure from Friends understanding of how the church should conduct itself.

> *Waiting for unity is a sign of obedience to the Holy Spirit, and trying to anticipate its guidance is a fundamental departure from Friends understanding of how the church should conduct itself.*

Christian worship must be offered in spirit and in truth, as scripture says. The preparation of Sunday worship on this basis is a matter for prayer and forethought, but we surely need to recognize that there are some things, like snake handling, that do not measure up to this standard. But there are more familiar, and no less deadly practices, like excessive concentration on charismatic preaching, Christian rock, and multi-media presentations. These things are not objectionable by themselves and have their uses, but they easily become a substitute for the moving of the Spirit. For Friends, open worship is a standing reminder of this danger. The curtailment of open worship is a sign that worship is becoming entertainment and something is going seriously wrong.

The early Friends were strongly critical of superficial worship because they rightly judged that it drew the heart and mind away from God and not toward him. Instead, they urged Christians to look inward, to wait and listen for the still, small voice that guided, empowered, and spoke with a direct authority that had to be obeyed. The whirlwind did not speak to Elijah, and no more do synthesizers speak to us. If Elijah had not first known God in his heart, he would not have heard the voice. One of the drawbacks of services built solely round the altar call and entry to the Christian life is that we neglect to teach growth in grace and the process of discipling our members. If we do not know and commune with Christ in our hearts, no amount of Christian music will be a substitute. Silence is not an irksome part of an unwanted heritage. It is a sacramental sign of the divine presence.

> *The early Friends were strongly critical of*
> *superficial worship because they rightly judged*
> *that it drew the heart and mind away from God*
> *and not toward him.*

These examples of departure from the tradition can be seen as unwelcome exceptions to the generally accepted standards of Quaker life, or perfectly permissible developments against which there is no argument in principle. Friends may even take the view that matters such as worship styles, business process, and willingness to offer baptism should be left for individual monthly meetings to decide, so it would be improper for a yearly meeting to assert its authority by saying that these go beyond what is permissible in a Friends Church. But one has only to raise the question to appreciate its importance. These things are either matters of theological indifference or else they go to the heart of the matter and reflect our basic convictions about the nature of the Church and define what it means to be Friends.

Challenges to the Tradition

The opinion is widely held, but not often explicitly stated, that the Quaker heritage should be discarded because it is more of a hindrance than a help. This viewpoint rests on three main claims. Some people simply say that the distinctives are not a part of the gospel and are an option we may freely relinquish. Others argue that they are an unacceptable addition to the gospel, like prayers to the saints or masses for the dead. Yet others question their utility. Preaching the gospel is more important than the cultivation of practices that divert Friends' attention from this task. Even if the distinctives are not superfluous or dangerous, it is said, they nevertheless represent a waste of time and an unjustifiable diversion of our energies from a greater purpose to a lesser.

To say that preaching the gospel should have absolute priority in the Church is surely correct. One cannot imagine George Fox disagreeing with that. But the argument goes too far because it is really a critique of denominational characteristics of all kinds, not just the Quaker variety. In fact, there are no influential evangelical churches without denominational characteristics. The Lutheran Church, Missouri Synod, and the Presbyterian Church in America are distinct precisely because they trace their roots to the national churches of the Reformation. Similarly, the Nazarenes, the Pentecostal Churches, and the Churches of God come from more recent movements like the holiness revival and fundamentalism, but they are denominations nevertheless.

These churches, which all have their own ideas about what discipleship involves, are not about to write off their origins and history because of some greater gospel they have only just come to recognize. They all exist because they have a specific theological emphasis, and in this respect they are no different from an evangelical Quakerism in full possession of its distinctives. Though we may not be comfortable with them, we have to face the possibility that denominational characteristics are a natural growth. Even new paradigm churches must decide the questions that the denominations have had to answer, and community churches generally recommend themselves on the variety of denominational experiences they are able to satisfy. Whoever heard of a non-denominational baptism? To decide between sprinkling and total immersion is inevitably, and essentially, to make a denominational statement.

The case for the distinctives, on the other hand, rests on the claim that they represent the truth. The reason for adopting and practicing them now is the same as it was when Quakerism began: we find them convincing. This does not mean that Friends are unable to fellowship with others and rejoice in the service of a common Lord, but it does mean that Friends who understand the distinctives are able to rely on a theological position as defensible as anybody else's. The critics fail to understand what this theological position is. The challenge to the distinctives is a clear indication that there are Friends who are so hospitable to outside influences that they have forgotten what they are supposed to stand for.

The distinctives do not represent the imposition of an extra and unnecessary burden. Christianity inevitably involves discipleship and a growth in grace and understanding. That has to be worked for. Each branch of the Church possesses a distinctive way of forming the Christian consciousness and bringing about its growth. Each has its own narrow way. The distinctives belong in this category. They express just such a path of discipleship and possess a unique power as a means of Christian formation, tried and tested for centuries. One might say that the Church as a whole, not just Friends, would be permanently diminished if they were to disappear.

Moreover, everything in the common life of the Friends Church, from its way of doing business to its yearly meeting structure and entirely lay fellowship, rests on the assumptions and the principles behind the distinctives. This is not a trivial matter. To relinquish the distinctives would create the immensely divisive task of asking Friends to rebuild their whole church from the ground up. In most places there is a clear consensus that Friends see themselves as Friends, and the most effective change will come from renewal and not from radical change. One only has to consider where the ulti-mate decision-making power in the church is to rest to see that nei-ther episcopal nor synodical government is consonant with Friends fundamental beliefs about the guidance of the Holy Spirit.

Finally, there is no generic evangelicalism available for dissatisfied Quakers to adopt. One only has to look at the existing scene. Some churches have a denominational affiliation, and some do not. There are Reformed and Lutheran evangelical churches, holiness, fundamentalist and Pentecostal ones. There is a new wave of non-denominational churches, but even they fall into certain patterns and types. Each of them has its own unique character, and there is considerable disagreement among them about fundamental matters of doctrine. While it will not be denied that there are problems connected with the maintenance of the distinctives, abandoning them is neither as simple nor as desirable as it might seem.

A church cannot be run on a pick and mix basis. Churches do not try out a variety of roles and identities until they find a suitable one. That is how adolescents behave. Historically we do not choose our convictions, they are forced upon us. Our choices are circumscribed by what we have and have not inherited; by our present situation, which renders some things possible and others impossible; by the fact that internal inconsistency within any religious group ultimately leads to its dissolution. That is as true for us as it was for the first Friends. We are called upon, therefore, to exercise wisdom and self-awareness when we face religious challenges. Change should be an orderly process, and to negotiate it successfully requires serious thought.

So the challenge to the tradition must be taken up. If the Friends Church declines to ask itself some fundamental questions about its identity, it will simply drift into oblivion or become the captive of every passing fashion. It can always reject its Quakerism, of course, but that leaves open the question of which kind of evangelical church it is then to become. The alternative is to return to history and theology and see how one can be Friend and evangelical at the same time. If these twin positions can be held without inconsistency, then each will enrich the other. Answers to our questions about the future have to be based to some degree on our past. We are products of the past, and one of the tests of consistency is continuity with it.

There is nothing discreditable in looking to the past. All modern evangelical Friends descend from the Gurneyites of the last century, and thereby inherit a great, if only dimly remembered heritage. Joseph John Gurney himself, while criticized harshly for his alleged departure from Quaker rectitude, sought to use all the powers of his mind for the preservation and the prospering of the Friends Church.[3] He knew the truth of John Henry Newman's words: "Depend on it, the strength of any party lies in its being *true to its theory*. Consistency is the life of a movement."[4] If these words are true, Friends will prosper if they look to their own heritage, instead of looking elsewhere for patterns to imitate that would ultimately turn them into something very different from what they are.

To produce a theory of evangelical Quakerism, therefore, is to reject a Christian eclecticism and provide a basis for the Friends Church that is theologically sound, consistent with the past, and internally coherent. Put another way, this means that any theory we devise must be required by, or consonant with scripture, consistent with Friends history, and corroborated, wherever possible, by experience. These are the basics. There is no inconsistency in trying to do this and at the same time giving proper attention to the formative influences that have made Friends what they are. It is a matter of attitude and outlook. No one would dream of playing football or baseball without a game plan, so what we will be looking for in the rest of this book is a game plan for the Friends Church.

The Formulation of Doctrine

To give an account of Quaker doctrine is not easy. Friends have no central authority able to speak for all yearly meetings and no generally recognized statement of belief. We have always had strong differences of opinion and have a testimony against creeds. Declarations of belief have been made at various times, but these do not possess a permanent validity like the Westminster Confession or the Thirty-nine Articles. Friends certainly issued statements of belief in response to particular historical circumstances, but these are not historical in the sense that they define the group or represent theological principles that bind Friends to their origins.

Given these circumstances, it is probably a better procedure to study the process of doctrinal formulation rather than an arbitrary selection of doctrines endorsed by one or other of the main branches of Friends. While it is true that early Quaker belief is not determinative of contemporary doctrine, original Quakerism became an enduring religious movement because it combined a convincing critique of the churches of its day with a dynamic message about the true nature of the Christian faith. That is something not easily ignored. Friends retain much of that vision, but they have also assimilated movements of renewal from outside their own denominational boundaries. What Friends teach today reflects this complex reality, and it should not be over-simplified.

Such a situation is not unique to Friends. All churches have to deal with the problems that arise with the passage of time, even those that have the sort of foundation document Friends lack. Such documents are usually written in response to particular historical circumstances. Among the enduring truths they reassert, there are also matters of solely contemporary importance. Inherited principles continually encounter new spiritual and intellectual challenges and are often found to have implications not realized when they were first articulated. Matters of crucial importance at one period of history may become insignificant in the next, and *vice versa*. Unless we think our church was perfect when it began, we will inevitably face the challenge of revision and doctrinal development.

> *Inherited principles continually encounter new spiritual and intellectual challenges and are often found to have implications not realized when they were first articulated.*

So an attempt to state the substance of Friends doctrine cannot be limited to a simple enumeration of what is and is not believed. Nor will it be a commentary on some early statement everybody once agreed with. An account of the original seventeenth-century doctrines is certainly an essential part of an examination of evangelical Friends faith, for they are the point of departure for a distinct line of development. But they need to be qualified. Doctrines have strengths and weaknesses, short-lived as well as enduring features, internal inconsistencies, and implications that unfold only as historical and theological circumstances change. These things all need to be considered, for without knowledge of the past we will have no signposts for the future.

This is why I have avoided the temptation to begin with arbitrary definitions or to regard historical movements as having an essence of some sort, which we can then compare with the essences of other movements. Doing that carries the risk that we shall end up dealing in definitions rather than ideas, and find similarities and differences where none exist in reality. By emphasizing doctrinal formulation rather than the content of doctrine, we shall be able to entertain the possibility that the evangelical and Quaker traditions may be compatible on some grounds but not on others, and also recognize that the terms of a reconciliation between them may depend on which particular interpretation of each we decide to use.

Doing this would be fairly pointless if it amounted to nothing more than showing the formal relations between two similar but partly incompatible sets of beliefs. That would be rather like trying to put pieces of a jigsaw puzzle into gaps they were not designed to fit. A better image would be to understand doctrine as developing like a flower that comes into bud and then matures slowly. Each unfolding petal has its own part in the organism, yet is vitally related to all the other parts, throughout the whole life of the plant. If we look at Friends beliefs and attitudes in this light, we shall be involved not just in doctrines, but an account of who held them, why, and what happened as a consequence. We shall therefore have a sense of the passage of time and the nature of extraneous influences, the life that comes from within and how the organism responds to stimuli. We shall then know, literally, what animates the Friends Church.

Broadly speaking, there are two ways in which we can look at the Friends Church. The first is to regard Friends as evangelical Christians who profess the main heads of evangelical belief, but possess in addition a number of denominational peculiarities or distinctives, which are not an integral part of the greater whole. The second is to agree that Friends are evangelical Christians, but to claim that they have independent historical access to the evangelical tradition since, through their Puritan heritage, they antedate it in its modern form.

One of the main drawbacks of the first kind of evangelicalism is that it is frequently individualistic. Quakerism, on the other hand, with its seventeenth-century background, possesses a strong doctrine of the Church. It is this doctrine that can give breadth and depth to its evangelical principles.

Quaker Understanding of the Covenant

One of the strands in Puritanism that shaped the early Quaker consciousness was its understanding of the covenant: that underlying and determining the whole range of human relationships with God there is a stable spiritual order that is neither arbitrary nor hard to understand. This is not to say that Friends adopted Puritan ideas about the covenant in their entirety, but that many of the doctrines and practices that came to distinguish Friends only make sense if they are seen to derive from one central principle. On this view, the testimonies, Friends principles of worship, church order, and personal morality—the distinctives, in a word—all stem from the covenant. A recovery of Friends covenantal vision does not require a return to every detail of traditional Quakerism, for that is both impossible and undesirable. But it would enable Friends to establish a realistic balance between the corporate and individual dimensions of the faith and thereby provide a significant counterweight to the excessive individualism often encountered in the wider evangelical community.

The covenantal ground plan of the Friends Church is still clearly visible, and outsiders can see it in the way Friends govern themselves. At the same time, there are places where it is not so obvious, because newer elements in Friends belief do not always combine easily with the old. This is part of the reason why Friends overall identity is not as clear as it needs to be. A re-examination of Friends original covenantal understanding of their faith is therefore very much in order.

> *One of the strands in Puritanism that shaped the early Quaker consciousness was its understanding of the covenant: that underlying and determining the whole range of human relationships with God there is a stable spiritual order that is neither arbitrary nor hard to understand.*

Friends and Other Evangelicals

In the nineteenth century, when Friends moved from a sectarian to a denominational self-understanding, the question arose about which doctrines and practices had continuing vitality and which could be conveniently abandoned. In view of what has happened since, we face the possibility that there are doctrines and practices that may have been abandoned unwisely or improperly at that time, which now need to be re-examined. The covenant is one of those doctrines.

The possibility that there may be important principles that we have lost comes into sharp prominence when we consider Friends relation to the other evangelical churches that trace their origins to the Great Awakening of the eighteenth century. That relationship is a complex one, partly because we have to make allowances for the changes that occurred when religious ideas moved across the Atlantic from the Old World to the Americas. Friends who are aware of the extent to which they have been influenced by the Wesleyan holiness movement often overlook that this is not the only form of evangelicalism in their genetic code. By common consent, the most important influence in articulating and establishing evangelical ideas among Friends was Joseph John Gurney, whose roots go back to the Anglican evangelical tradition of Cowper, Newton, Venn, and Charles Simeon.

This school of thought was the one that the first English Quaker evangelicals most closely resemble, and this is the form of evangelicalism they brought to America when they came as traveling ministers in the period before the separations. In a wide range of social and philanthropic activity, notably the campaign for the abolition of the slave trade, Friends enjoyed cordial relations with leading Anglican evangelicals, adopting their outlook and in many cases marrying into their families. The movement, as a whole, was doctrinally sound, intellectually vigorous, and seriously engaged in the betterment of society. However, the movement was not as ecumenical as might be thought. It was an élite faith, unsympathetic to Methodist enthusiasm, and hostile to the doctrine of holiness.

We need to appreciate, therefore, that the evangelicalism of the frontier revivals had a very different character from this and represents a second and tangential wave of evangelical influence on Friends. It was predominantly Wesleyan, quintessentially American, and entirely democratic. The revival movement developed rapidly among Friends after the Civil War and posed a serious problem for that group of evangelical Friends usually known as Gurneyites, because of their known or supposed affinity for Joseph John Gurney and his writings. Though they prevented Friends from becoming a holiness church, the Gurneyite leaders never really proposed a convincing alternative. If they had, we would not be where we are now.

They failed, in fact, to produce a lasting synthesis between Quakerism and the evangelical tradition because the form of evangelicalism they were confronted with was the Wesleyan holiness variety, and they faced the real possibility that their yearly meetings would be overtaken by it. There may not have been time and space for thought then, but times have moved on and the lack of such a synthesis is the basic reason for the present challenge to the tradition. Moreover, there are now newer forms of evangelicalism like fundamentalism and Pentecostalism to be considered, and they frequently put sharp questions to the older denominations. If one is an evangelical, one will sooner or later be called upon to answer some of these questions and one's church should be able to provide guidance on how to do so. Hence, we cannot give a comprehensive account of contemporary Friends doctrine without considering what is happening in the evangelical movement at large.

So is it possible to combine the evangelical and Quaker traditions in a convincing way? Probably not if we are unwilling to accept modifications to either of them. However, if we are willing to be flexible, we may find a number of possibilities emerging. First, a church claiming to be evangelical will obviously take scripture as the ultimate authority for its doctrinal claims, and the manner in which Friends do so will need to be explained. Second, the modern evangelical faith is rooted in the Reformation. This will inevitably give the Friends Church a certain perspective on history, and we will need to give an account of what it is. Third, since the most immediate and noticeable influence on the Friends Church has been the holiness revival, we know that our faith will be securely grounded in the personal experience of those who profess it and so we need to give at least some account of the nature of religious experience.

Scripture and Truth

The most important pillar of any theory of evangelical Quakerism will be its fidelity to scripture, because this is the main determinant of evangelical self-understanding. Christian doctrine is formulated on the basis of scripture, but over time, different modes of handling the text have emerged, and modern developments have influenced Friends in various ways. The maxim *sola scriptura* is deceptive. Although scripture may be our ultimate authority, it has not, in practice, yielded any uncontested interpretations. Allowances have to be made for this. It needs to be borne in mind that holding up the Word to the best, not the easiest, understanding we can give it is to endorse the principle of authority and not to compromise it.

> *The most important pillar of any theory of evangelical Quakerism will be its fidelity to scripture, because this is the main determinant of evangelical self-understanding.*

Two references will support this procedure. The New Testament itself says that the scriptures are able to make us wise unto salvation through faith in Christ, that they are inspired, and that they are useful for teaching, rebuking, correcting, and training in righteousness.[5] Drawing a corollary from this, Robert Barclay writes, "...whatsoever doctrine is contrary unto their testimony, may therefore justly be rejected as false."[6] While such a conclusion would be contested in some quarters, we shall assume that these two passages are in harmony with one another, and that the use of scripture as our court of appeal on matters of doctrine can be justified from both sides of the heritage. It needs to be remembered also that much of what the

early Friends wrote was commentary on scripture, not special pleading for Quakerism. It involved interpretation of a particular kind,
but it rested on an acceptance of the scriptures, not a rejection of
them.

We will therefore take it that the Bible represents God's revelation to us, rather than a record of our search for God. The God of the
Bible does not wait to be approached, but institutes relations with
his human creatures. Most of the stories in scripture are about what
people do when God speaks to them. They tell us of the nature and
will of God, and thereby instruct us as to who we are and what we
are to do. This instruction comes to us in many forms, including
prose, poetry, prophecy, and history. Sometimes it comes directly,
sometimes obliquely, but it is always revelation. Our task is to identify and act upon it, because that is the way God has chosen to com-
municate with us.

This places limits on what is generally called the historical-critical method, which seeks to put the biblical writings in the context of
their times and finds their meaning primarily in terms of how they
were understood when composed. Such information may be helpful, but it is not determinative. A theory of evangelical Quakerism
will regard meaning as flowing backwards through the scriptures.
This rests on the assumption that a full understanding of the significance of Christ only emerged as his death receded into history and
as the Holy Spirit came to guide and inform our collective understanding.

One can argue, for example, that when the servant songs in
Isaiah[7] were composed, they were intended to refer to some figure
other than Jesus Christ. Unless one has a prior commitment to Christianity, there is no reason to see them as prophecies of the atone-

ment. But *with* that commitment, the Bible acquires a different kind of meaning. The historical circumstances in which a particular passage was composed are of less importance than its place in the overall spiritual scheme of the Christian faith. In this scheme of things, doctrine is formed with reference to the overall meaning of scripture. This approach is inherently different from the historical-critical method because of these assumptions about the text and the conviction that the truth to be discovered has a divine, not a human origin. Although critical principles can be very helpful, evangelicals do not bring a critical ideology to the way they understand the text.

This point needs emphasis. There are schools of contemporary Christian thought, like liberation theology and process theology, that interpret scripture in terms of critical principles and ideologies that do not arise from within the faith, but are generated by currents of secular thought. There is no necessary reason why their conclusions should be rejected, but we are entitled to have reservations about their methodology. It is perfectly possible for a school of thought to be academically respectable, yet not actually able to illuminate the meaning of scripture. It is here that evangelical Friends will insist on Barclay's point that it is the scriptures, and nothing else, which are the only fit outward judge of controversies. It is necessary to be very cautious about theories that claim to shed helpful light on scripture, but ultimately become a substitute for it. By definition, that cannot be evangelicalism.

History and Belief

The second important element in any theory of evangelical Quakerism will be an explanation of how history influences the formation of belief. Christianity is not isolated from the cultures that surround it; it often reflects the tensions and conflicts of those cultures. It has proved very hard for the Church to remain pure in a fallen world. We must reject the opinion that says that all we need is the Bible and that if we only listened to what it said, we could put behind us the quarrels and separations that have disgraced the Church in the past. This is the sort of thing that underlies the criticism of Friends distinctives noted earlier. It is the fallacy of the fresh start. Idealists are always trying to set up communities that are free of the contaminations of the ordinary world, and they always fail. We are a part of history and cannot escape the consequences.

> *Christianity is not isolated from the cultures that surround it; it often reflects the tensions and conflicts of those cultures.*

Evangelicals ought to know this, because we are all, in one way or another, the children of the Reformation, which gives us our identity, our principles, and our mythology. When the two bishops, Ridley and Latimer, were being burned at Oxford in 1555, Latimer called across to Ridley as they were lighting the fire under him, "Be of good comfort, Master Ridley, and play the man; we shall this day light such a candle by God's grace in England as I trust shall never be put out."[8] In this story, two people, with whom we have a common faith, are doing something we hope we would have the courage to do in their circumstances. They are *our* people, showing us that what we have is so precious that they were willing to die for it. We identify with them.

Part of being human is to be moved by stories like this and enter into their meaning. They change us and make us better people. That is quite apart from the bald fact that, romance and emotion aside, their martyrdom was a significant part of the process that has resulted in our freedom to practice our faith in tranquility here and now.

So if Friends are tempted to say to themselves, "All we need is scripture," they might find that this is only temporarily a recipe for a quiet life and a solution to all their problems. As what we would call evangelicals, Ridley and Latimer probably thought the same thing, but that could not stop the world from dealing with them harshly, nor, one can imagine, making them ask in their last hours the significance of what was happening to them. This is a part of the tragedy and the nobility of the story. Like so many of the martyrs, who never set out to make the kind of profession that brought them to the deaths, these men were caught up in a set of circumstances that were beyond their own control. The Bible was not their license to avoid reality.

There is an analogy to be drawn here between individuals and the groups to which they belong, and this brings us to the question of character. Character matures when we are at ease with ourselves, knowing where we come from and where we are going. The martyred bishops, Ridley and Latimer, reached the point where they faced the consequences of all the decisions and choices they had made in the course of their Christian lives. The way they faced death revealed their true character. What is true of individuals is also true of the associations they form. Churches develop a character over time, largely out of the choices they are called upon to make, because they cannot be all things to all people, and no more could the bishops. This is the substance of history, and we shall therefore handle it primarily as the process whereby individual and corporate character is formed. If we believe that history is under the control of God, and its purpose to provide the means of salvation, this is the only possible principle to adopt.

Experience and Understanding

The third element in our theory of evangelical Quakerism will be experience. Friends, as well as the evangelical tradition in general, have always placed great emphasis on the importance of religious experience at the expense of theological speculation. It is a common mistake for critics of the evangelical faith to overlook how scriptural truth can be transmuted into intense personal experience. Certainly, studying the scriptures is a major evangelical preoccupation, but it is not an end in itself. Rather, it is the means whereby we can come to understand, to the fullest degree possible, the nature of God's dealings with us.

Conversion, the central experience of Christianity, also teaches an understanding of this in two significant ways. First, it re-orients life by giving the believer a different criterion of meaning and a different scale of values. Second, it opens the way to a different kind of spiritual experience and a new set of virtues. Experience in this context, therefore, means *Christian* experience.

We live in a period when the prevailing mode of explanation for human behavior is psychological, and this has a number of consequences. At one level, psychology helps us to understand ordinary life much better and to live more effectively. At another, it enables us to understand pathologies like alcoholism or criminality and provides a solid basis for social policy making. But there is also a level at which psychology encourages us to look at what it means to be human solely in terms of the dynamics of the human mind itself. Experience becomes a series of mental events defined by academic disciplines like psychology, sociology, or anthropology. It is personal, but it is also subjective, until the academic discipline sanctions generalizations about it.

There can be no doubt that experiences—our thoughts, feelings, desires, calculations, and decisions—are the raw materials out of which our lives are made. In an important sense we are all streams of consciousness, responding to stimuli and affecting the world though our own autonomous and self-assertive actions. But these are raw materials only. One of the ways we find meaning is to reflect on what happens to us and assess what we have learned, discounting, as far as we can, our own biases or self-interest. If we can do this, we might find that at the limits of the psychological mode of explanation there are more general and abstract truths about which both philosophy and religion have something to say. Theology and philosophy are dangerous elements in any non-theological or non-philosophical discipline, but they do provide a wider context within which the results of particular disciplines can be assessed.

If this is the case, then, our experience has a wider significance than just our own thoughts and feelings, because it is an experience *of* something. It is possible to explain Ridley and Latimer simply in terms of their own personal motivation, but that hardly exhausts the reality of what happened to them. They were characteristic figures of their time, so they have more than an individual significance. Why did they not recant and preserve their lives? The wider explanation is that they felt themselves to be under a religious duty, and that they had been placed in a particular position because God had allotted it to them as part of a series of events of much greater significance that we know as the Reformation.

It follows from this that while our personal experience may be vivid and informative, it is not self explanatory, but draws a significant part of its meaning from our place in a broader sequence of events. To interpret experience properly, therefore, we need to relate it to this broader setting. It is important to do this, because claims to personal experience are made with great conviction as a justification for all kinds of religious belief and conduct that we instinctively know are mistaken. So whenever someone makes a claim to truth based on experience, we have to look carefully to see what truth the alleged truth of experience is based on and how it is related to the broader picture.

There are various ways of doing this. Direct and reflective personal experiences are certainly means of encountering truth, but so are the teachings of scripture and the accumulated wisdom of the community. Genuine experience is an experience of the truth, and the truth is accessible to us through more than one medium. It does not follow from this that the evidence of our experience is inferior, however. History shows us that scripture can be misinterpreted and the community can be mistaken. While experience needs to be tested by external standards, those standards themselves need constant attention. Otherwise we allow circumstances to develop in which religious tyranny masquerades as the truth, as Ridley and Latimer discovered to their cost—or Mary Dyer and George Fox for that matter.

Earlier, we argued that conversion is an event that generates a new and specific kind of experience not available to non-Christians. If experience is purely subjective, that assertion is meaningless. But if part, at least, of the significance of our experience comes from beyond ourselves, we face the uncomfortable conclusion that there are two kinds of experience, that which comes to the redeemed soul and that which does not. In two places Paul speaks of the putting off of the old self and putting on the new, "...which is being renewed in knowledge in the image of its Creator."[9] This is in no sense a limitation of the principle of general revelation. What it means is that only redeemed experience will be capable of attesting truly to the nature and work of God.

The purpose of revelation is to give us this kind of understanding, and that is why we have to admit that experience is the most important element in our theory. Biblical and historical understanding can contextualize our experience and help in the process of discernment. They are each vehicles for revelation, as we have argued above. But there is equally no doubt that Christ seeks us individually, and Christianity is based on personal experience above everything else. Neither scripture nor a sense of history can generate conversion, though they can encourage it. Conversion is the work of the Holy Spirit, which does not leave the new Christian alone but is a loving and encouraging presence throughout the whole course of life. Experience of the Spirit is knowledge of God.

> *Neither scripture nor a sense of history can generate conversion, though they can encourage it. Conversion is the work of the Holy Spirit, which does not leave the new Christian alone but is a loving and encouraging presence throughout the whole course of life.*

In building a theoretical basis for the Friends Church, therefore, we have to give full weight to this reality. It is not enough to repeat the lessons others have learned; we have to go through the process of learning them for ourselves, both as individuals and as the Church. A comprehensive account of the work of the Spirit will necessarily include the experience of those with whom the Spirit dwells and also the experience of the congregations called together through the Spirit's ministry. It is through worship and prayer that we encounter the Spirit, and the conclusions we reach about the meaning of history and the authority of scripture have no value unless they reflect the Spirit's guidance. When they do, we may hope that the result is coherent, persuasive, and blessed.

Doctrine and Change

Evangelical Quakerism can be characterized as orthodox, biblically based, and spirit-led in the broadest terms. The significance of these principles can be seen by looking at their opposites, rather than in attempting to define each one more precisely. Evangelical Friends desire to be part of the historic Church, not a sectarian protest against it. They use the Bible as the touchstone of faith, practice, and innovation rather than the latest ideas of secular scholarship. They rely on the continuing guidance of the Holy Spirit in all things personal and communal, rather than deferring either to tradition or the human intellect.

Evangelical Friends are therefore essentially revisionists. Adoption of the evangelical faith was one of the ways in which Friends were able to relate to a much wider world when they emerged from their self-chosen isolation as the nineteenth century unfolded. As a preliminary to forming new relationships, the area of common agreement over matters of faith and conduct had to be established with the Christian community as a whole. This was not an easy process, but it had to be undertaken. The pace of social and intellectual development accelerated sharply during the nineteenth century making entirely new demands on religion and religious people. All Friends were bound up in this process of change, even though they had different opinions about its nature. Some chose the response of liberal Christianity and established a new identity by finding mystical awareness to be the central theme of the tradition. Evangelicals, preferring scripture, and thinking of themselves primarily as Protestants, found in the tradition the apotheosis of the Reformation.

Both responses were reasonable in the circumstances, because it is almost impossible to stand out against far-reaching social change. Every organized group of people needs to make an accommodation with forces beyond its control, and there is often bitter controversy in churches and political parties over the rightness of the compromises that emerge. But that is a question of practice, not of principle. Human beings do not behave the same way at seventy as they did at seventeen because they are older and usually wiser. They have developed their powers of understanding, discrimination and judgment, and change is the midwife of these qualities.

Change is inevitable, but hardly neutral. It can be very uncomfortable when it presents us with hard choices we are unable to avoid. Something of this was at work when Friends emerged from their isolation, and they did not always respond as they should have. They did not quite know where the process of adaptation had to stop. Their present predicament is the result. Earlier, we thought of change in biological terms, as the analogy of a plant coming into bloom. In this analogy change will be orderly, permanent, and in the nature of renewal rather than total innovation. The changes of the nineteenth century were the result of enthusiasm rather than forethought, and we are now in a position to ask whether they satisfy the proper conditions for organic growth. Some may and others may not. The hybrid we have called evangelical Quakerism can be expected to survive if the changes brought about by frontier revivalism meet the conditions for the orderly development of doctrine. Otherwise it will not be a hybrid but a mutation.

So when we look at the doctrine of a particular church, in this case, ours, how can we tell whether an innovation is likely to be beneficial, or harmful in the long run? We have to provide some kind of answer to this problem, because it represents the experience of the whole church in miniature. Orthodox Christian doctrine was formulated by the General Councils in the third and fourth centuries as a response to the theological controversies that preceded them. A process of development was at work in which the full implications of the gospel and the scriptural record only became obvious with the passage of time. If the decisions of the Councils represent the truth and are not just an arbitrary interpretation of the materials available to them, then there must have been a process at work that was under divine guidance. So it is with us.

Two things in particular need to be borne in mind when discerning the process of doctrinal change. One of the ways of testing the authenticity of a development is to ask whether it has been anticipated or prefigured in some way by earlier thinkers and writers. The second is to enquire whether the development is actually a logical extension of the older viewpoints and bears an organic relationship to them, not being just the outcome of chance. Organic growth is essential. So when we look at major doctrines like the nature of the light within or instantaneous perfection given as a gift of grace,[10] we are likely to find precedents for each of them in Christian history, operating like seeds, sprouting and coming to fruition when historical circumstances are right.

An example of this process is the assimilation of Wesleyan ideas and practices by Friends in the latter part of the nineteenth century. That the doctrine of the second work of grace is an innovation cannot be doubted. If it had been a cuckoo, and turned the Quaker fledglings out of the nest, or if it still had the potential to do that, we would need to regard it with suspicion, if not hostility. But the second work of grace may be compatible with our own tradition because it is related to it. If that is so, we might not wish to embrace it collectively, but may be willing to make a place for it within our more general scheme of doctrine. So continuity is important, as the image of organic growth emphasizes. There is plainly a continuity between traditional Quakerism and what is said and done in Friends churches today, and also, as we shall see, parallels between what early Friends called convincement and what Wesleyans understand as the second work of grace. The principle of development allows us to account for orderly change, and to see early Quakerism as a seedbed rather than the ultimate statement of religious truth.

In this way, over time, history arbitrates our disagreements, producing new developments out of old in such a way that few old ideas are entirely transcended, and few new ideas are entirely unprecedented. Indeed, Christian doctrine in general is in a state of constant development because of its continuing dialogue with a changing world. If it is to preserve its claim to truth it will need a theory of change that preserves as well as innovates.

Christianity teaches that the Holy Spirit is constantly leading the Church into an understanding of new truth, and therefore offers a theological, or spiritual explanation of our developing understanding. But at the same time, it sees the Spirit's continuing revelation working by increment and not substitution. Both perspectives have to be maintained, and that is not always easy. The process of doctrinal development is inevitably controversial and we should not be afraid of it. The best safeguard against error will be to recognize that this process has a spiritual as well as an intellectual process, and priority should be given to the former.

Continuing Revelation

The Friends Church has always been a living testimony to this standard. Historically, Friends have always believed that preoccupation with the niceties of doctrine leads smoothly to a coercive and persecuting spirit. In view of this we need to bear in mind the spirit in which doctrinal formulation is undertaken, as well as consider the intellectual process by which doctrine develops. It is easy to misunderstand what Friends mean when they say they look primarily to experience and only secondarily to doctrine. This way of putting it is not intended to downplay the significance or importance of doctrine, which is simply a formulation of the truth as understood by the community. Rather, it is an attempt to state the conditions under which doctrine becomes important. There are deep reasons, which relate to Friends' whole understanding of prophecy and the new covenant in Jesus Christ, for this emphasis on experience. The test of Christian commitment is not so much orthodoxy as obedience.

But experience never takes place in a vacuum. It is always an experience *of* something. While Friends value experience highly, they also give some clear guidance about what kind of experience they mean. If we have been saved, and are giving our testimony years afterwards, we will describe the significance of our conversion and the sort of new life it brought us. At the same time, our story will be an account of personal things such as our guilt, worry, decision, gratitude, wonder, and praise. All these things form our experience in the widest sense.

Friends are also realistic enough to recognize that such confessions can arise from social expectations as well as religious feeling. That is why Friends emphasize the inward processes of the soul rather than their public expression. The silence of open worship is a sign of this particular Quaker value. The truth Friends wish to assert is that we enter and sustain a relationship with God and with our whole self, not just parts of our personality like our emotions or our minds.[11]

Emphasis on this kind of experience lends support to what we have said about continuing divine revelation. A moment's thought will show us that experience is the medium through which we grasp the fact that the world is changing. We are faced with new intellectual and moral questions that demand a response. Sometimes these are old challenges dressed up in a new disguise, and the old answers are more than sufficient. But in another important sense, we are always entering a new world and the old guidelines apply only to the past. When the Israelites left Egypt, God went before them in a pillar of cloud by day and a pillar of fire by night. They were led by divine revelation, not by their own brainpower or moral strength.

And so it is, says the Quaker tradition, with individuals and the church. There is much that we already know, and evangelical Friends will say that the Bible is an entirely trustworthy guide to any of the emergencies life brings us. But God is still active in the world, in the church, and in the individual soul. There are divine purposes not yet accomplished, and we have a part in helping to bring them about.

We have to realize that, and so we have to believe in the possibility of continuing revelation. "Forget the former things; do not dwell on the past. See, I am doing a new thing! Now it springs up; do you not perceive it? I am making a way in the desert and streams in the wasteland."[12]

Experience and continuing revelation are, therefore, the keys to Friends particular understanding of Christian doctrine. We shall follow their implications in what follows. We shall see that the corporate life of the Friends Church has two sources, the gathered church tradition and the revival tradition. What these things have in common is that they are both reactions to the Protestant Reformation, one as a participant in those events, the other as a reflection on them. Evangelical Quakerism is perhaps preponderantly of the second kind, and it is through its lens, primarily, that we shall work.

Evangelical Quakerism will be presented as part of the continuing movement for the revival of the church throughout the generations. As Charles Finney wrote, "A revival is nothing else than a new beginning of obedience to God."[13] This, historically, was the origin of both traditional and evangelical Quakerism, and we shall now begin to see how the one emerged from the other.

NOTES

1. They are also referred to as the "programmed" or "pastoral" tradition.
2. Baltimore, Canadian, New England and New York Yearly Meetings.
3. Joseph John Gurney (1788-1847) of Earlham Hall, Norwich, England. Quaker banker, philanthropist, prison reform and anti-slavery campaigner. Brother of Elizabeth Fry. Controversialist and writer on Quakerism from an evangelical perspective.
4. John Henry Newman, *Apologia pro Vita Sua*, (1864) Norton Critical Edition, ed. David J. Delaura (New York: W.W. Norton & Company, 1968), p.197. Newman was born in 1801 and brought up an evangelical Anglican. He was converted to Catholicism in 1845, eventually becoming a Cardinal. He wrote extensively on the development of doctrine and died in 1890.
5. 2 Tim. 3:14-16.
6. *Apology for the True Christian Divinity* (1675), (York, England: William Sessions Ltd.) Prop.3 par. VI.
7. See Isa. 49:1-6, 50:4-9, 52:13-53:12, 56:3-8.
8. John Foxe, *Acts and Monuments of the Church*, (1563) see *Foxe's Book of Martyrs*, ed. G.H.Williamson (Pomfret, Vt.: Little, Brown, 1965), p. 311.
9. Col. 3:9-10 *cf.* 2 Cor. 5:17.
10. See Chapters 3 and 8 below.
11. Mark 12:30.
12. Isa. 43:18-19.
13. Charles Finney, *Lectures on Revival*, (1845) (Minneapolis: Bethany House, undated), p. 9.

2

Coming to Christ

2

Coming to Christ

To those who have found it, Christianity is the pearl of great price for which the merchant in the parable was willing to give up all that he had.[1] The jewel in the story is beyond compare. It symbolizes the Kingdom of God, the spiritual reality Jesus preached, which gives everything but demands all. The pearl is waiting to be found, but only by those who are willing to stake everything on getting it.

The Christian faith is therefore an all-or-nothing affair. It must be chosen consciously, with a full understanding of what is involved. The parable warns us that there is a condition for entry to the Kingdom. We have to place obedience to God above all of our own wishes and inclinations. A faith that cannot do this has failed to meet the condition on which the possibility of finding the pearl rests. It has not been genuinely converted.

In evangelical Christianity, conversion is the spiritual event by which an individual enters the Kingdom of God. It involves the recognition of one's sins, repentance, and confession of faith in Jesus Christ as one's personal savior and Lord. Conversion is brought about solely by the grace of God, and is the result of two underlying processes that change us fundamentally. By justification, God remits the penalty for our sin. By regeneration, God grants us new life, and we are born again. We are dealing with a complex matter in which there are both human and divine elements.

In this chapter we shall look at the process of conversion from a number of different angles, partly to show the complexity of the idea and partly to explain the Friends distinctive doctrine of convincement. We shall begin by discussing the nature of sin and then see how different views of the nature of conversion arise out of the Reformed doctrine of predestination and the Wesleyan doctrine of prevenient grace, as we have to do if we are to understand the strong affinity between Methodists and Quakers. This will put us in a position to examine what the early Quakers meant by convincement. This was the distinctive conversion experience of the early Quakers, and it has much to teach us about the cost of discipleship and the nature of personal commitment to Christ. The chapter concludes by suggesting what that teaching might be.

Sin and the Human Condition

Most people are familiar with tracts and pamphlets in which the gospel is presented as a series of claims on the attention of the reader followed by a text to back up the claims. They have a common pattern in spite of some surface variety. The texts chosen present a brief overview of the human condition, God's intentions toward us, what God has done in Christ, and how we should respond. The message is usually something like this: All have sinned and fallen short of the glory of God. The wages of sin is death, so unless we repent, we will perish. But God loves us and gave us Jesus, his one and only Son, so that if we believe in him, our sins will be wiped out and we will be saved.[2]

This short chain of texts contains a certain sequence of ideas. There is a pessimistic estimate of the moral capacities of human beings combined with an optimistic estimate of God's response. In the ministry of Jesus Christ, love is thrown into the balance against wickedness. But it is not an indiscriminate love because it requires a loving response, and this must be evidenced in the lives of sinners by repentance and belief. Those who accept the invitation the gospel makes are saved (that is to say, their sins are forgiven). They are empowered to overcome sin in their redeemed life, and they receive the gift of eternal life hereafter.

So what is sin, and how do we recognize it in ourselves? The most obvious way is to accept that from time to time we break the moral rules. We do things that are wrong, and the prick of conscience tells us so. In this sense, a sin is an action that contravenes a rule. But the idea of sin goes beyond formal disobedience to rules, because sin represents more than an individual transgression. Rules are not imposed arbitrarily. There are reasons for them, whether they are the laws of a country or the moral code of a religious community.

Scripture is clear that sin is not the breach of a conventional rule but a deliberate action contrary to God's will that breaks the relationship established by the covenant. It does not just involve the individual but undermines the cohesion of the community as a whole. A lie reflects on the reputation of the liar but also devalues the currency of trust throughout the community the liar belongs to. Even more than that, sin represents a direct challenge to the authority of God on whose continuing care and protection the community itself depends and who sustains the truth in the first place.

The effects of sin are evident. Although there is much in human history that is noble and inspiring, at the same time we can see a record of violence, theft, cruelty, and deceit. These things do not happen by spontaneous generation. They happen because there are people wicked enough to make them happen. While some people suggest social causes for these things, the Christian faith teaches that they happen because of sin. In other words, they originate in the human heart. If this is the case, we are faced with an awkward conclusion. Unless there are two distinct and separate kinds of people in the world, those who are open to these actions and those who are not, we are forced to conclude that sin is a propensity we all share.

Separation from God

Scripture teaches that sin is a tendency toward selfishness that is inherent in all of us and takes the form of desire, either for the possession of material things or the freedom to do what we wish without constraint or limitation. Because desire sooner or later conflicts with reality, it results in frustration and resentment, which find expression in the repudiation of the authority to which one is legitimately subject. This repudiation, says scripture, produces a state of mind alienated from God and enslaved to itself. It cannot see clearly into its own nature or the nature of the reality in which it lives. It is, therefore, a prey to pride, error, and immorality. It is lost, in all senses of the word.[3]

> *Scripture teaches that sin is a tendency toward selfishness that is inherent in all of us and takes the form of desire, either for the possession of material things or the freedom to do what we wish without constraint or limitation.*

This looks like a harsh and unrealistic account of the human condition. It has to meet a number of perfectly legitimate objections. One can say, for example, that there is also great good to be found in the world and that by concentrating on sin Christian theology has chosen the wrong point of departure. One can argue that this is far too lurid to be an accurate account of one's own experience. One can even concede that sin is latent in many, but at the same time believe that it is absent in many people too. What can be said in response to these criticisms?

It is certainly not very pleasant to be told that we are sinful when we are confident of our own righteousness. But the message of Jesus is clear that even when we have done everything good that we can, we have still done no more that we are required to do. There is reward, but no merit in the Kingdom of God. "So you also, when you have done everything you were told to do, should say, 'We are unworthy servants; we have only done our duty.'"[4] Unpalatable though these words are, they are at the root of the gospel and the foundation of our little chain of texts. One cannot have Christianity without them.

Sin is alienation from God, a condition that affects us all in different ways. It is our natural condition, as any textbook of psychology will show if you care to lend a little moral color to its conclusions. The consequence is that unless the power of sin is overcome we are unfit to be in relationship with God, because the essence of sin is to have rejected this relationship. Because the clarity of our judgment has been clouded over and the strength of our will fatally weakened, that relationship cannot be repaired from our side. We are morally imperfect beings in a fallen world. The absolute righteousness of God is so powerful that without divine assistance our sin will destroy us and we will never enjoy eternal blessedness.

The Need for Salvation

In evangelical thought, a denial of this proposition involves a higher estimation of human nature than the evidence warrants, or else a conception of God that rests on human reason and not the teaching of the Bible. Scripture teaches that we can be saved by the grace of God, not by our own efforts. "For it is by grace you have been saved, through faith—and this not from yourselves, it is the gift of God—not by works, so that no one can boast."[5] These words may be unpalatable, but they lie at the heart of the gospel. It does not follow from them that we are unable to do good. What is being insisted upon is that to be saved we need God. No matter what good we do, we cannot earn our own salvation.

But salvation from what? If part of the human condition is a seamless and inevitable transition from the trials and blessings of this life into the glories of the hereafter, the idea of salvation loses its meaning. But if sin is hateful to God, and if sin is our nature, we are in a very different position. We are under judgment, and unless there is some way of remitting the penalty that is justly ours, we face the prospect of hell—permanent alienation from God. Escaping from the coils of sin is the prime need of the human being. The message of scripture is that we have a choice between punishment and forgiveness, but forgiveness has to be on God's terms.[6]

And those terms are that we be converted, turn from our sinful ways, and accept Christ. In his nighttime conversation with the Pharisee Nicodemus, Jesus explains that behind the world of everyday life lies the world of the spirit. We are constantly in the presence of realities we do not see. He says that there is an absolute precondition for entry to the kingdom of God, and it is that we have to be reborn. No amount of scorn for born-again Christians outweighs the fact that spiritual rebirth is central to Jesus' teaching. Without new birth, the kingdom of God is closed to us. So we must be converted and believe the gospel.[7]

> *Escaping from the coils of sin is the prime need of the human being. The message of scripture is that we have a choice between punishment and forgiveness, but forgiveness has to be on God's terms.*

Turning to God

Conversion is simply the act of turning from what one *is* to become a follower of Jesus Christ. The root of the word in Greek is nothing more than that, "to turn." Although conversion stories are all highly individual, and inevitably so, they commonly follow a pattern. There is an emerging sense that one's life has gone seriously wrong, not just that misfortune or misjudgment has produced unhappiness. This is followed by a sense of guilt, which is paradoxically a blessing because it is a sign of the acceptance of moral responsibility. Then comes repentance, a rejection of the past and an earnest desire to change. Finally, as in the case of the prodigal son, there is the act of confessing one's sins and seeking pardon through the merits of Jesus Christ. It is the faith that we will be forgiven that restores our relationship with God.

Repentance and faith are, therefore, essential components of the process of conversion, though we also use this word to signify the point at which we actually make our appeal for forgiveness. It is somewhat artificial to try to separate all the different elements that are at work, and we should not be too arbitrary. Perhaps we should say that repentance and faith are the human side of an event in which God grants a sinner both rebirth into a new life and that justification is the forgiveness and setting aside of the consequences of sin. *Justification* is a term borrowed from the law courts. It means that from the moment of conversion God remits the penalty of our sins and we have an entirely new start. It does not mean that we are instantaneously made morally perfect.

The elements of conversion are laid out in the parable of the prodigal son.[8] The young man's initial assertion of his moral autonomy is followed by increasing degradation until he reaches the point of repentance and decides to go home. When he arrives, the young man acknowledges what he has done. He is met not with punishment but with forgiveness and celebration. The story is not only about the soul; it is also about the nature of God. The whole story revolves around a decision. As Luke puts it, the young man came to his senses and resolved to return to his father. He turned his back on all that he had done and sought to make amends. As a result he received a new life that went far beyond anything he was entitled to expect.

The story of the prodigal son is not only about the soul; it is also about the nature of God. The whole story revolves around a decision. As Luke puts it, the young man came to his senses and resolved to return to his father. As the young man knew, we cannot redeem the past. What is done is done, and we usually have little power to rectify our mistakes. In these circumstances, we might resign ourselves to fatalism, numbing our sense of what might have been and turning our backs on what could be. But then again, we might pick up the whispers of a new start that two thousand years of Christianity have placed somewhere along our way. Hearing the

Word and realizing that it is quite literally our salvation is the point at which conversion becomes a possibility. The gospel tells us that the path of forgiveness lies through accepting the cross of Christ, which is the measure of the pain our sin has caused God and the measure of God's love and forgiveness for us. With repentance comes faith, and the pearl of great price is given into our hands.

Repentance goes well beyond either regret or remorse. A conversion based merely on these two feelings is inadequate. Regrets are transitory and soon forgotten. We do not generally allow regrets to alter our conduct and attitudes. Unless a person claiming to have been converted shows serious evidence of the claim, that person's repentance is unlikely to last very long. Remorse is more serious than repentance and arises when we experience shame and fear at the consequences of something we have done. These emotions pass the test of seriousness, but can only mature into genuine repentance if they produce a willingness to recognize and accept the consequences of one's actions.

True repentance requires courage that comes from beyond our inner resources, because when we are converted we have usually exhausted them. This courage comes miraculously and paradoxically from God and depends solely on our willingness to accept that we need God's help because we can go no further on our own. It is similar to, if not the same as, faith: being sure of what we hope for and certain of what we do not see. In this sense, faith is a form of knowledge. It is trust in what is hidden, a practical knowledge of *how* things are rather than *what* they are. Such knowledge is essential to conversion. It only comes to people who are at the end of their tether and who have nowhere else to turn.

> *True repentance requires courage that comes from*
> *beyond our inner resources, because when we are*
> *converted we have usually exhausted them.*

The New Birth

Genuine conversion is transforming. In the parable of the sower, some of the seed withers away because it falls on shallow ground, and some is smothered because it falls on thorny ground. Not all the seed survives. Salvation has a negative side, in that we are saved from sin, but a positive side also, in that we are thereby called to an earthly life of virtue as well as an eternal life in glory. We are called upon to produce fruit. There is a strong tradition in Protestant Christianity that says that we can be saved from the power of sin as well as the consequences of it. Quakerism belongs to that tradition. Although conversion and moral change are usually presented as distinct processes, we should never forget that they are also indissolubly linked. A new relationship with God is established so that the righteous life can begin.

> *There is a strong tradition in Protestant*
> *Christianity that says that we can be saved from*
> *the power of sin as well as the consequences of it.*
> *Quakerism belongs to that tradition.*

The full gospel, then, requires that we give full weight to two New Testament principles, each of which is binding on us. Although we are saved by grace through faith, faith without works is dead.[9] Many will say that conversion is a process complete in itself, unconditioned in any way by what follows in the course of a Christian life.

Friends have never believed that, though they have always understood that salvation comes through faith alone. What Friends assert is that we are not just saved *from* something we are saved *for* something. The quality of our confession of faith has to measure up to the standards of Jesus Christ: "If you love me, you will obey what I command."[10] Obedience is not an option.

The second consequence of conversion is that the experience greatly widens our understanding of God. Robert Barclay, the early Quaker theologian, began his account of Friends doctrine with this very point. He begins his exposition by citing with approval two New Testament passages: "...no one knows the Father except the Son and those to whom the Son chooses to reveal him,"[11] and, "Now this is eternal life: that they may know you, the only true God, and Jesus Christ, whom you have sent."[12] Conversion occurs when we realize that these, rather than the conjectures of philosophy, are the fundamental principles of human understanding.[13]

We do not always grasp the corollary of this, which is that knowledge of God is not the same as our knowledge of the everyday world. The kind of persuasion and communication that we are normally used to is not the sort of persuasion God uses. As Paul says, "When I came to you, brothers, I did not come with eloquence or superior wisdom as I proclaimed to you the testimony about God. For I resolved to know nothing while I was with you except Jesus Christ and him crucified. I came to you in weakness and fear, and with much trembling. My message and my preaching were not with wise and persuasive words, but with a demonstration of the Spirit's power, so that your faith might not rest on men's wisdom, but on God's power."[14]

There is a warning here that we need to read, mark, learn, and inwardly digest. Eloquence and technique are not the gospel. Superficial persuasion is not conversion. Personal enthusiasm is not necessarily a sign of regeneration because the truth lies deeper than that.

The Quaker temperament has always stressed the importance of inward change, and it lines up with all the other interpretations of the Christian faith that do the same thing. These words of Paul to the Corinthians, pointing us to the inward power of Christ, are theologically sound from an evangelical point of view and fundamental to Friends understanding of where conversion begins. Conversion is not self-evident. It needs to be put to the test.

Conversion is the most important experience a human being can have because there is no way to salvation or to a full relationship with God without it. What we have just said implies that the decision we make goes beyond the exercise of any one of our faculties and involves the whole of our personality. Putting it like this is the only way to convey its comprehensive nature. But we also have to remember that it is a process, and the person making a decision for Christ has been led not just by the preacher's eloquence, but by the work of God in the heart, making preparation for this event often secretly over a considerable period. Regeneration, the new birth, is just as intimate and complex a process as conversion.

> *Conversion is the most important experience a human being can have because there is no way to salvation or to a full relationship with God without it.*

Birth and Growth

The analogy of birth must be taken seriously. Most of us take some time to come into the world. We have already been growing for nine months, and some of us go on for another ninety years. We also have a genetic inheritance that is not always to our liking. Certainly there is a time at which we emerge into the world, but that event depends on many others who helped to bring it about. To see birth only in terms of the date and time of a baby's arrival is pretty limited. So it must be with conversion. In the same way that a baby needs both heart and lungs, so the new Christian needs repentance and faith to be converted, and these things grow inside us.

It seems, therefore, to do no justice to the process of conversion to say arbitrarily that the new birth occurred to one soul at nine o'clock on Wednesday when the altar call was given, and that another soul who would have responded, but was killed by a truck on the way to the meeting, was lost for all eternity. That does not sound much like the tender concern of a loving God, but if we expect the various elements of conversion and regeneration to occur in a certain sequence, we may be forced into that position.

On the other hand, if God's time is not our time, we can envisage the situation in which souls may be reborn before their possessors know it, or give any visible indication to the rest of us. There seems to be no other explanation for many accounts in which people continue to be plagued by doubts and temptations well after they have received the first indications of divine favor.

What unites repentance, confession of faith, justification, and regeneration is not that they each have a place in a recognizable sequence of events, but that they all occur in the same organism— the soul. They have grown together, they work together, and they are each essential in the process of coming to the point of personal confession of Christ. To ask which has priority or to build one's preaching or doctrine on some concept of how these things ought to be and then to require that people measure up, is to misunderstand the spirit of Jesus' words about new birth. It is Nicodemus who wants things cut and dried, Jesus who says that the spirit blows where it wills.

Weak Faith and Temporary Conversions

The Puritan forebears of contemporary evangelicals wrestled with apparently weak faith, and what they called the "preparation for conversion." They realized as a pastoral matter that there were those unwilling to claim conversion whose lives exhibited the love of Christ. They knew that Christians in crisis went through an immense range of emotions of varying degrees of intensity and also that Paul wrote, "Accept him whose faith is weak, without passing judgment on disputable matters."[15]

Nowadays, however, the white heat of the camp-meeting conversion tends to be taken as the norm, without its dangers being fully appreciated. Emotionalism can lead to false conversions in which the whole person is not engaged, and it can persuade many who are working out their salvation in fear and trembling that they are not acceptable to God when in fact they are.

Ultimately, of course, every true Christian has to make a personal confession; for it is certain that we cannot be converted absent-mindedly. But that confession must be understood and taken seriously; devotion to Jesus Christ requires that we know and acknowledge what we are doing. Paul reminds us that if we confess that Jesus is Lord with our mouths and believe in our hearts, we

will be saved. Both elements are necessary. A bare confession is neither here nor there—it is belief that brings life. The confession can
be made in all sorts of ways, but until the belief in the heart has
been put to the test, there is no human way of telling whether it is
genuine. Preachers and pastors need to recognize that. Those who
are saved are those who endure to the end, not those in whom the
word springs up like seeds on rocky soil.

The gospel, then, is received inwardly. The particular strength
of Friends tradition lies in its understanding of this truth. Friends
have always insisted that the true interpretation of the scriptures
shows that we have to find within ourselves the things we read
about or are told. Knowing *of* Jesus or *about* Jesus is immaterial.
What makes a Christian is the encounter *with* Jesus.

> *Friends have always insisted that the true
> interpretation of the scriptures shows that we have
> to find within ourselves the things we read about
> or are told.*

There are many ways in which the good news can be presented.
There is an evangelism of emotion and an evangelism of reason.
Both are ways of making an appeal to people based on an important
human faculty. That is probably inevitable. But for Friends, that is
never enough. We need to be *convinced* of the truth in both senses of
the word.

Salvation and Grace

So far, we have concentrated our attention largely on the human, subjective side of the process of salvation. At this point we

should remember that throughout the process we are in the hands of God and are unable, because of the effects of sin, to choose our salvation without God's help. We do not begin from a neutral position from which we reason our way to a decision. We are under an insuperable handicap that has to be removed before we make our own genuine response. In Paul's terms, we are dead in sin until Christ brings us life.[16]

What then, is the human part in the process, if conversion is the gift of God? It has to be recognized that evangelicals differ about this. Some believe the soul is quite passive so that the grace of God may be emphasized to the full. Others, however, consider that we have some part in the process, although what that part is seems obscure. If free will is a fact of our existence, it is not of much value if we are denied its use at the most important moment of our lives. Historically, as we have already pointed out, there have been two broad answers to this question. Quakerism aligned itself with one rather than the other and thus determined in advance what kind of evangelicalism it would later be able to entertain.

Predestination and the Arminian Tradition

The two main theological traditions within evangelicalism derive from the seventeenth-century controversy over the doctrine of predestination, which states that God has decided in advance who is to be saved and who is to be lost. If we are predestined for salvation, God will do whatever is necessary to bring us to our reward. If we are not among those chosen, there is absolutely nothing we can do for ourselves. The gates of heaven are forever barred to us. Generally speaking, the Reformed tradition, which includes the Presbyterian churches, maintains the doctrine of predestination. The

Wesleyan Methodists and their offshoots do not. In this respect, Friends and Methodists occupy the same ground.

The doctrine of predestination is controversial because it has far-reaching implications for how God is to be understood, how the Bible is to be interpreted, and how the gospel is conceived and promulgated. On the one hand it envisages a God desiring to bring about our salvation. On the other, it sees the human soul totally depraved by sin and separated by an unbridgeable abyss from God; if the mechanism of salvation is to be put in motion, it cannot be done from the human side.

The problem arises because we are commonly supposed to have free will. That is why evangelists call for decisions. When people hear the altar call and step forward into a new life, is this a real decision, or was there never a possibility that they would not? The theory seems to suggest that their decision was always a foregone conclusion, regardless of the eloquence of the preacher. Consequently, there are those who are predestined to be saved and others who are predestined to be damned.

Opponents of the doctrine level their criticisms against both its particular elements and their cumulative effect. It is perfectly possible to maintain that conversion and regeneration are works of grace and not human merit without going as far as the Reformed tradition does. A doctrine of extreme sinfulness does not necessarily require total depravity. There is a strong line of texts that teach that Christ died for all and not just the elect. It is possible to join John Wesley in questioning the theological and spiritual consequences that often attend a belief in predestination. The central chapters in Barclay's *Apology* are just such a sustained attack on the doctrine of predestination.[17]

The Arminian tradition, to which both Wesleyans and Friends belong, now comprises those churches that reject the doctrine of predestination entirely. The name goes back to James Arminius, the Dutch Reformed theologian who wished to modify the force of the doctrine, and whose followers formed the minority party at the Synod of Dort in 1619. We might formulate his argument in modern terms by saying that God's justice is not satisfied unless there is a level playing field. If the unpredestined do not at least have an opportunity to be saved, one of the cardinal doctrines about God—that God is just—is infringed. Arminius himself claimed it as a divine decree that those who repent and believe will be saved, and that God has provided sufficient and effective means whereby people can come to repentance and faith.[18]

Those means are grace and its various means of expression. It is unlikely that people will have turned to God without some lengthy period of preparation, however sudden and dramatic their conversion might seem. There must surely have been deep dissatisfaction within the soul, painful acknowledgement of moral shortcomings, and some sense of the majesty and authority of God.

There is a pattern in all conversions. Although the individual undoubtedly turns to God, it is God who first utters the call to repentance, God who stands on the horizon, and God who upholds the sinner on the way. Without grace, we can do nothing, but with grace we can do things otherwise denied us. One of those things is to choose.

This is the solution to the problem of free will and salvation through grace alone suggested by John Wesley. He was uncomfortable with the doctrine of predestination because of its tendency to devalue the effects of preaching, destroy holiness, and provide no motive for change and amendment of life. On the other hand, he wished to preserve the instrumentality of grace. In his sermon "What is Man?" he writes, "And although I have not an absolute power over my own mind, because of the corruption of my own nature; yet, through the grace of God assisting me, I have a power to choose and do good as well as evil."[19]   Wesley therefore grounds his doctrine in experience, stating that he is conscious of his own liberty and has to find a place for this fact in his explanation.

Human and Divine Agency

Charles Finney[20] was of a similar mind and was characteristically blunt about the process of conversion. He went even further than Wesley and articulated what we should probably claim as a third tradition—that of American frontier revivalism and much of the modern evangelical movement. This tradition says, in Finney's words, "...Both conversion and regeneration are sometimes in the Bible ascribed to God, sometimes to man, and sometimes to the subject; which shows clearly that the distinction under examination is arbitrary and theological rather than biblical... The fact is that both terms imply the simultaneous exercise of both human and divine agency."[21]

We need take nothing away from the doctrine that salvation is the work of God to see the sense in Finney's words. We can all imagine the survivor of a shipwreck struggling in the surf that we know is going to overwhelm him. But somebody throws a lifeline. He still has no power to save himself, but he has the power to grasp the line. He has been put into the position where rescue becomes possible. On his own he can do nothing, but the line empowers him. He does not need to take it, but it is there. The point of this should be clear. It may be pretty circumscribed, but there is a human component in conversion.

We have a duty to ensure that our doctrine is scriptural, however, so the burden of thought and reflection is not one God has lifted from our shoulders. But we may seriously doubt whether our doctrine of human nature requires the epicycles of unconditional predestination, total depravity, and the ordering of the divine decrees. I find that the weight of scripture is against it. The idea of predestination occurs explicitly in only four texts in two books of the New Testament,[22] and against them we have to weigh the innumerable occasions throughout the Bible upon which human beings are invited to repent, return, listen, see, hear, obey, choose, follow, forsake, decide, or acknowledge the words and the works of God.

Each of these exhortations presupposes that people have the freedom to respond and fail to do so at their peril. It is perfectly possible to say this, and at the same time maintain the traditional position that we cannot do these things without grace. It is also possible to claim that the principles of theology underlying the doctrine of the new birth are not the least bit endangered if we use the language of experience to convey their truth rather than erect an ideal scheme for entry into the Kingdom of God to which every potential convert *must* conform. To be sure, we can scarcely be converted without repenting of our sins and having faith in Christ. Those are the theological minimum. But when we turn from *what* to *how*, it is altogether harder to insist that there has to be a common pattern.

The experience of convincement is just such an example. We shall now look at a number of early Quaker autobiographies that do not use the terminology that we have relied on up to this point. They come from a period much nearer the Reformation when the terminology was not so firmly settled. We are reading the words of radical reformers who were also trying deliberately to restate the gospel in words other than those used in what they considered to be a false and degenerate church. As we take a magnifying glass to our origins, we need to do so sympathetically, listening before we question.

Convincement

Early Friends did not use the word "conversion" as we use it today, so we must be careful when we look at their writings from an evangelical perspective. Without doubt they had been converted in our sense, but the spiritual autobiographies they have left us reveal an understanding of their salvation that does not always fit our familiar categories. The experience early Friends describe as convincement is part of a process that has certain characteristic phases. An analysis of them will show how the process as a whole relates to the more widely held understanding of conversion in Protestant Christianity.[23]

Most of the early Friends had received a sound religious upbringing, usually in Puritan circles, where religion was far from nominal. They report clear childhood experiences of God, but their adolescence was a time of great spiritual distress, which they explain in various ways: a sense of unrelieved sin, a sense of abandonment and dereliction, often an unending struggle against temptation, or an inchoate sense of unworthiness. This turmoil, or travail as they tend to call it, is an initial phase that prepares the way for the convincement experience itself.

The imagery these Friends use is sometimes quite dramatic. George Fox says, "...Now though I had great openings, yet great trouble and temptation came many times upon me, so that when it was day I wished for night, and when it was night I wished for day…"[24] Mary Penington describes years of trouble: "O the distress I felt at this time…but I was like the parched earth, and the hunted hart for water, so great was my thirst after that which I did not believe was near me."[25] Charles Marshall says, "So, in a deep sense of Man's miserable State, and particularly a sense of my own Captivity, and share in this unexpressible state of Darkness, Death, Bondage, Misery, Sorrow and Amazement, I fell to the Ground and cried to God for Deliverance and Redemption out of this State…"[26] John Crook reports the almost irresistible temptation to cry out in the midst of sermons, "I am damned, I am damned!" [27] These accounts all seem to follow a similar pattern.

From our point of view, these people were already Christians. They knew their Bibles, took part in the life of the Church, and knew what the faith is. In each case, the writer knew and acknowledged Christ, but had a deep sense of separation from him. They were desperate to overcome the barrier that separated them from the blessedness they read and heard about, but they could not find out how to do it. All the early Quaker autobiographies say the same sort of thing. We are not dealing with new Christians here, but intelligent experienced disciples for whom something is not going right.

So they looked for help. Most of them found their spiritual advisers to be Job's comforters and went through a period of solitary mourning. George Fox records that he sought out many reputable pastors, but none of them were of the slightest use. One man told him to take up smoking, another flew into a rage when he trod on a flowerbed. Francis Howgill was told simply that he would come to no harm if he carried out his formal religious duties like prayer and

Bible reading, listening to sermons, and going to communion. If he did that, he would be protected from harm, but it was unrealistic of him to think that he could ever get rid of his sin. He was not impressed. "...I said to myself, this was a miserable salvation."[28]

In due course, all these early Friends came to the second phase of the conversion process, the actual convincement. The following extracts capture the essentials. William Dewsbury says, "And then the Lord discovered to me, that his love could not be attained in any thing I could do...Then my mind was turned within, by the Power of the Lord, to wait in his Counsel, the Light in my conscience, to hear what the Lord would say..."[29] Joan Vokins gives one of the clearest of all accounts: "...the Spirit of Life and Light (which is the Spirit of Jesus) opened my understanding ...And also what Happiness might be received by taking heed to the Light that shined in my heart, which makes manifest, that the way to the Crown of Glory is through the daily cross to my own Will, and to take Christ's Yoke upon that Nature that would not be subject."[30]

We should not lose sight of the cognitive element in convincement, though. There is an intellectual clarity in what Joan Vokins writes, and also in the words of John Crook, who distinguishes the intellectual from the spiritual apprehension of Christ, referring to the latter as that "...which afterward I came to know and behold, as the appearance of the tried corner-stone laid in Zion, most elect and precious unto them that believed in him; whereby I understood certainly, that it is not an opinion, but Christ Jesus the power and arm of God, who is the Saviour...felt in the heart, and kept dwelling there by faith; which differs as much from all notions in the head and brain as the living substance differeth from the picture or image of it."[31]

The experiences described by these early Friends also imply an understanding of the truth of Christianity beyond just a sense of one's present condition as a sinner. They speak of truth in the sense we find in this scripture: "They perish because they refused to love the truth and so be saved... But we ought always to thank God for you...because from the beginning God chose you to be saved through the sanctifying work of the Spirit and through belief in the truth."[32] We shall see shortly that this idea of convincement by the truth was of immense importance to Friends' claim to carry the true message of Christianity to the rest of the apostate Christian world.

Convincement, then, was a profoundly transformative experience of God, very different from the partial and fleeting awareness of God's presence that belonged to the period of travail. It was direct and it filled the soul. It did not come through the operation of the intellect on religious ideas and doctrines. Convincement was wholly the gift of God, not something procured by spiritual discipline. Rather, the state of lostness, emptiness, and abandonment was brought to an end by an overpowering sense of presence. After this point in their narratives, our writers begin to use the concepts and terminology that we recognize as characteristically Quaker. Most important is the assertion that what they have experienced is the light in their conscience. Depending on the context, this can be understood as Christ, or God, the Holy Spirit, or grace itself. The early Friends were not particular. What they sought to convey was that the power of sin had been broken in them, and their lives thereafter were very different.

Convincement was wholly the gift of God, not something procured by spiritual discipline. Rather, the state of lost-ness, emptiness, and abandonment was brought to an end by an overpowering sense of presence.

But this experience, while certainly a conclusion, is also a beginning. Perhaps the third phase in the process is a second period of spiritual travail, which was not expected, and scarcely welcome. The first period was characterized by various spiritual states like sin, disobedience, confusion, and misunderstanding. There was a sense of being under judgment and failing the test. The second period of tribulation is different. The descriptions of it are much less individual. There is a clear understanding that at convincement the power of God in the conscience has been released with terrifying force. These Friends review their lives to see where they have fallen short, and they say that all their efforts are devoted to amendment of life, not in their own power, but in obedience solely to the will of God.

Following convincement, one's whole life came under condemnation, as every last secret was revealed. The instrument of this review was the light of Christ in the conscience, and the consequence was a highly painful sense of both judgment and punishment. In each case, rather than a battle with individual sins being carried on, there is a sense that the whole body of sin and death is under assault.[33] John Crook writes, "I saw now that the axe was to be laid to the root of the tree, and that there was an evil nature to be consumed in me, which had born sway long, notwithstanding my profession of religion..."[34] Francis Howgill is less restrained. He writes, "My eyes were dim with crying, my flesh did fail of fatness, my bones were dried and my sinews shrunk...All I ever did, I saw it was in the accursed nature."[35]

There is one last phase in this process that is not often remarked upon. Underneath the sometimes-opaque language, early Friends made very large claims. George Fox says, "Now was I come up in spirit through the flaming sword into the paradise of God...I knew nothing but pureness and innocency, and righteousness...."[36] John Crook says, "After this, I felt the spirit of truth to rule in me, and my spirit to be really in union therewith, as before I was in union with the spirit of this world;"[37] Edward Burrough says, "...so through the righteous Law of life in Christ Jesus, I was made free, and am from the body of sin and death...my Garments is *(sic)* washed and made white in the Blood of the Lamb, who hath led me...into the new Jerusalem where there is nothing enters that works abomination, or makes a lie."[38] Though the seventeenth century lacked the vocabulary, this looks like what we might call the second work of grace.[39]

The Redeemed Life

So what is the relevance of these accounts of convincement for us today? They are certainly of historical interest, and without them the Friends movement would never have begun. But are they more than just a part of the heritage? We can think of them as simply heritage if we want to, but we shall be the poorer if we do. Their voices speak powerfully and insistently about honesty and truth in religion, and this is (or ought to be) the basis of everything we say or do today. So let us take what they say about the process of conversion and the spiritual experiences surrounding it and see what light they can throw on our understanding of conversion.

We might begin with the sermon George Fox preached at Ulverston in the Furness district of Lancashire, England, in 1652. His text, from Romans, puts the nature of conversion like this: "A man is not a Jew if he is only one outwardly, nor is circumcision merely outward and physical. No, a man is a Jew if he is one inwardly; and circumcision is circumcision of the heart, by the Spirit, not by the written code."[40] There are echoes here of the passage in Ezekiel where God promises his people, "I will give you a new heart and put a new spirit in you; I will remove from you your heart of stone and give you a heart of flesh."[41] In both cases the writers use the imagery of radical transformation.

The sermon ends with a number of pointed questions, ultimately deriving from these texts. Fox concludes (at any rate according to the account given by Margaret Fell) by saying that an ability to quote scripture, even the words of Christ himself, is an outward thing and of no avail unless we know Christ in the heart. "Then what had any to do with the Scriptures, but as they came to the Spirit that gave them forth. You will say, Christ saith this, and the apostles say this; but what canst thou say? Art thou a child of Light and hast walked in the Light, and what thou speakest is it inwardly from God?"[42] His purpose is plain. The Church must maintain without compromise the standards of Paul and Ezekiel, who say conversion must be a complete and radical change. Nothing else will do.

Seeds of Change

So how do we know there has been a complete and radical change? The difficulty the early Friends had with imputed righteousness was that they believed it encouraged a lower standard of faith and conduct than they knew was possible and that they believed was the will of God as evidenced in scripture. William Penn asks with heavy irony, "If a man ask them, Is Christ your Lord? They will cry, God forbid else; yes He is our Lord. Very well; but do you keep his commandments? No, how should we? How then are you his disciples? It is impossible, say they. What! Would you have us keep his commandments? No man can. What! Impossible to do that without which Christ hath made it impossible to be a Christian? Is Christ unreasonable? Does He reap where He has not sown? Require where He has not enabled?"[43]

We must be clear that Penn is not arguing in favor of works righteousness. His sarcasm is directed not against genuine conversions but against the purported conversion that goes no further than comfort or emotional satisfaction, the kind of conversion that will weep over the sufferings of Christ but does not recognize that its own sins are the cause of that suffering. A genuine conversion can be compared to a seed at the very moment of its germination. It has not sprouted, much less borne fruit, but neither growth nor fruit will come unless the germination happens first. A genuine conversion enables spiritual and moral change, where a false one does not. The habits of the old life cannot be carried into the new.

> *A genuine conversion can be compared to a seed at the very moment of its germination. It has not sprouted, much less borne fruit, but neither growth nor fruit will come unless the germination happens first.*

True Conversion

In the gospels, Jesus' teaching about the new life emerges from his encounter with those who resist the consequences of what he has to say. The parables are a complex series of challenges. In them Jesus shows us the contrast between the life of the world and life in the kingdom and invites us to make a choice. The parables of the talents, the sower, the unmerciful servant, and the sheep and the goats show us what happens to the unrepentant.[44] The life of the early Christian communities also presupposes moral transformation. Timothy is advised, "Command them to do good, to be rich in good deeds and generous and willing to share." Hebrews invites us to consider "how we may spur one another on toward love and good deeds." Paul writes, "Do not be overcome by evil, but overcome evil with good." Plainly goodness is the will of God for us.[45]

So how do we become good? Conversion is certainly the beginning of the process, and its conclusion is a state of blessedness in the world beyond this. But neither the Church nor individual Christians are thereby absolved from moral endeavor in the here and now. Nobody can read the Sermon on the Mount without getting a lively impression of how Jesus intended his followers to live. The problem, as William Penn and the early Friends discovered, is that so many people make excuses for not adopting it and unscrupulous preachers provide justifications for infidelity. This is not what the doctrine of imputed righteousness is intended to do, but that is the effect it has.

Conversion, therefore, is not self-explanatory, and churches need to have a clear sense of how a genuine conversion can be discerned. In preaching the gospel it is necessary to make people aware of the consequences that come with following Jesus. Churches have to consider discipline and discipleship and have to know what sort of changes they are entitled to look for in the life of a convert. They must be able, as we have already suggested, to distinguish spurious conversions from real ones. The old concepts associated with convincement, the periods of travail and the rest, may no longer give us an adequate or acceptable account of conversion as they stand. But in them we can find four criteria that can give us very clear answers to these unavoidable questions.

The first criterion is that conversion must be an inward experience. We are linked to the world around us in all sorts of ways, through intellect, emotions, memory, desires, and preferences. Our unredeemed nature distorts these things and devotes them to purposes other than what God intends. So a conversion that is dependent on them is likely still to be tainted by sin. At the same time, the world itself is less than pure. The framework of understanding that we have acquired through our socialization, education, and general conditioning does not always present us with the whole truth or the reality of our situation. Thus, a conversion sought and procured by worldly means is a risky one. Christian history shows that in the long run Satan has used this reality as a means to subvert the Church. The early Friends were quite clear they were involved in a battle against him on precisely this issue.

Unless there is a source of religious authority that is pure, it is hard to see a way out of this impasse. But if conversion is a gift of grace alone, it will occur under the guidance of the pure principle by which alone the true and the false may be distinguished. If we rely on our unaided faculties we shall go wrong, but if we rely on grace, our understanding will be true and our conversion genuine. The precondition is that we seek grace first. Grace, since it has been constantly at work to bring us to the point of decision, will operate within us and enable us to discern the ways it has also been at work outside us. We must make this the first of our conditions for conversion. A true conversion, like convincement, is inward. This has an important corollary, that the task of preaching should direct the soul to this inward reality.

There are, however, different kinds of inward spiritual experience. Convincement was one specific kind reported by a number of people, each of whom came to it in their own way. All agree that it was primarily the direct appearance of God in the soul. Some came to it through preaching, others directly at the end of a failed religious search without, apparently, any human intermediary. We cannot say whether they thought God had always been present, but unrecognized, though there are reasons for guessing that this is what they would have said. Anyway, the intense personal experience is undeniable. God was present to them in their consciences, and they use the scriptural metaphor of seeing the light to explain it. It is hard to see what faculty brings us to conversion if it is not our conscience.

The second criterion requires that conversion must originate in the conscience, not the intellect. One glance at the story of the fall will show that at the instant that the apple was eaten, Adam and Eve were cursed with the pangs of conscience.[46] Our fallen condition is not so much that we possess moral responsibility as that we are no better equipped to exercise it properly than they were. The Second Adam visited us to free us from this condition. It is hard to see then where else we should look for the signs of moral and spiritual regeneration than in the faculty of conscience.

Repentance is one of the essentials of conversion, and it is in the conscience that we repent. But the conscience is a human faculty, conditioned by experience of a fallen world. The convincement experience has an important twist in it. It is not our conscience, which brings repentance, but God working on us *through* our conscience. A true conversion may be an emotional thing, but emotion is not of its essence. Convincement insists that the grace that saves us enters us through our understanding of right and wrong.

The early Friends described in their own experience what it is to take repentance seriously. One receives a sense not only of the wrongs that one has committed (sometimes quite an extensive list), but also the reasons why one has done these things contrary to God's will. That is the source of the deep sense of being under a terrifying judgment that we read in these accounts. In the seventeenth century, "convincement" meant the same as being convicted, nowadays, that is to say, being found guilty of a serious crime. We have to reach this point in the more familiar sequence of conversion also. So what is the appropriate and required response? Repentance, confession, and an appeal for God's mercy without reservation of any kind. But can we do that? The convincement sequence asks us whether we have held anything back and says that, if we have, it cannot be conversion.[47]

The third criterion requires that conversion be understood as the work of God. The second period of trouble was not one in which action, even spiritual action, was called for. Instead, it marked a phase in which early Friends learned to rely solely on the will and guidance of God and to resist any temptation to move away from it. This was a very difficult undertaking, as we have seen, because it was accomplished by contemplating the roots of our conduct and not the conduct itself. The process was described in various ways, but the upshot is the same. One stayed still. This is probably the genesis of silent worship and the culture of silence among Friends. The silence is sacramental. It represents the presence of God and our submission to him. For grace to enter and transform the individual, acceptance and submission must become realities. In traditional terms, one must have turned to the light. That is what conversion, properly speaking, requires.

The fourth criterion is that conversion is inevitably accompanied by an experience of the inward cross. When Jesus was in the Garden of Gethsemane he prayed, "Father, if it be your will, let this cup pass from me, but nevertheless, not what I will but what you will." His prayer indicates his clear understanding of what was about to happen. Less than twenty-four hours later he was carrying his cross. The inward cross, of which we have heard, is an emblem of resolution and faith, signifying the willingness of the believer not just to rely on the salvation brought by the Christ's cross, but to offer a sacrifice of his or her own life in return. It is certainly a blessed day when Jesus washes our sins away, but the occasion is a beginning and not an end. We need to be prepared for what is to come.

> *The inward cross…is an emblem of resolution and faith, signifying the willingness of the believer not just to rely on the salvation brought by the Christ's cross, but to offer a sacrifice of his or her own life in return.*

Though the carrying of the inward cross is traditionally described as something that happens over a period, the significance of the requirement does not depend on time. We cannot in fact know whether we will be able to bear the cross until we are put to the test.

An act of faith, whereby we undertake the task, is an essential of Christian discipleship. It is clear that to be converted in the conventional sense is to make that commitment. The traditional Quaker scheme probably takes us beyond that point into the process of sanctification. Nevertheless, the question it poses to our understanding of conversion needs to be faced. What sort of conversion fails to produce this experience? Not one that understands the true nature of the cross it has espoused.

It was because of considerations like this that early Friends were reluctant to use the word conversion in the conventional sense and preferred to apply it to the period of self-examination and amendment of life that followed a positive response to the convincement experience itself. In some ways it would appear that they believed salvation to be the culmination of the process rather than the positional change that came with conversion. We might say that they required that the potential released by the new birth be realized before one could claim salvation in the fullest sense.

We do not have to accept every detail of their doctrine to profit from it, however. I have tried to show that Friends tradition possesses a distinctive doctrine of Christian initiation, which is in many ways similar to the generally accepted understanding of conversion but goes beyond it in some respects. It emphasizes the processes of inward commitment and transformation rather than the external stimuli on which attention is usually concentrated and allows a period during which the reality of a possible conversion can be verified. I have sought to show that this process, while tangential to our present understanding, nevertheless conforms to evangelical principles. It is rooted in scripture and proven by human experience, and it upholds Christ and bases discipleship firmly on the reality of his cross.

We can take pride from the fact that the extension of Christianity throughout the modern world has come primarily from its evangelical churches because they offer a gospel of repentance and hope based upon conscience. To seek conversions, to bring new life to the lost is the greatest of vocations. Writing out of the experience of convincement and his understanding of the early Friends, William Penn wrote, "They were changed men themselves before they went about to change others. Their hearts were rent as well as their garments, and they knew the work and power of God upon them…The bent and stress of their ministry was conversion to God, regeneration and holiness."[48] These words are both evangelical and Quaker and represent both traditions at their best. We will now see where they might lead.

NOTES

[1] Matt. 13:45-6.
[2] Rom. 3:23, 6:23; Luke 13:3, John 3:16, Acts 3:19, 16:31.
[3] Rom. 1:18-25.
[4] Luke 17:10.
[5] Eph. 2:8-9.
[6] Mark 9:47-8, Matt. 25:41-5, Luke 16:19-31, John 3:16-18, Rom. 6:23, 1 John 5:11.
[7] John 3:4-5, Mark 1:15.
[8] Luke 15:11-24.
[9] Eph. 2:8, Jas. 2:20.
[10] John 14:15.
[11] Matt. 11:27.
[12] John 17:3.
[13] Robert Barclay, *Apology for the True Christian Divinity,* (1676), (York England: William Sessions Ltd.), Proposition I.
[14] 1 Cor. 2:1-4.
[15] Rom. 14:1.
[16] 1 Cor. 15:22, Eph. 2:4-5, Rom. 6:23.
[17] Barclay, *Apology*, Propositions V-VII.
[18] *The Writings of James Arminius,* Vol. 1, trans. James Nichols and W.R. Bagnall (Ada, MI: Baker Books, 1977), p. 247.
[19] John Wesley, *Works,* ed. A.C. Outler (Nashville: Abingdon Press, 1984), Vol. 3, p.154.
[20] Charles Grandison Finney (1792-1875). Leading American evangelist in the first half of the nineteenth century. Longtime professor at Oberlin College.
[21] Charles Finney, *Lectures on Systematic Theology,* (London: William Tegg, 1851), p. 407.
[22] Rom. 8:29-39, Eph.1:5, 11.
[23] The idea that one could apply some sort of stage theory to the convincement experience came to me when reading Francis Howgill's account years ago. I then came across it clearly articulated in William F. Medlin's extremely helpful book, *Born Again Quakers* (Hutsonville, IL: Quaker House, 1988), where it is attributed to T. Canby Jones. I have used some different references, but the idea seems to work in almost every case. However, it would be a mistake to think that we are dealing with a standardized set of experiences here, and what follows should read with some degree of freedom.
[24] George Fox, *Journal,* John L. Nickalls, ed. (Philadelphia, Pa.: Philadelphia Yearly Meeting, 1985), p.9.

25   Mary Penington (1616-82) *Some Account of Circumstances in the Life of...* (1821); see Garman, Applegate, Benefiel, Meredith, *Hidden in Plain Sight*, (Wallingford, Pa.: Pendle Hill Publications, 1996), p.218.

26   Charles Marshall, (1637-98) *Sion's Travellers Comforted & the disobedient warned* (London: T. Sowley, 1674), p. 3.

27   John Crook, (1617?-99) *A Short History of the Life of John Crook* (London: 1685), p. vi.

28   Francis Howgill, (1618-68) *The Inheritance of Jacob*, See Hugh Barbour and Arthur Roberts, *Early Quaker Writings, 1650-1700*, (Grand Rapids, MI: William B. Eerdmans, 1973), p. 171.

29   William Dewsbury, (1621-88) *The First Birth*, (1655). In *Works* (London: T. Sowle, 1689), p.50.

30   Joan Vokins, *God's Mighty Power Magnified*, (1691), in Garman, etc., p. 256.

31   Crook, p. xviii.

32   2 Thess. 2:10, 12.

33   Rom. 7:24.

34   Crook, p. xx.

35   Barbour and Roberts, p. 174.

36   George Fox, *Journal*, p. 27.

37   Crook, p. xxiv.

38   Dewsbury, ibid., p.53.

39   See Arthur O. Roberts, *Concepts of Perfection in the History of the Quaker Movement*, Nazarene Theological Seminary, M.A.Thesis, 1951.

40   Rom. 2:28.

41   Ezek. 36:26.

42   Britain Yearly Meeting, *Quaker Faith and Practice*, Extract 19.07.

43   William Penn *No Cross, No Crown*, (1682), *Select Works*, (London: Phillips, 1825), p.338.

44   Matt. 25:14, Mark 4:3, Luke 16:1, Matt. 25:31.

45   1 Tim. 2:3, Heb. 9:15, Rom. 10:8.

46   Gen. 3:7.

47   Acts 5:1-11.

48   William Penn, *The Rise and Progress of the People called Quakers*, (1694) ed. Bronner (York, England: William Sessions Ltd., 1993), p. 290.

3

The Light of the World

3

The Light of the World

W e revere the memory of the apostles because they are so like us. They came from all sorts of backgrounds, but they found their way to Jesus. They had a struggle to come to terms with the new way of life they had been called to, and if the record is true, they often misunderstood it or wished it were different from what it was. They deserted Jesus in the Garden of Gethsemane, and only one of them had the courage to stand by him at the crucifixion. Nevertheless, they were witnesses of the resurrection, and they were entrusted with the task of proclaiming the gospel to the world. In one sense it was easy for them. They knew Jesus in a way that we never can.

We know how some of them came to him, but not all. We hear about the fishermen and the tax collector, but not about the doubter, the zealot, or the betrayer. However, with the exception of Judas, we know that they were all present at the Ascension. This event marks a significant turning point in the history of Christianity. From then on, the number of people who knew Jesus in the flesh began an inexorable decline, and many who had not known its founder joined the Christian fellowship. Was the preaching of the apostles to be based only on memory, or was there some way in which those who did not know Christ in the flesh could nevertheless know him in the spirit?

The answer must be, both. Human relationships are sustained most strongly by shared experiences remembered in tranquility. That is the basis of friendship and family life. We are related to one another over the years by the things that have happened in them. We also bring a living sense of personal history to our memories of the dead.

So it is with the faith. Our collective memory of Jesus is sustained in various ways. We read the Bible, go to church, celebrate Christmas and Easter, and draw much of our identity from Christian history. Week by week, we experience the constant re-enactment of the gospel story in sermons, Sunday school activities, private prayer, and meditation. There are great traditions of Christian art and music for us to enjoy. These things have no other source than the memory of Jesus' life on earth and his departure from it.

But scripture also describes how it comes about that we can have a present and direct knowledge of him that is independent of our memory and imagination. Jesus gave fairly precise promises during his earthly life that need serious consideration. In terms of ordinary Christian experience we know the reality of the words, "For where two or three come together in my name, there am I with them," and, "… surely I am with you always, to the very end of the age."[1] These are certainly words of comfort, but can we interpret them as solemn promises? Is it possible for Christ to be with us though he is not here? What kind of God is it who is present to human beings but cannot be detected by their senses?

To answer these questions, we shall have to look in two directions: to the lessons of history and our present experience of God. I shall try to show that although memory and faith may be separate paths to one reality, they are both inspired by the Holy Spirit. In Friends understanding, the particular means the Holy Spirit uses is to endow every human being that comes into the world with a measure of spiritual light, by which they may *see*; that is, understand

and comprehend their own spiritual condition, recognize their need for salvation, turn to God in repentance, and thereafter lead godly lives. As Paul writes in one place, "I pray also that the eyes of your heart may be enlightened in order that you may know the hope to which he has called you, the riches of his glorious inheritance in the saints..." and in another, "For God, who said, 'Let light shine out of darkness,' made his light shine in our hearts to give us the light of the knowledge of the glory of God in the face of Christ."[2]

Understanding the Light

I shall begin examination of the doctrine of the light by examining its source, the promises Jesus made to his disciples at the last supper: that although he had to leave them, he would also return to be with them in spirit. I shall claim that this is possible because there is a harmony between the physical world and the realm of the spirit, and, therefore, between what God tells us in the intimacy of prayer or Bible study and what we learn in reasoned reflection about our experience of the world. The light within is our most reliable guide to the real nature of the created order. Christ the Word was instrumental in the creation, and Christ the Comforter dwells in the hearts of all those who invite him to come in—the two are one. My purpose is to establish that the doctrine of the light is not a Quaker peculiarity of any general application but to assert boldly that the light within is a reality. It is one of the modes of the Holy Spirit's activity and is therefore consistent, rational, universal, and capable of scriptural proof.

> *The light within is our most reliable guide to the*
> *real nature of the created order. Christ the Word*
> *was instrumental in the creation, and Christ the*
> *Comforter dwells in the hearts of all those who*
> *invite him to come in—the two are one.*

From this standpoint we shall see how early Friends saw the light as the very means of salvation. In their arguments with the Puritans over predestination, they upheld the claim that God desired all to be saved and had provided a sufficient means for all to come into that condition. They certainly did not believe that any who rejected Christ could be saved, but the doctrine of the light enabled them to show how those who had not and *could* not have received an outward offer of salvation might nevertheless be redeemed through the presence of Christ in the heart. For the doctrine of the light to bear this weight, I have to show that it is rooted in scripture. I will do so by examining what the New Testament has to say about Christ as the light and Christ as the word of truth. Finally, we need to recognize that we are on unfamiliar ground and examine what can be said about some of the questions the doctrine inevitably raises.

The Counselor

In the account of the Last Supper given in John's Gospel, there is no mention of bread, wine, or the foundation of the new covenant. Instead, we have a series of discourses in which Jesus describes what will happen when he has returned to the Father. He stresses the inevitability of his departure, but also that his disciples will not be left alone. In some mysterious way, he promises to come back to them. During the course of his teaching he makes reference to an elusive figure that he calls the Paraclete.[3] In Greek, this word stands for a companion, who comforts and consoles us, and stands by us as a representative or advocate when our integrity is questioned, as when we stand trial in a court of law. A good, but not complete modern translation would be "Counselor."

The Counselor is a spiritual figure with whom the disciples are to have an intimate, personal relationship. As in other parts of John's writings, we move quickly from the familiar to the mysterious, and hidden implications are drawn out of ordinary words in surprising ways. Jesus assures the disciples that they know the Counselor because he is with them already, but at the same time says that the Counselor will come to them only after he has gone. This contradiction is apparent rather than real, because there is only one Counselor. At the supper, Jesus is present in the flesh. With the passage of time, he will be present in spirit. The Counselor is the mode of his continuing presence.

The Work of the Counselor

Jesus describes the work of the Counselor in some detail, and three of the activities mentioned in connection with him bear close examination. The first is that the whole focus of his work is to bring to fulfillment the purposes of the Incarnation. He will therefore testify to Jesus. The second is to teach us "all things," by which we might suppose the fullness of spiritual truth. The third activity, which presupposes the disciples' acquaintance with the scriptures of the Old Testament, is to remind them, and thereby us, of everything Jesus said to them during his time on earth.[4] It is important to note that the reference in these promises is to Jesus' public ministry, and they should not be spiritualized in such a way that they lose that connection.

The language in these passages is somewhat opaque, because Jesus uses a number of different terms in combination with one another to build up the full implications of his continuing spiritual presence in the world. He speaks successively of the Holy Spirit, the Spirit, the Spirit of Truth, the Counselor, the Father, and himself, and we find ourselves asking how these terms are related to one another. However, there is order underlying this apparently confusing terminology. If we begin with the conception of truth, we find that the role of the Counselor is to teach or witness to the truth and is called the Spirit of Truth. Jesus has already called himself the truth and said that he is one with the Father, so these terms can be taken to refer to one reality, so that to speak of one is automatically to refer to the other.[5]

The Universal Spirit

There is yet another equivalence that we should note. Apart from the occasional liturgical reference, we seldom hear the words Comforter, Counselor, and Spirit of Truth because they are generally subsumed under a third, all-embracing term, "Holy Spirit."[6] These two words enable us to express a full sense of mystery in speaking of God. But at the same time, their imprecision allows some to give them a meaning that goes beyond the teaching of the farewell discourses. It is necessary to remember at this point that in scripture there is a condition precedent to the presence of the Counselor in the believer—that the one in whom he dwells should both love Christ and obey his commands.[7] The presence of the Holy Spirit, therefore, does not seem to be universal. It is confined to those who have crossed over the threshold of conversion.

There is a puzzle here, because elsewhere in scripture the Spirit is seen to have a wide-ranging sphere of operation covering all kinds of circumstances, two of which call for special comment. First, the Spirit of God was instrumental in the creation, hovering over the waters and speaking the word by which the world came into being. Second, the Spirit of God is present in every part of the created order. The Psalmist laments, "Where can I go from your Spirit? Where can I flee from your presence? If I go up to the heavens, you are there; if I make my bed in the depths, you are there. If I rise on the wings of the dawn, if I settle on the far side of the sea, even there your hand will guide me, your right hand will hold me fast... How precious to me are your thoughts, O God! How vast is the sum of them! Were I to count them, they would outnumber the grains of sand. When I awake, I am still with you."[8] Quite obviously there was a sense in which the Spirit was granted before the coming of Christ, and the Nicene Creed says so without equivocation.

The fact is only hard to grasp if we forget the cumulative nature of revelation. It would be stretching reason beyond the breaking point to argue that the Spirit of God and the Holy Spirit is not one and the same thing. The words of Jesus, as they stand, are quite compatible with the claim that the Holy Spirit has been active in the world since the very beginning. There is a progressive revelation in scripture in the sense that later events reveal the full meaning and implications of what has gone before. Hence, our understanding of the Holy Spirit as redeemer could not be articulated until the passion of Jesus Christ. This conclusion does not gainsay the antecedent work of the Spirit in the world, but simply points to the purpose of that activity.

There is a progressive revelation in scripture in the sense that later events reveal the full meaning and implications of what has gone before. Hence, our understanding of the Holy Spirit as redeemer could not be articulated until the passion of Jesus Christ.

Christ and Creation

The redemptive work of the Spirit can be seen as a natural consequence of creation. Creation presupposes intention, as scripture indicates by using such terms as "plan," or "decree," for the designs of God. Events, including the emergence of the Church, develop in accordance with God's design. "For he chose us in him before the creation of the world to be holy and blameless in his sight. In love he predestined us to be adopted as his sons through Jesus Christ, in accordance with his pleasure and will..."[9] There is a clear indication here that God intended to give a certain character to the creation before it came into being, and designed it to develop in a certain way.

That design is described in the Prologue to John's gospel, which teaches that Christ both has a part in, and lends his character to, the creation.[10] It is essential, therefore, to read this passage in conjunction with the farewell discourses. The term "word," or "logos," provides the link between the creation and the incarnation. With reference to the creation, it signifies the character, the ground plan—the program, so to speak—on which the universe took form. With reference to the Incarnation, it indicates the ultimate significance of Christ as the self-expression of God. So, if the universe had a distinct point of origin, what has developed is part of the self-expression of Christ. What we know of Christ will be borne out in our experience of the created world, because it bears the imprint of his character and we can therefore move easily between concepts of Spirit, Paraclete and Christ with ease and without error.

The Character of Grace

Now if all created things display the character of Christ, they will display his love, which comes to us in as many different ways as the Spirit can gain entrance to our lives. Perhaps the most appealing form of Christ's love is what the New Testament calls grace, a reality hard to define in abstract but unmistakable in experience. Grace signifies the special character of the divine love we receive in great abundance though we do not merit and cannot earn it. This love is spontaneous and there are no preconditions that we have to meet before we can receive it. Grace is characterized by the simultaneous presence of mercy, forgiveness, blessing, and joy. Grace is what defines the character of the Counselor.

> *Grace is characterized by the simultaneous presence of mercy, forgiveness, blessing, and joy. Grace is what defines the character of the Counselor.*

Because of the need to talk about grace, there is a temptation to speak of it in the abstract, as if in some sense it could be separated from its source, the Holy Spirit, or that the work of the Spirit could be severed in some sense from that of the Father and the Son. This temptation must be resisted. God is one, and the character of God is likewise one. We must therefore understand grace as representing the fundamental character of God and the expression of that character in his relationship with us. But this relationship is not form-less. The Comforter comes to us so that we can be channels of grace, not just recipients of it. That requires a change in our nature.

The Transforming Nature of Grace

By what means, then, does the grace of God change our nature and make us suitable ambassadors for Christ? Friends have always answered this question by speaking of the light of Christ within. William Penn suggests that this transformation can come about because God has placed what he calls "a principle" in the human heart. Elaborating on what he means by this word, Penn uses a number of phrases, including: the manifestation or appearance of Christ, the witness, or seed of God, the seed of the kingdom, wisdom, the word in the heart, truth in the inward parts, the spiritual leaven, the spirit given to man to profit withal. He says that these are figurative but scriptural expressions, though Friends prefer "the light of Christ within man, or light within, which is their ancient, and most general and familiar phrase...."[11]

It is strange that Penn should use the word "principle" in this connection, because the term marks a lapse from early Friends objections to theological terminology not derived from scripture.[12] One could scarcely imagine a more abstract term than "principle," so we should approach Penn's explanation of the light within with some caution. He speaks of a principle of light, life, and grace and says that it is *one with the Holy Spirit*. He seems to envision a functional distinction between these three things and concentrates on light because light is the means of perception, understanding, and choice. "For they (Friends) say it is the great agent in religion; that, without which, there is no conviction, so no conversion, or regeneration;

and consequently no entering into the kingdom of God. That is to say, there can be no true sight of sin, nor sorrow for it, and therefore no forsaking or overcoming it, or remission or justification from it."[13]

It is not necessary to follow Penn's analysis in every detail to substantiate the claim that the light is a spiritual and theological reality. Penn distinguishes the functions of grace, light, and life while simultaneously asserting their common origin. Nowadays, we would probably not want to make such a hard-and-fast distinction, and, indeed, it has been argued above that grace has logical and theological priority. Nevertheless, the prologue to John's gospel has to be the foundation of any Christian metaphysics, and on this basis, it is very hard indeed to rebut Penn's claims about the light. He claims that one of the Spirit's fundamental properties has to do with understanding and moral choice and that scripture uses the concept of light to convey that truth.

The answer to the question about how we are to become transformed so that we can become channels of grace is precisely this: The light shows us how and then gives us the capacity. Light is, therefore, not a metaphor. It is the means of salvation and the spiritual reality by which God intends us to live.

The Reality of the Light

The light, then, is a reality and not a figure of speech. Scripture gives some clear guidance as to the nature and functions of the light, and we must now begin to generalize about them and set them in some sort of order. Perhaps the most important feature of the light is that it is of the essence of God. When we speak of God's house or God's servants, we are talking about external possessions by analogy. When we speak of the glory or wrath of God, we are describing divine attributes that are not always expressed. But when we talk about the love, peace, and grace of God, we are referring to the qualities of the divine character. The light is of a piece with these qualities. If it were no more than a term of convenience, it would be no foundation for a specifically Quaker theology. In fact, it is the means of salvation.

Any discourse about the light, therefore, will have all sorts of implications that derive from its nature. The universe in which we live is more than titanic forces and infinitesimal particles; it is the place where life has been bought forth and where spirit is present. Two sentences stand next to one another in scripture to tell us this: "Through him all things were made; without him nothing was made that has been made. In him was life, and that life was the light of men."[14] The doctrine of the Light within, therefore, unites the creative and the saving work of Christ. Very often, creation and redemption are treated separately, but the full significance of each only emerges in combination with the other. If we keep this dual perspective, we can enhance our understanding of the processes of salvation. Let us consider two examples.

The Role of the Light in Conversion

First, the mechanism of conversion. Earlier, we noticed that Protestants do not have a common view on this, so there is no reason in principle why a Quaker position should be regarded as any less acceptable than anybody else's. In that discussion, I drew a distinction between the conversion of a soul and that soul's comprehension of what has happened to it and gave reasons for the distinction. I did this to emphasize that there are claims to conversion that can be seen to be false and other instances where people who are obviously saved are reluctant to make that claim. Neither case fits the usual scheme, because the usual scheme is based on a strict temporal sequence and assumes that claims to conversion are self-evidently true.

Second, we turn to those who have never received an effective offer of salvation. There is certainly no other name by which we are to be saved, but Christians differ about whether those who have never heard the gospel because they lived in the remote past, have never been reached by missions, or whose understanding has been clouded by false gospels will be denied the opportunity to be saved. If salvation is dependent on the written word alone, it is hard to see how they can be. It is also hard to see how such a judgment would reflect the character of a loving God. If we endorse the view of Joseph John Gurney, that "all men are placed, through the redemption which is in Christ, in a real capacity for salvation," we face the problem of explaining how, in the absence of the word, an effective offer of salvation *can* be made.

The doctrine of the light provides an economical answer to these problems, provided it is correctly formulated. It is necessary to begin with the three elements that have to be satisfied for a person to be justified: a sense of sin, an act of repentance, and an appeal to God for forgiveness in reliance upon Christ. These are primarily matters of personal morality, and that is why the point was made earlier that the early Friends believed conversion to be a matter of conscience rather than the intellect. Because a sense of moral failure is not a Christian peculiarity, we are entitled to regard it as a general feature of human experience and part of that preparation for the gospel we have already mentioned. The first function of the light is to give us a sense of sin prior to any understanding of where that conviction might lead. No conversion that omits this stage is genuine.

The Universality of the Light

Those who repent of their transgressions (in contrast to those who experience only regret or remorse) have begun the process of moral regeneration or turning to the light, as Friends usually call it. This is not merely a moral change in response to the demands of our conscience, but a change in our self-awareness. That is why the imagery of light is so crucial. Early Friends knew that in different cultures the conscience spoke in different voices and that universal moral principles would need to transcend these limitations, as would our ability to apprehend them. The element of universality is essential. We all have the light in our conscience, and we also have some conception of the universal moral rules. The second function of the light is to inspire us to act on the former and obey the latter.

> *Those who repent of their transgressions (in contrast to those who experience only regret or remorse) have begun the process of moral regeneration or turning to the light, as Friends usually call it. This is not merely a moral change in response to the demands of our conscience, but a change in our self-awareness.*

Unless the light were universal in both senses, it would not be able to accomplish the redemption of those who turn to it. This is why we have been at pains to argue that *through* the Holy Spirit the world bears the character of Christ and that *by* the Holy Spirit also the capacity to respond to Christ, subject to grace, has been placed in the heart. These two things are systematically related. This means that Friends reject the conception of the universe as neutral or hostile to human concerns. They also believe that it makes no sense to claim that Christ died for all unless an effective offer of salvation has been made to all. We shall add concepts of sin and judgment to this picture at a later stage, but for now we simply need to register our rejection of a dualistic view of the universe and a predestinarian view of redemption.

So let us return to the situation of those who, for whatever reason, have never received an effective offer of salvation. This is the condition of those who lived in Patagonia or Outer Mongolia at the time of Moses, those parts of the world today where the light of the gospel has never shone, and those enmeshed in all sorts of quasi-Christian cults. It is quite contrary to our idea of a just and merciful God to think that the possibility of salvation will be withheld from them. But on the other hand, the third of our conditions for justification requires a conscious, or explicit acknowledgment of, or decision for, Jesus Christ in the way evangelicals are familiar with. So how can this dilemma be resolved?

Salvation by the Light

The first part of an answer follows from what has been said so far. To see the light solely as an individual entity, a spark of the divine, as mystics say, is a fundamental mistake. There is one light, and it is Christ. Therefore, there is more to the doctrine than making individual choices under the guidance of God, through impulse, taste, psychological need, intellectual conviction, spiritual leading, or discernment. All those things are relevant to conversion, but it is the light that makes them operative. We also need to remember that the capacity to choose is not all there is to it. The doctrine of creation sketched here provides that the range of choices we have open to us is fixed by God's command as part of the act of creation itself. They are fixed by divine decree.

The second part of the answer returns us to what has been said about the nature of conversion itself. The offer of salvation is accepted by our willingness not just to repent, but to turn to God who judges not just ourselves, but also the presuppositions we habitually make about the world. The key to the process is faith. Because faith emerges from moral awareness and issues in a reformed life, what is known as turning to the light is properly seen as the act of faith by which we are justified. This is exactly what Jesus called for in his hearers. It also provides a way of reconciling the two assertions of scripture that give some people difficulty, but that have never bothered Friends: that we are saved by grace though faith and not because of our own good works, and that unless our faith is accompanied by good works, it is dead. On this analysis, it is possible to lead a Christian life, even if one has not heard of Christ.

This is an awkward conclusion, and though it may be inevitable, granted the premises of the argument, it must be carefully circumscribed. It means that those souls who have been brought to repentance and reliance on what they know of God within will be saved. To be sure, all who sin apart from the law will perish apart from the law, but it is also written, "Indeed, when Gentiles, who do not have the law, do by nature things required by the law, they are a law for themselves, even though they do not have the law, since they show that the requirements of the law are written on their hearts, their consciences also bearing witness, and their thoughts now accusing, now even defending them. This will take place on the day when God will judge men's secrets through Jesus Christ, as my gospel declares."[15]

It is crucial to distinguish the process we are discussing and the individuals involved in it from those to whom the gospel is accessible but who resist its call. This is a very different matter. In modern western countries, there are many who profess sympathy with Christian values but who refuse to commit themselves to Christ for a variety of reasons. People claim that the history of Christianity stands in their way and prefer to see the negative side of that history to all the good the Church has accomplished down the centuries. They dislike what they see as doctrinal rigidity, moral judgmentalism, and a lack of respect for the convictions of others. But what they really object to are the doctrines and the morals themselves, upright souls though they may be. This is not the operation of the light within.

The Light in Convincement

We can now see how fundamental the difference is between conversion in the usual sense and what Friends call conversion. If justification requires, as it does, an acknowledgment of the cross of Christ, what actions on our part will meet that requirement? A profession of faith is required, but that of itself amounts to nothing.[16] It has to be heartfelt. The importance of the convincement type of conversion is that it inevitably carries the requirement that repentance is carried through to the taking up of one's daily cross and an experience of what that involves. Those led by the light to this decision have testified by their actions to the truth as it is in Jesus, though they cannot put a name to the power in which they act.[17]

The consequences Quakerism has drawn from this analysis are

as follows. We shall see that there is a Quaker critique of Christian history that says that it is possible to think of oneself as a Christian and to be considered as such by others and yet to be very far from the kingdom of God. The critique argues that when the gospel is used to require conformity to creeds and doctrines, intellectual conviction will replace faith and persecution will follow, because this is the means Satan uses to subvert the Church. Consequently, only the light can show us the difference between true and false Christianity. It follows from this that there are those who appear to be Christians and in fact are not, and there are those who do not appear to be Christians, having never heard of Christ, who in fact are. The difference between the two groups is the encounter with the light—true conversion.

Christ the Light

The New Testament texts teach quite clearly that the light is the agent of salvation. There is a sense in which light can be used as the opposite of ignorance and superstition, but in scripture it always indicates the power by which alone evil can be defeated. As William Penn pointed out, Christ came to save us from our sins, and it is the light that shows us what our sins are.[18] Both Paul and John use light language in this sense and say almost the same thing. Paul writes, "The god of this age has blinded the minds of unbelievers, so that they cannot see the light of the gospel of the glory of Christ, who is the image of God." In the words of John, "Everyone who does evil hates the light, and will not come into the light for fear that his deeds will be exposed. But whoever lives by the truth comes into the light, so that it may be seen plainly that what he has done has been done through God."[19]

There is a dualism here, as there must be, between God and all that resists his will. This is why those people who profess sympathy with what they see as the values of Christianity but are unwilling to accept its disciplines are mistaken. Perhaps the most dramatic example of the power of the light is in Paul's account of his conversion as given to Agrippa. He describes his experience of a light from heaven greater than the sun, from which a voice speaks identifying itself as Jesus. Finally, he receives his commission as an apostle. He is sent to open people's eyes, to turn them from darkness to light, and from the power of Satan to God. It is an almost irresistible step, though only one text uses the idea, to say that turning to the light is identical with entry into the kingdom of God.[20]

The Light Brings Us to Faith

Forgiveness, then, and justification, begins with the light, which manifests sin and gives life and understanding.[21] It would be hard to underestimate the significance of these things. To face the fact of one's sin and to repent of it is to open oneself to grace. If we then inquire what that grace produces, one of the major fruits is spiritual understanding, which of course is the basis of all other kinds of understanding too. Thus the light is instrumental in bringing us to faith and giving us the understanding to come to terms with what it entails. This was the experience of Paul. Moreover, as we have seen, it is a fundamental feature of early Friends understanding of convincement.

The light is that which we may trust,[22] and it is also a touchstone for the reality of our conversion, as we have already argued. As John points out, if we love others, we are in the light, but if we claim to be in the light and still have hatred in our hearts, then we are still in the realm of the prince of this world. Paul also sees the light as part of the spiritual struggle in which Christians are engaged, not only within themselves, but as citizens of the end time. The night is almost over, he says, so we must put aside the works of darkness and put on the armor of light.[23] It is the light that clothes us in righteousness. These scriptural passages are often used in discussions of the end times, and they are certainly relevant to what is to come. But to confine them to this is to overlook the powerful counsel they have for us about how to live here and now.

This advice is essential, for Christians are always at risk. At one point, Paul warns the Church of the dangers of involvement with the world, and by implication, its ways and standards. He instructs his hearers not to be "yoked with unbelievers." (Sectarian Quakerism with its "hedge" took this with extreme seriousness.) He then inquires rhetorically what fellowship light can have with darkness.[24] There is so much about the background to Paul's letters that we do not know. One wonders what historical reminiscence lies behind the words, "Remember those earlier days after you had received the light, when you stood your ground in a great contest in the face of suffering." [25] The obvious conclusion of this is that the light is both the instrument and occasion of spiritual struggle. It is necessarily evangelical and necessarily divisive, as Christ was in the flesh and as his word is in the contemporary world.

> *The obvious conclusion is that the light is both the instrument and occasion of spiritual struggle. It is necessarily evangelical and necessarily divisive, as Christ was in the flesh and as his word is in the contemporary world.*

The Light in Scripture

We can measure the neglect the biblical doctrine of light has received by the surprise that meets any attempt to restate it. References to light are commonplace in hymns, worship, and prayers, but one seldom encounters an explanation of the scriptural basis of these things. The word "light" is often used in connection with the experiences and reflections of mystics. That might encourage us to believe that it is too general to be given any particular significance except as a means of referring to the otherwise inexpressible. It is unnecessary to go that far, however, and it is unlikely that the early Friends did. They certainly emphasized the importance of religious experience, but they also had a clear idea of what kind of religious experience was important. It was not an experience of an undifferentiated ultimate; it was an experience of the God of the Christian scriptures.

Long before the emergence of Quakerism, the conception of light was common currency among the Orthodox, who gave prominence to the Transfiguration because it is the point at which God clearly reveals the identity of Christ to the disciples. Some have even spoken of Orthodox "light spirituality." While the word "light" appears in the Transfiguration narratives only once, it is perfectly plain that the disciples were dazzled by their experience.[26] That is not to be wondered at. Paul had the same experience. We can find a measure of what happened in First Timothy, where there is a description of God "who alone is immortal and who lives in unapproachable light, whom no one has seen or can see."[27] Sin and our natural condition render such vision an impossibility.

In view of this, we would expect to find much in scripture about the light. Paul uses the word in connection with both the Christian community and the individual Christian's destiny, urging the Ephesians to live as children of light, and in reminding the Colossians that they will share the inheritance of the saints in the kingdom of light, as we saw earlier. In John's books, references to the light are to be found in abundance. In the First Letter we read, "This is the message we have heard from him and declare to you: God is light; in him there is no darkness at all."[28] In the gospels, as we also saw, the most immediate and obvious example is Jesus' proclamation on two occasions that he is the light of the world and that his followers would not walk in darkness but have the light of life. Such exaggerated talk is absurd unless its meaning transcends the particular circumstances in which it was uttered.

The manner of this transcendence is a matter of debate, though. There are Christians, including both liberals and fundamentalists, who believe that our only link with Jesus is through the records of his life or the specially privileged access available through scripture. Both positions reflect a prior understanding of what the scripture is saying, rather than being based on the claims it makes and the kinds of experience it offers. The doctrine of the light, however (which has strong parallels with Pentecostal teaching in this particular respect), is based on the principles laid down in the farewell discourses that say we can know Christ through personal, spiritual acquaintance not dependent for its reality on those other modes of communication. This is a vital distinction, and what follows will be based upon it.

Christ the Word

What is at issue is the manner of our salvation, which goes beyond the simplistic idea that all we have to do to be saved is to accept Christ on the basis of the text, "...if you confess with your mouth, 'Jesus is Lord,' and believe in your heart that God raised him from the dead, you will be saved."[29] The context of this promise is a discussion of the outward morality of the law as opposed to the inward righteousness of faith. It is a situation exactly analogous to that of the liberals and fundamentalists referred to above. In the position of those who sought righteousness through the law, there are those who are intent on interpreting the faith through the historical-critical method or by insisting that only fidelity to the written word will bring us salvation. Paul is arguing the contrary case: that morality arises from inward experience and not in obedience to a code.

If we piece together the details of Paul's argument, we find that at the end of the preceding chapter he is making one of his characteristic paradoxes: that there are Jews who sought righteousness through the law and failed to find it; whereas there are Gentiles who ignored the written code but found it through faith. One cannot understand Christianity unless one grasps the significance of this. The Gentiles have what the Revised Standard Version translates as "righteousness based on faith." This is what enables us to escape from our bondage to the letter. The word, says Paul, is near us. It is in our mouths and in our hearts. If we are willing to confess it, we shall be saved.

So what is "the word"? In this connection it is plainly the instrument of our salvation. It would be tempting to leap to the conclusion that what is being referred to here is the scripture, but that is not the case. Words and scriptural words are extremely important, of course. Words are the vehicles by which meaning is conveyed. They are expository, interpretive, persuasive, and useful for whatever function the speaker or writer intends. But scripture itself goes beyond grammar and often gives the word "word" an extended and figurative meaning, as when it is made to stand for news, a message, or even a text. When we ask what the word is, then, we shall look in the scriptures for an answer, but the answer we receive will be one to which the scriptures point, rather than one they explicitly teach.

In the Old Testament, the prophets receive the word of God, and then articulate and proclaim what was originally a private communication. The actual words they used are immaterial, for otherwise, we should need to master ancient Hebrew before we could hear the word. Obviously we do not. What matters is that we grasp the meaning of what has been said. The point is reinforced by the parable of the sower.[30] The Word will save, but there are obstacles in its way. It has to be *allowed* to save. The parable presupposes two things: a correct understanding of the message and a proper response to it. It is noteworthy that we cannot grasp the meaning of the parable unless we already know what the word is.

> *The Word will save, but there are obstacles in its way. It has to be allowed to save.*

In the New Testament, the word that matters is the gospel because it is the instrument of our salvation. Although it is customary to call scripture the Word of God, it should not lull us into thinking that the gospel is tied solely to what is written. It is hard to see what other conclusion can be drawn from Jesus' words, "...the Father who sent me has himself testified concerning me. You have never heard his voice nor seen his form, nor does his word dwell in you, for you do not believe the one he sent."[31] This is about the word of faith in the heart, not the verbal articulation of a message. James says the same thing. "Every good and perfect gift is from above, coming down from the Father of the heavenly lights, who does not change like shifting shadows. He chose to give us birth through the word of truth, that we might be a kind of firstfruits of all he created."[32]

We might be able maintain that the references here are to the preached word were it not for the Prologue to John's Gospel. In a series of interlocking verses we read the widest and most profound statement in scripture of the nature of the Incarnation. In the very first verse, Christ is described as the Word, that by which all things came into being, the ultimate source of all meaning, and the ultimate reference of all language. Then it is asserted that in him was life—the spiritual reality we have been at pains to locate in the heart and mouth of those who confess him as Lord. He is called "the light." He enlightens all who come into the world, whether or not they realize or respond to the fact. The word in the heart and the light in the heart are the same thing.

Describing his memories of the Transfiguration, Peter pursues the theme of the presence of Christ the light. He recalls the voice of God acknowledging his beloved son, and testifies that he, James, and John heard it. He then goes on, "And we have the word of the prophets made more certain, and you will do well to pay attention to it, as to a light shining in a dark place, until the day dawns and the morning star rises in your hearts. Above all, you must understand that no prophecy of Scripture came about by the prophet's own interpretation. For prophecy never had its origin in the will of man, but men spoke from God as they were carried along by the Holy Spirit."[33]

The symbolism of this passage is complex. The day and the rising of the star are plainly part of the theme of light in the New Testament. The context indicates that they are a reference to the *parousia*, the dawning of the messianic age, the time when light triumphs over spiritual darkness.[34] "The word of the prophets made more certain" is sometimes interpreted in a mystical sense to indicate the inward presence of Christ. Although that is a powerful idea, it needs qualification. The morning star rises but, in the course of history, not the heart of the believer. But surely the farewell discourses teach us that we can anticipate that event. If Christ's promises given there are taken literally, the inward presence is a reality. Whatever else we may like to say, there can be no theoretical or practical objection to the conclusion that this passage also supports the claim that Christ enlightens us personally, individually, and directly. This is the substance of the Friends doctrine of the light of Christ within.

The Doctrine Justified

Nevertheless, the doctrine of the light has difficulties that need to be recognized and put in proper perspective. Friends are a small denomination with a particular historical origin and have not made a theological impact on the Church at large. In these circumstances, our positive doctrines have usually appeared (and it has to be said, often been presented) as reservations over particular matters in the general tradition, rather than commentary and amplification of what is already there. All doctrinal systems require glosses of various kinds, and Quakerism is no exception. So some qualification of the doctrine of the light is perfectly in order.

There is a risk, for example, of it being articulated in an overly philosophical way so that the connection between the light and Christ is weakened or severed, and it develops in a deistic or Unitarian direction. Opinion is divided among Friends about the consequences of Robert Barclay's *Apology,* but there is no doubt that in defining the light as the *vehiculum dei* he was attempting to give the doctrine expression in philosophical terms that would carry weight in seventeenth-century intellectual circles. This is, of course, entirely laudable. But thereafter, Friends who chose to articulate the doctrine in terms of the philosophy rather than the scripture from which it was derived transformed the doctrine into something it was never intended to be.

Nevertheless, to say that salvation is possible without an explicit knowledge of the nature of Christ's sacrifice and a personal acceptance of his saving grace, is *prima facie* contrary to evangelical principle, and without more being said, the possibility of there being an evangelical Quakerism collapses. However, if the doctrine of the light is limited in two directions, it is altogether more difficult to dismiss it. The first limitation is that the light must be identified with the historic and risen Christ and not be interpreted as a philosophical abstraction. The second limitation is that the atonement is a condition precedent to any saving experience of God, and the light, which is to all intents and purposes the same as grace, is the only means by which to appropriate the benefits of Christ's sacrifice. But the sacrifice comes first.

These limitations preserve the principle that there is no salvation by the light unless the light is Christ. Hence, those who experience the light while ignorant of the historical facts of the atonement are nevertheless saved, while those who claim a saving knowledge of the historical facts of the atonement while foreigners to the light, are not saved. The gospel offers salvation, but on its own terms entirely. It is hard to see how any person who has heard its claims and rejected them can be saved. It is equally hard to see how someone who has been exposed only to a spurious gospel can seriously be said to have heard the real thing. The doctrine of the light explains how God does not withhold the offer of salvation from such a person.

This doctrine does, however, seem to render unnecessary the preaching of the cross, and by extension, the significance of the crucifixion as the event that determines the destiny of every human being in the world. No evangelical can accept for a moment any interpretation of Christianity that detracts, even slightly, from the importance of Christ giving himself for us on the cross. While the doctrine of the light can be interpreted to mean this, such a conclusion is by no means compelling. Once more it has to be emphasized that what saves is a real encounter with the living Christ. If we grasp this, we can see that the light is the means of the encounter, no more, no less. It can come to us through our intellectual understanding of the gospel story, but the doctrine preserves the truth that, without inward transformation, that is insufficient.

There is no necessary conflict between asserting the universality of the light and claiming that salvation is only possible though faith in Jesus Christ. As we have seen, the light is the indwelling presence of Christ, not an impersonal power or force. The doctrine outlined here claims that his presence is in all people, but is not so naïve as to assume that all will welcome him in. It claims simply that nobody is outside Christ's personal concern or love, or in a position in which it is impossible for that person to know and act upon the moral demands Christ makes upon him or her.[35] We have not been afraid to accept that the concepts of "light" and "grace" are often indistinguishable. However, I have preserved the possibility that they are not quite identical in order to prepare the way for a later argument that the light can also be an agency of intellectual as well as moral understanding.

In due course we shall see some of the consequences of the doctrine of the light. The light is instrumental in conversion, as we have already seen, but it is also the distinguishing feature of Friends doctrine of the covenant and is the basis of the Friends understanding of morality in general and discipleship in particular. It is the Friends covenantal understanding that provides a framework for understanding the light within. Our first experience of it is necessarily personal, but we are called out of the world into the Church. Though it dropped out of use quite soon, one of the first names Friends ever took for themselves was "children of light." This, according to scripture, is what all true Christians are called upon to be.[36]

The great merit of the doctrine of the light is that it is true to the scriptures and to experience simultaneously. In this way it serves as an antidote to excessive literalism and excessive individualism together. It is characteristic, if not unique to Quakerism, but has always been represented as what the scriptures teach all Christians, not just the historically conditioned claims of a small sect. Perhaps the difference between other parts of the Society of Friends and its evangelical branch lie in the words of Joseph John Gurney, who disclaimed and affirmed his tradition at one and the same time when he wrote, "Were I required to define Quakerism, I should not describe it as the system so elaborately wrought out by a Barclay, or as the doctrines or maxims of a Penn, or as the deep and refined views of a Pennington; *(sic)* for all these authors have their defects as well as their excellencies. I should call it the religion of the New Testament of Our Lord and Saviour Jesus Christ, without diminution, without addition and without compromise."[37]

> *The great merit of the doctrine of the light is that it is true to the scriptures and to experience simultaneously.*

The doctrine of the light within is, therefore, central to the Friends understanding of the Christian faith. It seeks to describe the main channel of grace that is open to us and arises out of Christ's promise to be with us in spirit as recorded in John's Gospel. We experience the light as individual believers, but also, since that promise was given to the disciples at large, in the regular worship and ordinary fellowship of our churches. The light signifies the real presence of Christ, and is as tangible and solid as bread and wine to those who have experienced it. I have noted some of the complications of the doctrine and some of the ways in which it can be both misunderstood and criticized. It is necessary to be clear about what the doctrine involves, because it is at the root of Friends understanding of both personal discipleship and the nature of the Church. Before we go further into these matters we must turn to a matter of fundamental importance that has been the source of considerable controversy among Friends: the relationship between the light and the scriptures, which we will discuss in the next chapter.

NOTES

1. Matt. 18:20, 28:20.
2. Eph. 1:18;, 2 Cor. 4:6.
3. See John 14:15-20, 25-26; 16:7-10, 12-15; 1 John 2:1.
4. John 15:26, John 14:26
5. John 14:17, 15:26, 14:6, 10:30.
6. John 14:26.
7. John 14: 15-17.
8. Gen. 1:2, Deut. 34:9, Judg.14:6, Ezek.11:13, Hag. 2:1, Ps. 139: 7-10, 17-19.
9. Eph. 1:4-5.
10. John 1:1-18.
11. William Penn, *Primitive Christianity Revived*, (1696) ed. Bronner (York, England: William Sessions Ltd., 1993), p.229.
12. Penn does not allow his opponents the same liberty in his earlier attack on the doctrine of the Trinity in *The Sandy Foundation Shaken*, (1669).
13. Ibid. p.230.
14. John 1:3-4.
15. Rom. 2: 14-16.
16. Matt. 21:28-31.
17. Matt. 25:44-55.
18. In part this argument makes use of Penn's *The Christian Quaker* (1672).
19. 2 Cor. 4:4, John 3:20-21.
20. Acts 26:13, Col 1:12-13.
21. John 3:20. 8:12, 12:46.
22. John 12:36.
23. 1 John 2:9-11, Rom 13:10-14.
24. 2 Cor. 6:14.
25. Heb. 10:32.
26. See Matt. 17: 1-8, Mark 9:2-8, Luke 9:28-36.
27. 1 Tim. 6:16.
28. 1 John 1:5.
29. Rom. 10:9.
30. Mark 4:1-20.
31. John 5:37-38.
32. James 1:17-18.
33. 2 Peter 1:19-21. For a discussion of the text see *Word Biblical Commentary*, Vol. 50. (Waco, Tex.: Word Books, 1983), p.225.

[34] See the development of the star motif through Num. 24:17, 2 Pet. 1:19 and Rev. 22:16.

[35] John 1:12-13.

[36] Eph 5:8, 1 Thess. 5:5.

[37] J.J.Gurney, *Brief Remarks on Impartiality in the Interpretation of the Scriptures*. Printed for private circulation only, Norwich, (1836), p.16. See David E. Swift, *Joseph John Gurney* (Indianapolis: Wesleyan Publishing House, 1962) p. 178.

4

The Word of God

4

The Word of God

E vangelical Friends identify themselves by their name. Both words in their self-description have honorable associations, and together they produce a unique identity. "Evangelical" identifies them as children of the Great Awakening, while "Friends" places them in the gathered church tradition. These two formative influences are often in harmony, but have certain points of divergence. In the early nineteenth century, when evangelical ideas began to exert a strong influence on Friends, there was bitter controversy over the nature of the Bible and the way the authority of scripture was understood and applied. Some Friends were willing to change their position, but others remained committed to the traditional view.

The argument was about authority. For evangelicals, scripture is the authority from which there is no appeal. Friends' tradition certainly concurs that scripture has a higher authority than human reason or tradition. However, as Robert Barclay puts it, the scriptures are "a declaration of the fountain, and not the fountain itself." He says, "Nevertheless, as that which giveth a true and faithful testimony of the first foundation, they are and may be esteemed a secondary rule, subordinate to the Spirit from which they have all their excellency and certainty; for as by the inward testimony of the Spirit we do alone truly know them, so they testify that the Spirit is that guide by which the saints are led into all truth; therefore, according to the scriptures, the Spirit is the first and principal leader."[1]

On the surface, these two positions look as if they are mutually exclusive, and historically Friends took issue with one another over them. However, the question arises as to whether they are in fact as inconsistent as they appeared to be when tempers ran high. Neither finding an adequate working definition of the term "Holy Spirit" nor finding an uncontested way of using scripture to validate theological propositions is as easy as it looks. We may find on analysis that we are not obliged to draw the contrast in anything like as stark a manner as was previously done. By securing a proper balance between our ideas of scriptural authority and our understanding of the Holy Spirit, we may go a long way to reconcile the two.

The problem arises from the use of the word "authority." Barclay's formulation implies a potential conflict between the teachings of scripture and those of the Holy Spirit and provides that in such cases the guidance of the Spirit must be followed. This appears to imply the possibility that the scriptures can err. Now if Barclay and the early Friends believed this, their doctrine would clearly be incompatible with evangelicalism. But if, as Barclay also claims, the scriptures possess "certainty," conflicts are, by definition, illusory. They must, therefore, arise from human error in failing correctly to discern the meaning of the text or the insight into it granted by the Holy Spirit. Because the Spirit both inspires scripture and guides our understanding of it, it is clearly the primary authority. But the question of correction does not arise, for there is nothing to correct.

> *Because the Spirit both inspires scripture and guides our understanding of it, it is clearly the primary authority.*

Barclay's formulation seems appropriate to a different case. This is where an individual Christian, or a branch of the Church, is faced with a decision about a matter of faith or practice where there is no clear guidance in scripture. Either no guidance can be discerned or else there is no precedent to be followed. Problems of this kind have often arisen during the course of Christian history because scripture does not provide obvious answers to many of the questions on which we might want guidance. Persuasive interpretations are relatively easy to devise, but Barclay's point is that we can decide which is right only by appeal to the Holy Spirit, which therefore enjoys logical priority.

In this chapter we shall focus on how the authority of scripture is related to the authority of the Holy Spirit in order to clarify the terms on which traditional and evangelical Quakerism can be reconciled. I shall begin by examining the twin concepts of revelation and inspiration, because the authority of scripture rests on these two principles, which together provide saving knowledge of God. Scripture is also a human instrument, sanctioned by God as a true record of all the doctrines and precepts that Christians are obliged to believe and observe. Its truth is not self-evident, and its authority has to be recognized. The formation of the canon in the early centuries of Christianity came about precisely because the Holy Spirit led the Church into this understanding. I will argue that to understand the scriptures truly we must recognize this dual inspiration. The Holy Spirit inspires scripture with meaning, but also inspires us to find that meaning. Both conditions must be satisfied for revelation to occur. Finally, we will consider the questions of infallibility and inerrancy and see what the Quaker tradition can add to a consideration of these matters.

> *The Holy Spirit inspires scripture with meaning,*
> *but also inspires us to find that meaning.*

Revelation

The authority of the Bible arises out of the Christian belief that God reveals himself to us without prior request. There is much that we can know about God, but we cannot work it out for ourselves. If we could, it would not be revelation. Revelation occurs when we realize the meaning of something we did not know before. Our minds do the realizing, but the content of what we realize comes from God. In scripture, all kinds of people receive revelation—usually in person but sometimes through intermediaries. Revelation comes in the form of dreams, visions, and words, and it is given to people in all kinds of circumstances, ranging from quiet contemplation to imminent, life-threatening danger. There are messages of instruction, support, command, guidance, correction, blessing, and many other things. Sometimes these messages are general and are about the broad range of religious truth. Sometimes they are specific and relate to God's plan of salvation.

> *Revelation occurs when we realize the meaning of*
> *something we did not know before. Our minds do*
> *the realizing, but the content of what we realize*
> *comes from God.*

The Bible is the record of these events and our means of access to the self-revelation of God. It would be naïve, however, to think of what is revealed in scripture as a series of discrete messages often separated by many centuries. Scripture contains a variety of different genres, shows evidence of extensive editing and arranging, and is unified by a number of complex general themes. The evangelical tradition has generally supposed that revelation comes through the terms and concepts of scripture and that it conveys propositional truth. That is a position we will wish to maintain. At the same time, our understanding has been enhanced by the recent discussion of literary forms, mythology, historical narrative, and personal encounter as vehicles of divine revelation.[2]

It is important to maintain a balance. I will suggest that the traditional evangelical understanding of how scripture works is in need of re-examination and that this can be done in such a way that scriptural authority is strengthened. Hermeneutics, the study of meaning, has shown us that we do not just read the meaning of the Bible off the top, as if it were a billboard. We bring to its interpretation ideas that we have already absorbed from our own convictions, our church communities, and our wider culture. In fact, God engages us in dialogue when we read scripture, and the meaning of what we read is the outcome of this dialogue. We need to recognize the complexity of this process if we want to move on from the milk of the gospel to the meat.

So we can look at hermeneutics in two ways. We can regard it as a way of reading into the Bible what we would like to think it says, or we can see it as a devotional exercise in which God speaks to us, as meaning is constituted, and revelation takes place. "Now what I am commanding you today is not too difficult for you or beyond your reach. It is not up in heaven, so that you have to ask, 'Who will ascend into heaven to get it and proclaim it to us so we may obey it?' Nor is it beyond the sea, so that you have to ask, 'Who will cross the sea to get it and proclaim it to us so we may obey it?'

No, the word is very near you; it is in your mouth and in your heart so you may obey it."[3]

A distinction is generally drawn between two kinds of revelation. First, there is general revelation, in which the activity of God in designing, creating, and sustaining the world comes to us through our contemplation of the creation. God opens our understanding generally as well as through specific testimony to particular people. God has made many truths accessible to us simply through the operation of our own minds, should we wish to find these truths. They are no less revelatory for being generally available to the human mind, Christian or not. This kind of revelation may provide knowledge of God, but is not sufficient to produce salvation. There is a unique quality about saving knowledge that is not generally available because it demands a particular kind of response.

Special revelation, therefore, is the name given to those truths necessary for salvation, the things we have to realize before we are in a position to be converted. The crucial significance of the Bible to the Christian faith is that this is where we find out what those truths are. To be sure, they have been articulated through Christian thought and experience into the great doctrines of creation, incarnation, atonement, and the last things, but scripture is the root and foundation of all doctrine. Without the written word we would have no access to that part of God's revelation that can bring us salvation. That is part of what makes special revelation, by definition, special.

Our definition of special revelation must be slightly qualified, however. We should bear in mind, first, that God's direct and intimate special revelation to us continues. Prayers are still answered, people are still called, visions are still seen, prophecies are given, and there are healings and speaking in tongues. We do not record these events in scripture, but they are surely no different from the incidents which scripture does record. Second, it appears that there has been special revelation not recorded in scripture, like lost Pauline epistles, or the book of Jashar.[4] Hence, the logical category of special revelation is slightly wider than what we might call "biblical" revelation, that part of it that is written down. The difference is minimal, but we need to know that it is there in order to see scripture in the right perspective.

Revelation is a form of communication, so we must now ask, in general terms, what is communicated through it. It needs a conscious or attentive recipient, so it is plainly a specific form of human knowledge. But of what kind? For present purposes we need to draw a distinction between knowing and understanding. There are certain matters about which we have specific factual knowledge. When we read about the Exodus, for example, we are presented with a detailed narrative of an historical event. But an ability to answer a series of multiple choice questions about it does not imply that we have understood its meaning. Saving knowledge goes beyond factual information.

Saving Knowledge

We come by divine revelation when our minds, each with its particular character and general capacities, seek to interpret the meaning of the experiences (including what we read and think) that are God's means of communication with us. This is not as simple a process as it might seem. These experiences are shaped in part by who we are and in part by the general conditions of our environment, like our education and inbred assumptions. It is improbable that revelation is a separate form of divine communication that can by-pass these realities. We have to take full account of them, because it is through them, not apart from them, that God speaks.

It follows that revelation will accommodate itself to human capacities and a full account of its nature will necessarily include a theory of knowledge of some kind. This is not the place to enter into great detail about what such a theory of knowledge might involve, but it is important to state what its foundations are. We are concerned here with the character of the divine knowledge transmitted in revelation, and we need to ask whether simple comprehension of it is sufficient to save or whether more is required. The clearest answer is given in Jesus' prayer before the Passion, where he says, "Now this is eternal life: that they may know you, the only true God, and Jesus Christ, whom you have sent."[5] The reference is hardly to factual knowledge. "Know" in this context is not that of understanding how to fill out a tax return but that of knowing a relative or an intimate friend.

In other words, knowledge of God requires more than intellectual apprehension. A proper understanding is certainly an important element in saving faith, but it is necessary rather than sufficient. In the fullest sense, knowledge of God establishes a relationship and moves us to respond. When we receive it, we have to follow its implications. Returning to Jesus' prayer, the word "know" makes most sense if it is construed to mean this practical, relational knowledge of God. It is quite consistent with this to say that such knowledge is available only through the mediation of Jesus Christ and that it is impossible for human beings to obtain it through their resources and abilities. Knowledge of God is not just factual. We have to accept the consequences along with the knowledge.[6]

Knowledge of God requires more than intellectual apprehension. A proper understanding is certainly an important element in saving faith, but it is necessary rather than sufficient.

This is the principle that distinguishes false from genuine knowledge of God and deals with the case of people who claim to be converted, Bible-believing Christians but who act in ways that bear no resemblance to the true faith. Are they in possession of this saving knowledge? The answer depends on the definition of "knowledge." What is known intellectually to the individuals in such cases is identical with what is known to truly converted souls. They both know the nature and mechanics of conversion and the requirements of the Christian faith. But in one case there is an understanding of the relational and performative dimension of this knowledge. In the other, it is by definition absent. We might define saving power by analogy as a spiritual charge possessed by religious knowledge that will transfer itself only when the right conductor is present.

So we are not obliged to go along with those theories that say that there is a distinct form of spiritual knowledge that cannot be reduced to other kinds of understanding and that consequently there is an additional hidden faculty within us that gives exclusive access to a certain kind of knowledge, as if we had a special revelation gene to deal with special revelation. That borders on Gnosticism. An incarnational religion like Christianity must be willing to stand on the principle that we know God with the same minds that give us knowledge of the beauty of the landscape, the love of family, or the proof of the theorem of Pythagoras.

The basis of this kind of knowledge is trust, not intellectual assent. Knowing God is like knowing a person, not like knowing a theory. Divine knowledge comes to those who know they are not self-sufficient, that they are in need, and that there is nothing they can do to help themselves. It is plainly a consequence of conversion. The true nature of the knowledge of God can be measured by the seriousness of Jesus' words, "All things have been committed to me by my Father. No one knows the Son except the Father, and no one knows the Father except the Son and those to whom the Son chooses to reveal him."[7]

The Bible is a book of revelation, and we have seen a little of what this involves. But for evangelicals it is more than a record of revelation. Although it contains an account of God's decisive actions in history and possesses the capacity to inspire faith, these qualities do not exhaust its revelatory significance. There is a marked difference between the Bible and the myths and legends of the cultures among which it came into being. Its subject is not human experience, but the nature of God. It does not explain, it invites and commands. The scriptures are indivisible from the material of which they are made up, and they are a part of the revelation itself. Scripture is the standard whereby we may take the measure of our own destiny.

Inspiration

There is a sense in which everything we know is revealed to us, because God, the creator of all, is the only possible source of knowledge. We have already argued that the universe bears the character of its creator and that this is discernible by the ordinarily reflective person. "The heavens declare the glory of God; the skies proclaim the work of his hands. Day after day they pour forth speech; night after night they display knowledge. There is no speech or language where their voice is not heard. Their voice goes out into all the earth, their words to the ends of the world."[8]

Although the object of this knowledge is religious, it has the same character as our non-religious knowledge, because there are limits to what it can convey about God. What it cannot do is to lead us into the kind of relationship that God desires to establish with us. For that, we need the kind of knowledge not generally available, the saving knowledge given in special revelation. "But as for you, continue in what you have learned and have become convinced of, because you know those from whom you learned it, and how from infancy you have known the holy Scriptures, which are able to make you wise for salvation through faith in Christ Jesus."[9]

The knowledge derived from general and special revelation has only one source, because each derives from the activity of the Holy Spirit. The knowledge that comes from special revelation has a distinct character, however. So what is the quality of the knowledge that inclines us to hear the gospel and accept the scriptures? What is it in ourselves that enables us to recognize it when we encounter it? Does it possess a sound, a taste, and a fragrance? Not in those terms perhaps, but Christianity teaches very clearly that this special knowledge of God does indeed possess a special quality. That quality is inspiration.

The Nature of Inspiration

Using sensuous terms to portray the substance of special revelation redresses the balance of our discussion somewhat. We have used abstract terms to chart the relations between what God wishes to convey to us and what we are able or wish to hear. But as we move to the concept of inspiration, we need a different vocabulary. We have suggested that the difference between those who read the Bible and are unmoved and those who read it and are transformed is that the latter are receptive to the spiritual potency, or charge, the Bible contains. They rise to its vision; they hear its call. They have a sense that there is life in the words it uses. That life is its inspiration. Its fruit is not so much understanding as joy.

The scripture itself says, "The law of the Lord is perfect, reviving the soul. The statutes of the Lord are trustworthy, making wise the simple. The precepts of the Lord are right, giving joy to the heart. The commands of the Lord are radiant, giving light to the eyes. The fear of the Lord is pure, enduring forever. The ordinances of the Lord are sure and altogether righteous. They are more precious than gold, than much pure gold; they are sweeter than honey, than honey from the comb."[10] This is a very subtle passage. The writer uses very simple words, many of which are adjectives. He uses the comparative, but conveys the superlative degree. The capacity to induce this reaction is one of the marks of inspiration.

Webster tells us that "to inspire" means to fill with an animating, quickening, or exalting influence. A person or a community that is inspired has come to life because something has happened to it. Hence, inspiration is that which arouses thought, feeling, or sentiment. It can be seen as either the power possessed by the inspiring person or idea, or it can be seen as the influence produced in the one inspired. There is also a sense of the word that means to bring about or cause something to happen. We have to be careful to preserve this double meaning. Inspiration is both the power that animates and the animation itself. It is one thing with two appearances.

Scripture as Inspired Writing

Now as everybody knows, "All Scripture is God-breathed and is useful for teaching, rebuking, correcting, and training in righteousness."[11] This is the only occasion in which scripture uses the word "inspired" to refer to itself, but the text gives a graphic illustration of the process by which the Bible acquires the power to transform the minds of its readers. We have just suggested that revelation is the communication of God's will to us in the form of human knowledge. The grace, the glory, the tenderness, the reproof, and the love of God come to us when our conversion brings us into the kingdom of which Jesus spoke, and we encounter the covenantal community of which the Bible is the story. What distinguishes the Bible from all other religious writings is that it alone possesses the power to do this.

In modern times, the status of scripture as inspired writing is taken for granted. It is hard for us to think back to a time before the canon of the New Testament was closed. Yet we need to do so for two reasons. The first is that it took time for the Church to set aside a specific number of books recognized as inspired and referred to as "scripture." The books finally included in the canon were chosen because they were believed to have special revelatory power. But many other ancient books, often of profound spiritual insight, are not included in the list. So we need to know why we have the canon we do. The second reason arises out of this process. The Church believed the Holy Spirit guided it in making this selection. We need to understand the implications of the fact that the Bible does not tell us what books are inspired. That knowledge comes from somewhere else, as Robert Barclay understood.

The Canon and the Holy Spirit

The process of forming the canon, the list of books to which reference may be made in the process of doctrinal development, took nearly four hundred years, and the debate over what to include kept pace with the doctrinal controversies of the early period. Significant intellectual movements (of which Christianity is one) generally begin well and gain adherents on the basis of their original claims. Then they go through a period of controversy in which inconsistencies are pointed out and criticisms leveled, often in circumstances of acrimonious debate. Finally the original idea is stated in a mature form after a lengthy process of assimilation, consolidation, and then systematization. Consensus eventually arrives, but not without cost.

We can see this happening to the early Church. Out of the process emerged orthodoxy, heresy, and schism. The controversies surrounding Marcion and the Montanists are well documented. In recent years considerable attention has been given to the extent of gnostic ideas and localized forms of the faith in early Christianity.[12] Without doubt there were historical factors at work in the process of forming the canon, and the process obviously reflects power struggles and conflicting personalities. Nevertheless, doctrinal controversy required some objective standard by which competing opinions could be assessed, and the canon of scripture came into being to satisfy the need for such a standard.

> *Without doubt there were historical factors at work in the process of forming the canon, and the process obviously reflects power struggles and conflicting personalities.*

Criteria for Canonical Books

Three criteria were used in settling this standard, perhaps not formally, but in effect. To begin with, a book had to have been written by, or in association with, an apostle. This requirement obviously rests on the special status of the apostles rather than the specific content of what they taught. Then, a book needed congruity with the tradition. Early in this period the phrase "rule of faith" appears, to signify the general experience and doctrine of the Church, which a book needed to reflect clearly before being regarded as having authority. Finally, there had to be general acceptance. There is in fact very little difference between the books that the Third Synod of Carthage in 397 AD ultimately recognized as authoritative and the sources quoted in the controversial writings of Irenaeus about two hundred years earlier.

From the standpoint of faith, the historical circumstances do not exhaust the significance of the process. Where a secular historian might see a process of debate and disagreement in which the outcome is decided in favor of the most powerful forces, the committed Christian will see the Church discerning and testing its leadings as the Holy Spirit completes the work of bringing scripture into being. We must resist the temptation to view these events simplistically. The historical circumstances are part of the process. At the same time, evangelicals need to grasp the extent to which their belief in the authority of scripture rests on the direct inspiration of the Holy Spirit. Unless there were revelations outside the canon of scripture, that canon would never have come into being.

> *Evangelicals need to grasp the extent to which*
> *their belief in the inspiration of scripture rests on*
> *the direct inspiration of the Holy Spirit.*

The formation of the canon, therefore, involved an extensive process of discernment. The books included in the canon were recognized to be inspired, but there was an additional qualification they had to meet. The standard for inclusion was not so much that they were inspired (though they were), but that they constituted the apostolic witness in literary form. It was later that the category of "inspired" works was limited to them.[13] Thus, the fact that other, non-canonical, works were considered to be inspired was not a reason for their inclusion in the canon. In fact, the principle of inclusion thus formulated would require their *exclusion* unless they met the other criteria also.[14]

These considerations are important for two reasons. First, it is possible in theory for other books to be added to the canon provided they meet the criteria. There seems to be no objection to this on principle, provided the requirements of apostolic origin, conformity with tradition, and general agreement are met. This is by no means a far-fetched suggestion, because in recent years there have been remarkable finds of documents that might theoretically meet these standards. Both the Dead Sea Scrolls and the Nag Hammadi manuscripts contain canonical and non-canonical, but previously unknown, material. The well-known Gnostic Gospel of Thomas, for example, is a mixture of both in one document. The possibility that books will be added to the canon is unlikely, however.

Because there is no scriptural authority for the canon, then, any decision as to the status of a newly discovered book, say, Paul's Third

Letter to the Corinthians, or any other book mentioned in the scriptures themselves, could be decided only by a convocation of the whole of the Christian Church. Quite apart from the practical difficulty that there is at present no body able to speak for Christians as a whole, there is no scriptural warrant for how to proceed or what conditions, over and above those of history, to which to appeal. Unless we are to take the secular historian's view of the process of canon formation, we have no alternative but to see it as the work of the Holy Spirit, as Barclay's principle requires.

Particular books are capable of becoming scripture because a number of prior conditions have been satisfied. The first condition is that they must meet the three qualifications for inclusion in the canon, which represents the books on which faith and practice must be based. The second condition is that these books must be inspired. They must be of a slightly wider class of writings that were considered by early Christians to reveal the character and will of God in a unique way. The third condition is that they represent divine revelation. Although we are permitted to discern something of God by using our own reason and imagination, the scriptures tell us what God wants us to know and has not disclosed to us in any other way.

Recognizing Inspired Works

This looks like a simple scheme, but let us ask some questions that will illustrate its complexity. Why should connection with the apostolic teaching be determinative of scriptural status, thus limiting the number of books we now call inspired? By what means was this list adjudged to be canonical? How was the early Church able to distinguish books that were inspired and not canonical and decide on the status of books that were obviously not inspired? Why are the canonical books revelatory to some people and not to others? How it is possible for converted Christians seriously to misread the meaning of canonical scriptures? And what about the Apocrypha? If revelation led to inspiration and inspiration to understanding, there would be a smooth transition at each point, and we would not need to debate these questions.

There is no such smooth transition because, as I have argued, there are loose ends at each point of transition. For example, some of the forms of immediate revelation mentioned in scripture continue to occur to individual people today, so we narrow our understanding of the process if we confine revelation to an approved text. Then there is the point that revelation is conveyed in a variety of literary forms, not just in propositional statements. The way we interpret scripture needs to take account of this. Moreover, the concept of inspiration is ambiguous, involving both God's action in revelation and the content of that revelation. Unless we realize this, we run the risk of confusing the two. There is also the temptation to put all our intellectual eggs in one basket. A certain kind of inspiration has been codified in the canon of scripture and is collectively binding on us. But it is not autonomous. Its authority depends on its place in the wider scheme of revelation.

The bearer of revelation is, of course, the Holy Spirit, and the solution to all the problems we have been raising lies in the work we understand the Spirit to perform. The end and purpose of revelation is the salvation and perfection of the individual, Christian soul, as we have already seen in our discussion of the Counselor. Let us remind ourselves once more that Jesus promises his disciples that the Holy Spirit will dwell within them, that the Spirit bears witness to him, and that the Spirit will lead us into all the truth. The scripture also tells us very clearly that the Spirit gives us wisdom and knowledge, and that there will be those who hear but do not understand, and those who have the semblance of religion but are really corrupters of it.[15]

> *Let us remind ourselves once more that Jesus promises his disciples that the Holy Spirit will dwell within them, that the Spirit bears witness to him, and that the Spirit will lead us into all the truth.*

Recognition of the Bible as an inspired and revelatory work is, therefore, one of the fruits of the Spirit and should be understood as such. It follows that only those whose lives are guided by the Spirit will be able to understand what scripture is saying. Its message is spiritual, and only the spiritual can hear it. This has to be true on principle. One understands scripture because one has been converted. People are not converted because they read the scripture. It may bring them to the point of conversion, but from then on the Holy Spirit is in control and actually performs the work of bringing them into the kingdom. Possession of the Spirit is a precondition to understanding the meaning of the Bible. Our intellects are essential to this process, but only bring us truth when the Spirit enlightens them.

It is for this very reason that early Friends so consistently used the language of illumination. The light of Christ within drew us to our convincement, brought about our conversion, empowered us to amend our lives, gave us discernment in spiritual matters, and opened the meaning of the scriptures. Light is that spiritual agency which enables us to see properly. As we have noticed above, scripture itself foresees the probability that there will be those who do not see properly and therefore do not understand. We are entitled to conclude from this that only those inspired by the Spirit can understand the inspired writings.

Scripture and Spirit

The Bible is accepted by Christians as an inspired book and as the ultimate guide in matters of religion. In some branches of the Church, reason, tradition, and the inherent authority of the Church itself augment this principle. Early Friends, however, took a new position. They insisted that the final authority in matters of faith was not scripture but the Holy Spirit. At Nottingham, England, in 1649, George Fox heard a minister say that the scriptures were the touchstone and judge by which to try all doctrines, religions, and opinions. He cried out in denial that that it was "the Holy Spirit, by which the holy men of God gave forth the Scriptures...for it led into all Truth and so gave the knowledge of all Truth."[16] We must now examine this position carefully, because on the surface it clearly conflicts with the evangelical principle that the final authority in matters of faith is the scriptures, as noted at the beginning of the chapter.

What sort of question could form the basis of an appeal from Holy Writ to the Holy Spirit? A number of candidates come to mind straightaway. Inerrancy, predestination, slavery, episcopacy, war, and peace are all matters where the churches, in possession of one Bible, have come to very different conclusions on the basis of the same Bible's authority. How can this be possible? One answer is that where the scriptures appear to support a number of equally well-considered possibilities, there is no scripturally convincing reason for preferring one possibility to another. If this is so, the right course must be to approach the question spiritually rather than exegetically, in other words, to seek the guidance of the Holy Spirit. This is not a matter of correcting scripture or admitting contradictions. It is a matter of interpretation led by the Spirit.

Let us consider a concrete historical case that raises these matters, namely, the meaning we should attach to the Richmond Declaration of Faith of 1887, the standard statement of evangelical Quaker belief. The Declaration was originally promulgated to express a consensus of opinion among the so-called Orthodox yearly meetings, on the nature of Friends faith, but it was also, and inevitably, political in view of the controversies of the day. Although all the evangelical yearly meetings except one include it in their Disciplines as a generally accepted account of what contemporary Friends believe, its status is still problematical. Nevertheless, it is clear, concise, soundly based in scripture, and much more traditional, in Quaker terms, than some of its critics think.

Section Four of the Declaration deals with the scriptures and asserts (along with the plainly false historical claim that what it says has always been the belief of the Society of Friends) that they "were given by inspiration of God; that, therefore, there can be no appeal from them to any other authority whatsoever, (and) they are able to make wise unto salvation through faith which is in Jesus Christ." It also asserts that the scriptures are "the only divinely authorized record of the doctrines which we are bound, as Christians, to accept, and of the moral principles which are to regulate our actions." Nobody can be required to believe anything that is not contained in them, and "whatsoever anyone says, or does, contrary to the Scriptures, though under profession of the immediate guidance of the

Holy Spirit, must be reckoned and accounted a mere delusion."

The context is significant here. The Section goes on to link these statements about authority with some general observations about the relationship between the Testaments. It asserts the importance of the Old Testament and claims that when read in the light of the New, the whole would display the "many-sidedness and harmony of its testimony to Christ." The Declaration continues, (with late Victorian grandiloquence, perhaps, though with Quakerly insight), "The great Inspirer of Scripture is ever its true Interpreter. He performs this office in condescending love, not by superseding our understandings but by renewing and enlightening them. Where Christ presides, idle speculation is hushed; His doctrine is learned in the doing of His will and all knowledge ripens into a deeper and richer experience of His truth and love."

Fifty years earlier, London Yearly Meeting had issued a similar statement usually taken to indicate the high water mark of evangelical sentiments in that body. The London Epistle of 1836, like the Richmond Declaration, reflected the circumstances of the time, in which the yearly meeting was wrestling with the publication of a controversial booklet, *A Beacon to the Society of Friends*. The author of this work, Isaac Crewdson, was in some ways a similar figure to Elisha Bates of Ohio. A Friend in good standing, Crewdson found that with the passage of time, he was unable to square his evangelical principles with the doctrines of the Society of Friends and relinquished the latter. Crewdson declared the doctrine of the light within to be a "delusion."

The London Epistle needs to be read against that background. Its authors produced a strong statement on scriptural authority, but actually declined the opportunity to repudiate the doctrine of the light within at a time when, in other Quaker circles, it was being used in a manner inconsistent with the scriptures. The Epistle certainly rejected the idea of "any principle of spiritual light, life or holiness" in the human being except under the influence of the Holy Spirit imparted in "various measures and degrees" through Christ. But the Epistle also asserted "the precious doctrine of the Holy Ghost" which it regarded the Society of Friends as having "cherished...from its first rise to the present day," and advised Friends earnestly to submit themselves to the "free and immediate visitations of the Holy Spirit." It is clear from the text (to say nothing of the circumstances) that this doctrine of Friends was also in danger from the advanced views of the Beaconites. The yearly meeting, however, while strong in its evangelical principles, wanted none of them.

Is Evangelical Quakerism a Real Possibility?

There is in fact very little difference between the Epistle and the Declaration, and the Declaration often repeats the Epistle word for word. They are good examples of evangelical Quakerism in practice and show the continuing acceptability of certain ideas and formulations over a fifty-year period. In view of the position of primacy held by London Yearly Meeting in the middle years of the nineteenth century, this is what we might expect. What we might not expect is that the Richmond Declaration remains the standard statement of evangelical Quaker faith while the nature of evangelicalism has changed in a number of significant ways.

Of the evangelical character of the Declaration, not much needs to be said. If it had not asserted the scriptures to be the final authority in matters of doctrine and morals, it would not be evangelical at all. But is it Quaker? That depends on what the word "Quaker" means. There is no doubt that original or traditional Quakerism did not hold scripture to be the final authority in matters of faith and morals. If that is to be the criterion, then it is hard to see how the Declaration can be considered a "Quaker" document. This is the usual criticism, and it has considerable weight in theory. Those who advance it, however, usually overlook how much of the traditional faith and practice actually is reflected in the Declaration.

Indeed, Robert Barclay is quite explicit on this point. Although agreeing that the scriptures contain reliable records of prophetic, doctrinal, and historical matters, he nevertheless argues that they are only a secondary source of religious truth and inadequate as a primary rule of faith and practice. This, he says, is because the primary source of revelation is the Holy Spirit, and that is what the scriptures actually teach. If he correctly articulates early Friends position here, and he does, it is very difficult to square Friends traditional teaching with the Epistle and the Declaration, both of which say there can be no appeal to the scriptures to any other authority whatsoever. This is the *prima facie* case against evangelical Quakerism: it departs from the tradition in the most fundamental way possible. It has substituted an alien conception of authority.

The Question of Final Authority

The question that faces us, therefore, is whether, in accepting the final authority of scripture, evangelical Quakerism is a fundamental departure from the tradition or simply a legitimate extension of it. We need to understand that there is more than one articulation of Quakerism and also different varieties of evangelicalism. It would be easy to find grounds to judge either that evangelical Quakerism has taken itself outside the Quaker tradition, or that its residual Quakerism prevents it from being truly evangelical. I argue that neither conclusion is inevitable and that, on certain assumptions, it is possible, desirable, and necessary to be both.

> *The question that faces us, therefore, is whether, in accepting the final authority of scripture, evangelical Quakerism is a fundamental departure from the tradition or simply a legitimate extension of it.*

To begin with, Barclay's formulation of the superior authority of the Holy Spirit may actually be stretching a point, and what he means may amount to rather less than what he says. Evangelical Friends will assume with justification that when he talks about the Spirit he is using that word in its scriptural sense. He says, "And because the Spirit of God is the fountain of all truth and sound reason, therefore...it cannot contradict either the testimony of the scripture, or of right reason..."[17] It is a reasonable deduction from this to say that we may rely on the scriptures as an authority greater than any human authority because they are given by the inspiration of the Spirit. It is hard to see how in effect this is different from what the London Epistle and the Richmond Declaration say.

In addition, this formulation would seem to preclude an appeal to the Spirit either for claims to personal illumination that run counter to scripture, or to the interpretation of scripture in terms of some contemporary theological model or theory which can be shown to do the same thing. The Epistle and the Declaration are simply saying that if such things are in accordance with scripture they can be seen to be inspired, and if not, they are not. This is not a denial of the ultimate authority of the Holy Spirit, but it is a means of protecting the Church against ideas that appear to have religious authority but are dangerous in the long run. It also places the scriptures higher than any human authority, and that is exactly the heart of the evangelical position. There is nothing inherently "un-Quakerly" about that either.

It is always possible to argue, though, that the "right reason" Barclay talks about is really the same as what the most up-to-date scholarship and scientific research is telling us, because all knowledge is a vehicle for the Holy Spirit. If this is so, the historical-critical study of the Bible will provide a more secure understanding of Christianity than one based on the sense that it is inspired and in some sense sacrosanct. Liberal Friends usually make this move when they seek to deny the legitimacy of evangelical Quakerism. This point of view may be consistent with traditional Quakerism, but is not obviously required by it, as it would have to be if the criticism were to be sustained. We are therefore not obliged to give up evangelical principles in order to remain Quaker.

Indeed, there are other statements by Barclay with which evangelicals find themselves in agreement and which liberals find altogether more difficult to accept. One of the reasons why evangelicals do not accept liberal theological principles has to do with the degree of trust we should place in the innate capacities of human beings. Early Friends were optimistic about the possibilities of redeemed human nature, but by no means as confident of it in the natural state. Barclay, for example, describes human beings as corrupt and fallen and unfit to take one right step to heaven.[18] George Fox, (almost in passing) observed, "all were concluded under sin, and shut up in unbelief as I had been."[19] William Penn wrote, "The soul of man, however living in other things, is dead to God, till he breathe the spirit of life into it..."[20] To place the interpretation of scripture in the hands of those who do not live a redeemed life is therefore running a greater risk than evangelicals are by and large willing to undertake.

Evangelicals find themselves in agreement with these words not because they come from the tradition, but because they represent a necessary corollary of the doctrine of sin. This is a good illustration of the origin of the word "sin" in the Hebrew word for missing the mark. In the same way that an arrow is bent, or someone's aim is false, human nature has a tendency to go wrong, particularly in thought. The reason for insisting on the authority of both the Holy Spirit and scripture is that neither of these things suffers from this deficiency. Barclay in fact has a startling comment to make about those who place private illumination over the guidance of the Holy Spirit. "We shall also be very willing to admit it as a positive, certain maxim, That whatsoever any do pretending to the Spirit, which is contrary to the scriptures, be accounted and reckoned a delusion of the devil."[21]

These statements operate, then, not as a denial of the ultimate authority of the Holy Spirit, but as a means of protecting the Church against ideas that appear to have religious authority but are actually extremely harmful in their implications. They also place the scriptures higher than any human authority and that is exactly the heart of the evangelical position. (It is interesting to note in passing that the phrase, "delusion of the devil," is printed in italics in earlier editions of the *Apology* so as to add greater emphasis. It is noteworthy also that in the Epistle and the Declaration, where it finds an echo, the entire phrase has dropped out of sight.)

Spirit and scholarship is not necessarily the same thing. Such a comment might easily be mistaken for anti-intellectualism, but in this context it has a narrower significance. Friends have always taken the position that it is the scriptures that are authoritative for doctrinal formulation, not commentary upon them. Barclay says, "...we do look upon them (the scriptures) as the only fit outward judge of controversies among Christians; and that whatsoever doctrine is contrary unto their testimony, may therefore justly be rejected as false. And, for our parts, we are very willing that all our doctrines and practices be tried by them; which we never refused, nor ever shall, in all controversies with our adversaries, as the judge and test."[22] Barclay clearly envisages that the body with access to the Holy Spirit is the Church and not the Academy.

Trust in the Word

The question we face, and the early Church faced, is that Christian experience knows two realities and two authorities, the Holy Spirit and the Scriptures. The problems arise when we consider the scope and relationship of the two. Innovators of all kinds throughout Christian history have leaned to the former, and their movements have been short-lived. Similarly, in modern times, there have been those who lean to the latter, without giving sufficient attention to the freedom the Spirit inevitably imparts. Evangelical Christianity is prone to do this and needs the constant reminder that the authority of scripture is spiritually discerned and not intellectually apprehended. An evangelical Quakerism that denies this has probably parted company with its Quaker component. It will be unable to endorse George Fox, who stated the Quaker position classically in a sermon at Ulverston, in England in 1652.[23] His question bears repeating, "...what had any to do with the Scriptures, but as they came to the Spirit that gave them forth?"

Evangelical Friends have always had to steer a middle course between the two different schools of thought that they superficially resemble. There are the non-evangelical Friends who give a great deal of attention to the workings of the Spirit but neglect the authority of the scriptures, and then there are the fundamentalists who adhere rigidly to what is written but leave little space for the Spirit's continuing guidance. The influence of fundamentalism has been so strong that it is now difficult to stand out against it. That evangelicals believe scripture to be a sufficient guide to all religious perplexities is axiomatic. But how that quality in the inspired word is to be described is a matter about which there can be legitimate disagreement. However, it is a contemporary evangelical shibboleth[24] that one should be able to assert that scripture is inerrant.

Understanding Infallibility

The principle of inerrancy is based on the historic and perfectly acceptable claim that scripture is infallible. This is a reasonable inference to draw, if "infallibility" and "inerrancy" mean the same thing. On analysis, however, this appears not to be the case because of an ambiguity in the word "infallible." On the one hand, infallibility stands for the quality of being absolutely trustworthy. On the other, it denotes the quality of being exempt from error. The ambiguity occurs because these two concepts are logically independent; one of them relates to the cognitive faculty that governs our understanding, the other to our moral sense that tells us who or what to trust. Although the two concepts have certain things in common, they are not identical.

So before we are willing to allow the fundamentalists to decide whether we may cross the fords of the Jordan, let us examine the relationship between infallibility and inerrancy a little further. Both words describe ways in which the authority of scripture is exercised, so we must begin by examining the concept of authority itself. An authority can be a person or body whose pronouncements we obey, a principle of reason to which we customarily defer, or a guide whose recommendations we follow when we are uncertain or undecided. Authorities operate in a number of different ways, and can inform, warn, order, advise, encourage, assist, or persuade with varying degrees of emphasis. Experience shows that the best of them operate by consent rather than coercion.

An authority can be a person or body whose pronouncements we obey, a principle of reason to which we customarily defer, or a guide whose recommendations we follow when we are uncertain or undecided.

Now the authority of scripture is widely felt because it is based on trust, and this is what the word "infallible" signals. There is a tendency to limit its importance to providing guidance on disputed matters of doctrine, but that is to place a quite unnecessary limit to its scope. People possess Bibles and use them for a wide range of purposes in connection with the spiritual life. Some of these uses have to do with public or church matters; others relate far more to the individual lives of the readers. One size does not generally fit all, and the variety and scope of scripture enables it to meet a wide range of conditions. Whether or not its guidance is followed, we would expect its advice to be sound in every case because in principle it is never misleading. It is therefore infallible in the sense of being perfectly trustworthy. Scripture itself says, and Christian experience echoes the claim, that God's faithfulness never fails.[25]

The Question of Inerrancy

So, in response to the eternally loving and faithful character of God, we approach the infallible scriptures in an attitude of trust. Fundamentalism, however, prefers to see infallibility as inerrancy and rests its explanation of why we trust scripture on its inherent authority. This leads to the claim that scripture is accurate in every detail and if we were to find it mistaken in one place, we could never be confident that any other part of it was trustworthy. Providentially, it has been preserved from error and is therefore perfectly inerrant. The logic of this argument is appealing, but can it be sustained? It is important to come to terms with it because there are churches that think that Friends *bona fides* as Christians rests on the answer. Let us take the question head on.

The main argument against it is one of principle. The Christian religion is based upon the life and work of Jesus Christ, and it is his gospel that we proclaim. He is a real presence among us through his Holy Spirit, advising and guiding us in everything we do, accepting our personal prayers and our corporate worship. We have direct, unmediated access to him. Whatever authority individuals, churches, and, yes, the scriptures themselves possess, comes from him. This particular defense of the principle of inerrancy requires the premise that our only access to Christ is through the scriptures and that we have no other guide to the truth but the written word. This is itself contrary to the scriptures, and there is no reason why any conservative evangelical Friend should feel obliged to accept it.[26]

Then there are the practical objections. The Bible contains surface errors and anomalies of various kinds, some grammatical and some involving the use of scriptural sources by the human authors themselves. There are problems connected with the transmission of the autograph copies of the original texts. Where there are variant manuscript readings, which is to be considered authentic and why? There are also the issues of genres, idioms, and styles of writing, which raise the question of what is to be considered an error. Literary devices often convey truth by being less than strictly accurate, and the line between statement and interpretation is often very hard to draw. Although fundamentalists say they accept this in principle, they do not seem to do so in practice.

There are further objections based on the irrational consequences of the doctrine in its rigid form. If we regard what is written as our guide to every reality, we shall find ourselves fixed with a cosmology that sees the earth as the center of a three-decker universe in which disease is caused by demons, not viruses, bacteria, and parasites. Many evangelicals are not willing to countenance such obscurantism. They have also been taught that the Holy Spirit used faithful human instruments to compose the inspired scripture and then they find that the inerrancy principle encourages them to interpret scripture in such a way that the individuality and humanity of the writers is effectively ignored.

Finally, we need to note the claim that the doctrine of inerrancy is a modern development and is not necessarily an essential item of evangelical belief in its own right.[27] This is a fertile field of controversy that we shall not enter, but it is worth remarking that although the infallibility of scripture has always been a feature of evangelical biblical interpretation, the doctrine has manifested itself in more than one form. As a denomination, there seems to be no reason why Friends should accept one rather than another or leave individual Friends free to make up their own minds.

There is, in fact, a moral danger in the doctrine of inerrancy that needs to be recognized and neutralized before the principle can be employed. In searching the scriptures, one must pay heed to their complications and be vigilant for the guidance of the Holy Spirit in understanding them. This is not a criticism of the principle; it is an indication that it can lead to serious error if not observed with extreme caution. The Spirit guides us into the truth, but sometimes over considerable periods of time. It was, for example, many centuries before Christians came to understand that slavery is incompatible with the faith. One welcomes the Southern Baptist Convention's recent gesture of confession and reconciliation over slavery and racism as a process in which the Holy Spirit, working with the Baptists' experience of the world, taught them the true meaning of scripture. But it has to be said that they had the inerrancy principle all along— and it did not teach them this lesson.

To perceive the truth in what is written, we have to be under the influence of the Holy Spirit. Reliance on the truths of scripture frequently means a major re-orientation of our ways of thinking and basic philosophy of life, as we have seen in the case of the Southern Baptists. Our priorities are inevitably changed, and the process of discerning what the written record means is a collective as well as a personal process. We have our own tradition, church, and individual ways of thinking.

As the world changes and develops there is a constant need to formulate and test what we think scripture is saying to us. Proposed guidance will be qualified, interpreted, and discussed before it is accepted. The spirits have to be tried.[28] In studying scripture, those spirits are sometimes ours.

George Fox's handling of scripture is a good illustration of this principle. He constantly emphasized that only those who knew Christ, the incarnate Word, were able to understand the message of the written Word. In Wales, in 1657 he said, "So I opened the Scripture...to them and turned them to the spirit of God in their hearts, which would reveal the Scriptures to them and lead them into all the truth of them..." In Northumberland in 1653, he asserted that "...he that had the Son of God, he had life eternal and he that had not the Son of God, let him profess all the scriptures from Genesis to the Revelation, he had not life."

The clearest statement of his doctrine is in his famous sermon on Firbank Fell in 1652, which ends with these words, "And so I opened the prophets and the figures and shadows and turned them to Christ the substance...And so turning the people to the spirit of God, and from the darkness to the light that they might believe in it and become children of the light, and turning them from the power of Satan which they had been under to God, and that with the spirit of Truth they might be led into all the Truth of the prophets', Christ's and the apostles' words." This is in no way a challenge to the authority of scripture. On the contrary, it is an indication of the proper basis of that authority. [29]

This attitude must be sharply distinguished from liberalism, which evangelical Friends reject, and which did not exist when the Quaker movement began. There is no sense whatever that a critique of the principle of total inerrancy implies a weakening of evangelical principle, though many of the keepers of the fords of the

Jordan think it does. If the line between evangelicalism and fundamentalism is clear, the line between evangelicalism and liberalism is clearer. For evangelicals of all kinds, scripture is a specific revelation, the meaning of which is determined by its divine author and not by the desires and inclinations of its recipients. There is therefore a fundamental antagonism between secular culture and religious truth, because in many quarters, resistance to revelation is far more common than the search for it.

This resistance is evident in all those theologies that rest the authority of doctrine on its manner of reception rather than its origin and interpret doctrine in terms of a secular rather than a religious understanding of history. In broad terms, therefore, what differentiates the liberal and the evangelical mind is where each reposes its trust. The instinct of the evangelical is to trust the scriptures, the Church, and the guidance of the Holy Spirit. The instinct of the liberal is to look for what the latest scholarship can say. These are bald, and in some circumstances misleading, characterizations because there are many people who do not fit neatly into them. Nevertheless, there is enough truth in the generalization to make an outright denial of it uncomfortable, and therein lies the line.

But there is also a line between fundamentalist and non-fundamentalist evangelicalism. The keepers of the fords have numerical and psychological superiority in the evangelical community, and they expect their lead to be followed. However, to question the doctrine of total inerrancy does not amount to the liberalism that they fear. Reservations about total inerrancy are an inevitable element in any form of evangelicalism that gives due weight to the activity of the Holy Spirit and emphasizes Christ, rather than a text, as the source of meaning in the Christian religion. The tradition of the Friends

Church is here. It looks to scripture as the infallible record of Christ's life on earth and the significance that attaches to it. But its ultimate trust is in Christ, the Word made flesh. It knows his presence in its assemblies and the lives of its members. This is the source of its evangelical integrity.

> *Evangelical Friends, then, need courage and fortitude if they wish to maintain the traditional link between their doctrine of the Holy Spirit and their doctrine of scripture.*

Evangelical Friends, then, need courage and fortitude if they wish to maintain the traditional link between their doctrine of the Holy Spirit and their doctrine of scripture. Some Friends will wish to adopt fundamentalist principles and other Friends will not, and our understanding of the freedom of the gospel ought to allow us to live with this situation. To adopt a fundamentalist position on scripture officially would have such consequences for Friends concepts of church order and government, personal discipleship, ministry, and evangelism that it would effectively terminate the tradition. It would make the Friends Church into something those who founded it and have devoted their lives to it for three hundred years never intended it to be.

NOTES

1. Barclay, *Apology,* Proposition III.
2. See, for example, David H. Kelsey, *The Uses of Scripture in Recent Theology,* (Minneapolis, Minn.: Fortress Press, 1975), and Avery Dulles, *Models of Revelation* (New York: Doubleday & Co., 1983) p.27.
3. Deut. 30:11-14.
4. Col. 4:16, Josh 10:13, 2 Sam. 1:18.
5. John 17:3.
6. See e.g. John 8:28, Gal. 4:8-9, Eph. 3:18-19, 2 Cor. 10:5, Col. 1:9-14, Tit. 1:1-3.
7. Matt. 11:27.
8. Ps. 19:1-4.
9. 2 Tim. 3:14-15.
10. Ps. 19: 7-10.
11. 2 Tim. 3:16.
12. See, e.g. Elaine Pagels, *The Gnostic Gospels* (New York: Random House, 1979): Robin Lane Fox, *Pagans and Christians* (New York: Alfred A. Knopf, Inc., 1987).
13. See Bruce Metzger, *The Canon of the New Testament* (New York: Oxford University Press , 1987).
14. Ibid. pp. 254-257.
15. John 14:16-17, 15:26, 1Cor 12:4-11, 2 Pet. 2:1, Matt. 13:15, Matt.7:15-16, Acts 20:29.
16. George Fox, *Journal,* (Nickalls), p.40.
17. Barclay, *Apology,* Proposition II, par. XV.
18. Barclay, *Apology,* Proposition IV, § II.
19. George Fox, *Journal,* (Nickalls), p.11.
20. William Penn, *No Cross, No Crown,* (1682), *Select Works* (London: Phillips, 1825), p. 374.
21. Barclay, Apology, Proposition III, par. VI.
22. Barclay, *Apology,* Proposition III, par. VI.
23. p.44 above.
24. Judg. 12:1-6.
25. Ps. 100:5.
26. John 5:39.
27. See Jack B. Rogers and Donald K. McKim, *The Authority and Interpretation of the Bible* Harper & Row (1979) and John D. Woodbridge, *Biblical Authority—A Critique of the Rogers/McKim Proposal* (Grand Rapids, Mich.: Zondervan Publishing House, 1982).
28. 1 John 4:1-2.
29. George Fox, *Journal,* (Nickalls), pp. 303, 167, 109.

5

The Covenant of Light

5

The Covenant of Light

A promise is an undertaking we make to somebody else, who accepts it in the confidence that we will carry it out. There are simple promises, like agreeing to take our children to the park, and serious promises, like commercial contracts that can involve billions of dollars. What these two examples have in common is that they each depend on the promisor being someone who can be relied on, and the promisee being willing to trust the person promising. We do not make promises in a vacuum, but on the assumption of order and continuity. As far as possible we make allowance for inevitable risk before giving our word. In ordinary life we do not give our word at random. We may assume that God is not going to do so either.

In this chapter we shall be concerned with God's promises as revealed in scripture and how Friends distinctive practices of worship, discipleship, church government, and personal conduct are directly traceable to them. We shall begin with the divine decrees, the fundamental decisions God has made about the nature of the created order. From the decrees flow God's benign intentions toward us and the promises of the covenant, which give form and shape to our relationship with God. Where the Puritans characterized this as the covenant of grace, Friends preferred to talk about the covenant of light. By extending the range of the "offices" or roles of Christ, they extended the range of possible relationships Christians might have with their Lord. Our purpose is to show that the Friends Church is a covenantal church and that its distinctive features are integral, and not marginal to its identity.

What early Friends said needs to be qualified. We know now that early Christianity was not a uniform movement, so it is no longer possible to look to "the church of the apostles" as a model for what *we* should become. Instead, we live in the age of the ecumenical movement and face the problem of accounting for the common interests we have with members of other churches, while wanting to preserve our own heritage at the same time. We conclude by suggesting a solution to this problem. If we are not simply to say that others only grasp the nature of the covenant to the extent that they agree with us, we must ask what *we* recognize in the life of *other* churches as being true to what we ourselves understand the covenant to involve.

The Divine Decrees

A covenantal understanding of the Christian faith begins with the assumption that the universe was created to give effect to the purposes of God. These purposes are creative and benign and give meaning to human existence. They are usually called "God's plan." However, we should not take this to mean that God worked from some heavenly blueprint or architectural drawing in creating the cosmos. Rather, the phrase refers to God's methods and objectives. In the act of creation, God laid down moral and physical laws by which the creation is governed, brought the human race into being, granted us free will, anticipated our fall and its consequences, and provided the means of our redemption.

> *A covenantal understanding of the Christian faith begins with the assumption that the universe was created to give effect to the purposes of God.*

God, therefore, deals with us in an orderly and predictable way. This is how he has decreed the world should be so that it is possible for us to discern the general principles of divine action in the world. Reformed theology makes specific mention of the divine decrees as the principles governing what is to happen in the created order. The *Westminster Shorter Catechism* (1646) defines the decrees of God as, "...his eternal purpose according to the counsel of his will, whereby, for his own glory, He hath foreordained whatsoever comes to pass."[1] While some might think it presumptuous or idle to inquire as to the nature of the decrees, it is hard to see how any definite statements of Christian doctrine can be made unless there is clarity about the first principles that underlie those doctrinal statements.

The "decrees" represent those first principles because they originate in the mind of God. They express God's will revealed in his purposes. These purposes are eternal, good, and unchanging.[2] They provide order in the universe because they determine what is possible, what may or will happen, and conversely, what may not. "The reason, therefore, why any event occurs, or, that it passes from the category of the possible into that of the actual, is that God has so decreed."[3] The divine decrees represent a predetermined scheme for the unfolding of human history because they determine the outcome of the creation. They represent an exercise of the sovereign will of God and also indicate what that will requires.

The doctrine of decrees is one of the cornerstones of Reformed theology and is used to substantiate the doctrine of predestination. Indeed, the decrees seem never to be discussed in any other connection. Friends and Wesleyans, who reject the doctrine of predestination, generally find that the Reformed understanding of the decrees leads to an unacceptably rigid account of the nature of God, the significance of history, and the possibilities before the human race. But it is not necessary to follow the Reformed doctrine in every detail to accept that there *are* divine decrees. It is generally agreed among Christians that the universe exists solely because of God's intention to create and to order it, and whatever shape or structure we may find in either the cosmos or the world of human experience, therefore originates in what God has ordained.

We live and encounter the consequences of the divine decrees in time. Astrophysics and theology both concur that time had a beginning and will have an end. The doctrine of decrees, however, speaks of realities that transcend these limitations and finds in the decrees the causes and purposes of what happens within the realm of time. Such explanations are beyond the scope of science, by its very nature, and require revelation to be understood. On the surface, the Bible can be read in purely historical or literary terms, but it becomes scripture when it is regarded as an expression of the divine will. It is the necessary outcome of the divine decrees. The decrees provide the framework within which the whole meaning of scripture emerges.

> *On the surface, the Bible can be read in purely historical or literary terms, but it becomes scripture when it is regarded as an expression of the divine will. It is the necessary outcome of the divine decrees. The decrees provide the framework within which the whole meaning of scripture emerges.*

Because the decrees originate in the reality beyond space-time, we know them primarily by their effects—how we experience them in ordinary life and in the story of salvation. The manner of our salvation is one of the primary provisions of the decrees.[4] The Puritans were very clear that the decrees found their primary expression in the terms of a covenant, a set of reciprocal promises that give form and structure to the process of salvation. The *Westminster Confession* states, "The distance between God and the creature is so great that although reasonable creatures do owe obedience unto him as their Creator, yet they could never have had any fruition of him as their blessedness and reward but by some voluntary condescension on God's part which he hath been pleased to express by way of a covenant."[5] Covenant is one of the fundamental concepts in scripture. Consciously to respond to God is to enter the covenant.

We have been discussing items of Reformed theology because most of the early Friends had been Puritans before they rebelled against their upbringing. Although they consciously rejected predestination, imputed righteousness, and other doctrines, their own thought was shaped by what they had jettisoned. It might not have had a Puritan content, but it had a Puritan form, for the covenantal theology of the seventeenth century provided a comprehensive framework for Puritan and Quaker alike. Broadly speaking, this theology argued that God had originally concluded a covenant of works with Adam, which failed because Adam proved unable to keep his side of the bargain. God then instituted the covenant of grace that reached its fulfillment in two stages. As we shall see shortly, Friends extended this idea in a completely new way.

Hence, the division of the covenant of grace into old and new dispensations provides a basic structure for the whole gospel story. The reciprocal themes of prophecy and fulfillment, law and grace, sacrifice and redemption, and sin and forgiveness all have a vital significance to the story scripture tells. But such is their richness and variety that they need a unifying idea by which they can be coordinated and properly related to one another. Their full meaning will only emerge when they are related to one another by one central conception. Covenant provides this coordinating element. The covenant of works and the covenant of grace give expression to the divine decrees and order all the elements in the religious lives of believers and the possibilities faced by nonbelievers. The covenants, therefore, take a central place in the whole scheme of Christian doctrine.[6]

The Covenant of Grace

In the Old Testament, there are accounts of several specific covenants like those made variously with Noah, Abraham, Moses, and David.[7] Though these covenants are each made in specific circumstances, they are all properly seen as deriving from the one central covenant by which God makes Israel his chosen people. The terms of the covenant are, broadly speaking, that God will protect his people and in return they will carry out his will. This means that the people will make the sacrifices, observe the rituals, keep the law, and preserve the Temple. The system works well some of the time, but in the long run it collapses because Israel neglects her promises. There are periods of renewal,[8] but out of the Exile, the idea emerges that perhaps God has it in mind to institute a new covenant.

By this time, the prophetic understanding of God's purposes has broadened considerably. Isaiah proclaims God's promise of an everlasting covenant if Israel will live up to her destiny as example to the whole world. Jeremiah proclaims God's promise of a radically new covenant, in which sins will be forgiven and the law is to be written in people's hearts so that they will not need to exhort and teach one another. These are radical departures from the old understanding. The covenant remains the basis of Israel's relationship with God, but the prophets begin to see something more momentous. In the servant songs of Isaiah we can discern the emergence of a Messianic figure who will be given "as a covenant" to the people and whose rule, by implication, will fulfill the prophecies of an everlasting covenant.[9]

Christianity is based on the conviction that this prophetic vision is fulfilled in the person of Jesus Christ. On the night that he was betrayed, Jesus blessed the cup and said, according to Mark, "This is my blood of the covenant, which is poured out for many..." This basic statement is extended in two directions, by Matthew, who adds the words, "...for the forgiveness of sins," and by Luke who uses the form, "...the new covenant in my blood, which is poured out for you." In the earliest documentary evidence of the event, Paul uses the words that later appear in Luke.[10] Here we have a prophetic action signifying that the new covenant would come into being when the Passion had accomplished God's purpose. John records that on the cross the following day, Jesus was given a drink. When he had taken it, he said, "It is finished."[11] And he died. Christianity claims that from then on there was a complete change in the basis of human relations with God. The new covenant had come into being.

The Essentials of the Covenant

The most complete account of the nature of the new covenant occurs in the Letter to the Hebrews, which roots the new conceptions of Christianity in the soil of contemporary Judaism. It understands the essentials of a covenant from the human side to include repentance, an amended life, and participation in an act of sacrifice to obtain the benefits of the arrangement. Although Hebrews arises out of a Jewish experience and pays close attention to the significance of ritual, it presents the new covenant as an inward, unseen, spiritual reality and fulfillment of the prophecies of Ezekiel and Jeremiah about the new heart and the law within.[12] Consequently, the rituals of the old covenant have lost any power they might have had precisely because they were not conducted in a wholly repentant spirit.[13] One of the central arguments of Hebrews is that we are always prone to avoid our moral responsibilities by the observation of outward forms. To avoid this outcome, religious observance must depend on faith rather than meritorious ritual actions.

Faith is an inward quality, and if it is central to the covenant, we necessarily have to see our obligations in spiritual, rather than ritual terms. One can hardly understand the teaching of Hebrews otherwise. In our day and age, we participate in Christ's sacrifice on two conditions that we tend to forget. First, we are saved as heirs to the promise because we belong to the covenant people. We belong not through anything we have done, even the confession we make at our conversion. The promises are made to the Church in the first place and only secondarily to us. Second, faith is not self-authenticating, and we must safeguard our understanding of what it is. The only kind of faith that matters is a union of trust, love, and hope.[14] When evangelists call for decisions, they are following Christ's command. But we need to remember that decisions not backed by commitment are subjective and external. They do not measure up to the standards laid down in scripture.

Faith is an inward quality, and if it is central to the covenant, we necessarily have to see our obligations in spiritual, rather than ritual terms.

Sacrifice is essential under both covenants, so participation in sacrifice is a condition that must be fulfilled before the covenantal blessings are available. The Letter to the Hebrews presents Christ as the final sacrifice because only he has the power to procure these blessings. "Gather to me my consecrated ones, who made a covenant with me by sacrifice,"[15] reads the older tradition. But the newer one says, "Therefore, brothers, since we have confidence to enter the Most Holy Place by the blood of Jesus, by a new and living way...let us draw near to God with a sincere heart in full assurance of faith."[16] Those who are like children, those who seek the Kingdom of God, must come to the foot of the cross in order to enter the community of the new covenant.

So it is reasonable, at the very least, to suggest that covenant is the fundamental category in which to interpret the meaning of Christianity, covering and integrating, as it does, the other major themes of creation, redemption, and judgment. The covenant shows us the form God's activity takes. It gives directions for worship, ethics, and all the other features of the religious life. It defines the channels of revelation and grace and takes us beyond the experience of the individual to an understanding of the destiny of the race. Scripture reveals the major dimensions of the covenant, but in turn the covenant shows us the fundamental terms by which we may understand scripture.

The New Covenant

The death of Christ is instrumental in bringing the new covenant into being. We enter a new relationship with God through it and acquire new obligations. In the Reformed tradition, this relationship was structured through what are called the offices of Christ, the threefold role he plays in the drama of our salvation. As priest, he sacrifices himself to reconcile us to God.[17] As prophet, he proclaims God's will for us.[18] As king, he is, and will be the ruler of the whole of creation.[19] The priestly office is the most significant. It is Christ's sacrifice of himself that delivers us from the power of sin and the prospect of destruction and has an objective reality quite apart from its effect in the lives of those who have been converted and are regenerate.[20] This is our only means of entry into the covenant of grace.

> *It is Christ's sacrifice of himself that delivers us from the power of sin and the prospect of destruction and has an objective reality quite apart from its effect in the lives of those who have been converted and are regenerate.*

Quakerism emerged in part out of the Puritan understanding of the covenant, which can be summarized as follows. At the beginning of human history, God covenanted with Adam to provide him with care and protection in exchange for obedience. The arrangement failed because it was beyond Adam's power to obey, and God was obliged to institute another covenant, based this time upon faith rather than works, the covenant of grace. The covenant of grace has two components. The dispensation of law was the period of prepa-

ration for the coming of Christ. We now live in the period of fulfillment. Though we customarily talk of the old and new covenants,
we should remember that they are both parts of one overall covenant of grace. Although Puritan divines debated the details of this
scheme, they broadly agreed on the outlines.[21]

Tensions in the Puritan Understanding

The covenant of grace, however, contained a tension that divided the Puritans and that the Quakers solved in their characteristic way. The problem involved the channels of grace within the covenant and can be put like this: If grace alone is the means of our
salvation, what is the place of human religious endeavor? Some
believed that grace came through instruments that belong to the
created order, like the scriptures, the ordinances, and the guidance
of the Church. Others thought that grace came through direct inspiration, overruling and transforming natural capacities and human
institutions. There were mutual recriminations. One party accused
the other of antinomianism, the rejection of all forms and standards.
In reply, it was said that the accusers were guilty of works-righteousness, the idea that in some way salvation can be earned.[22]

Being of the Reformed faith, both parties to the Puritan dispute
shared a belief in imputed righteousness. By this doctrine, we are
acceptable to God though we are still sinners because the righteousness of Christ is imputed to us to make up the deficit between what
we are and what we ought to be. This makes it difficult to reconcile
the purity of the covenant of grace with the presence of sin in the
individual. On the one hand, it can be argued that sin will produce a
descent into immorality where there is too much freedom; this is
the danger of antinomianism. Alternatively, it can be claimed that

sin can corrupt our zeal for righteousness and turn it into intolerance, legalism, and religious tyranny.

Friends, however, did not find themselves in this particular dilemma. They preached that convincement was not just conversion; it signified a victory over sin, not an accommodation with it. This was exactly the quarrel Francis Howgill had with his Puritan advisers. He was unable to contemplate the presence of sin within the covenant of grace, and the Puritans were because the doctrine of imputed righteousness allowed them to.

Friend's covenantal understanding was therefore very different from the Puritans, and they spoke instead of the "covenant of light." In this form of words, covenant is a Christological term and is used as an equivalent of Christ, or the light. James Nayler writes, "That faith we own and witness is that which stands in Jesus Christ, the everlasting covenant of light, who is the light of the world, and this light we believe and follow; and by this we are led out of all the ways, works and worships of this dark world, and the effects of this light we witness by faith...What covenant have you who deny the light of Christ to guide you? Was he not given for an everlasting covenant to both Jew and Gentile?"[23]

George Fox customarily equates Christ, the light, and the covenant. He writes, "Ye that have felt the light, and have been turned to it, in that light feel the covenant of God, who is light, which gives the knowledge of Christ, your salvation and redeemer, by which light and covenant ye are turned from darkness and the power of Satan that separated you from God who was the enemy that when you had not peace."[24]

We do not need to enter into George Fox's game of endless equivalences to see the force in what he says. Our safeguard against antinomianism and works-righteousness lies in our direct experience of Christ the light. This experience creates a relationship with Christ at the level of our very being, not one based simply on obedience to his will. Hence, if we understand the covenant as an external principle or arrangement that mediates grace and which we have to grasp intellectually, we go wrong. Different consequences flow from the two ways of regarding the covenant. But the covenant is one. The covenant of light is the covenant of grace, properly understood.[25]

> *Our safeguard against antinomianism and works-righteousness lies in our direct experience of Christ the light.*

The Covenant of Light

The covenant of grace is not superseded, then. Rather, the concept of a covenant of light draws out its full consequences. Grace is experienced primarily in our moral and spiritual lives, but the Christian community receives grace also and structures the forms of worship and discipleship within which we realize our personal experiences. But it is not a substitute for them. Harmony between the individual and the community becomes a possibility when we submit to the guidance of the light, both in our personal lives and in the lives we lead as church members. This is how the covenant of light finds expression. The presupposition, however, is that we are liberated from sin, have the patience to wait for liberation if we have not got it, or have the humility to accept correction. Obviously Quakerism replicates the tension within Puritan ideas of the covenant of grace, but in a different way. Historically this is what has led to the distinctive Friends institutions and practices.

> *Harmony between the individual and the*
> *community becomes a possibility when we submit*
> *to the guidance of the light, both in our personal*
> *lives and in the lives we lead as church members.*

However, history is not all. Friends also need to provide reasons based on scripture and in terms of experience for their distinctive doctrines and ideas. The question is not how the tradition emerged from a particular historical milieu, but whether it commands our agreement now. The new covenant is experienced inwardly and inwardly only, because the types, figures, and prophecies of the older dispensation—the worship, sacrifice, priesthood, and law—are the schoolmasters that lead us to Christ, whose real presence in the covenant of light fulfils the law and the prophets. This is not a gospel, but *the* gospel. It does not require us to say others are in error, but allows us say what it really means to exalt the cross.[26]

The Work of Christ

We noticed earlier that it was customary among the Puritan forbears of the early Friends to characterize the work of Christ under three heads, the offices of prophet, priest, and king. While not adhering too strictly to this classification, we need to note that the offices summarize neatly a great deal of the scriptural teaching about Christ and allow us a degree of structure in seeking to understand how Christ relates to the Church and to us. In view of what has been said above about the role of Christ in initiating the covenant through his sacrifice of himself, it would be hard to deny the claim that the office of priest is the most significant.[27] The cross is the greatest illustration of God's love, and that is why it is at the heart of the faith.

At the same time, our understanding of the cross must give due weight to its purpose as well as its nature, for it marks a beginning, not an end. Salvation, in the fullest sense, includes experience of the Christian life in all its aspects, including perseverance, sanctification, and glorification and deals with what is to come as well as what is past. Christ imparts this fuller salvation to us through his activity in the Church, the covenant community, for this is the means by which his continuing work in the world is carried on, and this is how we come to experience him in all his offices. Because the outward drama of the atonement is so compelling and essential to the gospel, there is always a temptation *not* to "...leave the elementary teachings about Christ and go on to maturity..."[28] But we must. The full strength of the Christian religion does not rest on Christ's priestly work alone but his activity as the life that fills the Church.

Chiefly, Christ fills the Church in his second office, that of king. Christ is the ruler and arbiter of all that is, and as his disciples we are called out of the world into his kingdom. He was crucified beneath an inscription that called him a king. He governs the Church, and he will one day judge the world. These are no small claims to make, and they indicate the nature of the Christian faith. To be a Christian is not to adopt a philosophy of life, but to come into obedience to the will of Almighty God. The most important spiritual injunction carried over from the old covenant to the new is this: "You shall have no other gods before me." Jesus is no less forthright. He said to his disciples, "If you love me, you will obey what I command." [29]

To be a Christian is not to adopt a philosophy of life, but to come into obedience to the will of Almighty God.

Then there is the office of prophet. We know that Jesus was recognized as a prophet and that he accepted this description of himself, although the authorities were apprehensive that their own authority would be undermined if he were.[30] But his prophetic significance extends beyond this. Just before what we might see as the altar call in his sermon at Pentecost, Peter claims Davidic descent for Jesus not through the royal blood, but as David's successor as a prophet. Later, in the sermon following the miracle at the Beautiful Gate, Peter says, "For Moses said, 'The Lord your God will raise up for you a prophet like me from among your own people; you must listen to everything he tells you. Anyone who does not listen to him will be completely cut off from among his people.'"[31]

Understanding the Offices

It is necessary to maintain the threefold distinction with tenacity, but also with caution. Scripture uses these terms, and they give coherence and order to the ways we understand Christ to be at work among us. On the other hand, they can be a source of danger. Undue definition of the offices may cause us to think of Christ as if he is playing certain clearly defined roles, and then confine him to them. We may then portray him through inward conceptions and outward images increasingly at variance with reality. One modern commentator has remarked that a rigid application of this threefold distinction is "artificial and scholastic," and "The result is a clouding over of the dynamic and personal character of Christ's work."[32]

This insight was anticipated at the beginning of the Quaker movement. On the assumption that Christ does work through his offices, it can be asked whether the list is closed or whether there are other offices, modes of Christ's continuing presence, that we should think about. George Fox was brought up a Puritan and knew about the decrees, the offices, and the covenant. They were integral to his way of thinking, and he developed them in novel ways. In his writings, he speaks of Christ as bishop, king, shepherd and counselor, and occasionally, commander, overseer, and teacher.[33] We have to approach this extension to the list of offices with caution, because it would be easy to find an office of some sort in every name given to Christ. But Fox knew his Bible. There is scriptural warrant in each case.[34]

The list of offices can be extended because they show us Christ in action, both generally, and in his particular relationships with us. This is why we should not try to be too precise about them. Christ possesses a sovereignty that is not exhausted by this terminology. We encounter him in the offices, and we learn of him by taking part in what he does. Thus, the offices give form and structure to Christian discipleship. In ordinary life we enjoy a wide range of relationships. We are friends, neighbors, children, parents, husbands, wives, employees, employers, and many other things. In each relationship there is an appropriate range of privileges, responsibilities, and common interests, but within that range we all have our particular pattern. So it is with our discipleship. It is shaped by our experience of Christ in his offices within the general framework of the new covenant.

The offices are therefore the means of our entry into the covenant. They also give form to our continuing life within it and allow us to think of God's purposes, the work of Christ, and our own discipleship as parts of an integral whole. The offices provide order and significance and show us what to look for if we want to understand our relation with God here and now. They provide a structure for our corporate Christian life and give understanding and a sense of security to the individual Christian.[35] George Fox always emphasized this corporate dimension of our salvation. "Now the congregation of the living...are alive by Christ Jesus and are so gathered together by him, the heavenly man, as he is in the midst of them...to exercise his offices among them...as a shepherd and a bishop and a prophet etc. And these are the living members who have a living head, Christ Jesus...and he is their head and counselor to order them."[36]

It was for reasons of this kind that George Fox believed that reliance on the priestly office alone was insufficient for salvation. Being fully in Christ meant that Christ's other offices conditioned our relationship also. In part, this opinion was due to his sense of the fullness of Christ. In Colossians we read, "...and you have been given fullness in Christ, who is the head over every power and authority."[37] In Ephesians, one of Fox's favorite epistles, we read of the Church being built up "until we all reach unity in the faith and in the knowledge of the Son of God and become mature, attaining to the whole measure of the fullness of Christ." Fox himself, always fearful of cheap grace, wrote, "So Christ is over his great house, an enlightener, a quickener, a savior, a redeemer, a counselor, a leader, a captain, a prophet to open, a shepherd to feed, a bishop to oversee, and a king and lord to rule, order and govern..."[38]

Friends and the Offices of Christ

At this point, the Friends Church is going to have to distinguish itself from some other forms of the evangelical faith if it wishes to be true to the Quaker part of its heritage. There is no earthly reason why it should not be willing to do this, because plenty of other churches are in exactly the same position about one item of faith or another. In their understanding of the offices, Friends have a point of great substance, which deserves to be much better known. What the tradition says is that we do violence to the faith if we narrow it down to one experience and one experience only and give the impression that all that is necessary to be a good Christian is to have been washed in the blood. That is a beginning and not an end, and those who do not understand this and teach it are not in possession of the full gospel.

George Fox also gave great emphasis to two particular offices by means of which Christ leads us to a fuller salvation and that are exercised in the body of the Church—the offices of teacher and counselor. One might call them the intimate offices. In one of his most appealing utterances, Jesus says, "Come to me, all you who are weary and burdened, and I will give you rest. Take my yoke upon you and learn from me, for I am gentle and humble in heart, and you will find rest for your souls."[39] Jesus was a teacher, and is universally addressed as such.[40] But the way he teaches is easily misunderstood. During the last week of his life, when he was under increasingly sharp attacks from his enemies, he said to his Disciples, "But you are not to be called 'Rabbi,' for you have only one Master and you are all brothers... Nor are you to be called 'teacher,' for you have one Teacher, the Christ. The greatest among you will be your servant. For whoever exalts himself will be humbled, and whoever humbles himself will be exalted."[41]

In the new covenant, therefore, Christ is our teacher—our only teacher. Obviously we still need formal education to prepare us for the practical and intellectual demands of life, and we need teachers for that purpose. But that is not what these passages mean. Christ is saying that he is our spiritual teacher, and whatever we do in our own name is at our own risk if we do not do it as he would. At the Last Supper, he took the opportunity to speak about himself when he washed the disciples' feet. He matter-of-factly accepted the titles of Teacher and Lord, which they had given him, and confirmed that, indeed, that was what he was. But he went further, saying that he had set them an example of what they should do for one another.[42] The washing of feet, then, is a symbol for what a Christian teacher does. It is an exercise of service and not authority.

> *Christ is saying that he is our spiritual teacher, and whatever we do in our own name is at our own risk if we do not do it as he would.*

The Church, then, is the body of Christ and the community of believers. We can recognize it precisely because it experiences the fullness of Christ. Friends have always claimed that they are of this company and thus belong to the universal Church—the church of the apostles. Their assertion is by way of a testimony that nobody can deny them that title, as many, throughout history, would have done. The Friends claim rests upon a clear understanding that, in George Fox's words, "There is no true Church but where Christ exercises his offices in and amongst them."[43] The corollary of this statement is deceptively simple. It means that experience of Christ in his offices, not some kind of mystical succession or outward identity, is what defines the true church.

Throughout this account of Friends doctrine there are examples of how the Friends Church understands this spirit to be expressed in its common life. Its worship, discipleship and church government are based on the principle that if we widen our experience of Christ, we shall narrow proportionately the scope of our own self-centered desires. The Church becomes Christ's to the extent that we are willing to do this. Arising out of Friends' particular historical experience there is the judgment not that Friends way is the only way, but that properly understood it contains everything necessary to preserve the Church in health and protect it from all those subtle human influences that cannot, or will not distinguish their own interests from those of God.

This, then, is the source of Friends' plainness in all things, for which they believe they have the sanction of scripture and church history, as we shall see. Looking at the society of Christians portrayed in the New Testament, Friends do not find elaborate worship, human authority, outward ordinances, personal ambition, or morally compromising behavior. Instead, they see communities of Christians with a minimum of outward identity but an intense awareness of the presence of the Holy Spirit. In the enthusiasm of the seventeenth century they looked back to these golden times, perhaps with some naiveté. Whether it is possible to recreate the circumstances of the first century is doubtful. But that the early Church provides the model which we should strive to emulate cannot be doubted. That part of Friends inheritance is not negotiable.

The Early Church

This understanding of the covenant and the Church, which forms the basic reason for separate identity of Friends, needs qualification. Although Friends corporately claimed the same power and spirit the apostles were in, they also distinguished between the visible society of the Church and the wider community of those who are obedient to the light within but remote from the outward expression of the Christian faith.[44] They distinguished, as it were, the visible from the invisible Church. Again, while scathing in their condemnation of the churches of their day as being out of the power and spirit of the apostles, they had to find ways of accommodating their theory to the undoubted existence of good Christians who were not about to become Quakers.

Early Friends reasoning tended to run along the following lines. The premise was that it is inconsistent for a church to claim to be a successor to the church of apostles and at the same time not to display the character of the church of the apostles. To find out what the apostolic church was like, one referred to scripture and then asked, in any given case, whether those precedents were being followed.[45] If they were, the church in question passed the test. If they were not, its claim failed. I have argued so far that among the main features of the New Testament church are its awareness of the nature of the covenant, its inwardness, and its experience of Christ in his offices. These were perfectly realistic standards for early Friends to apply in making their own theological and spiritual judgments, and they remain valid for us.

We must take care, however. In the period following the death of the apostles, and even while they were still alive, there was considerable diversity in teaching and emphasis among the widely scattered Christian communities. We must therefore relinquish the idea that there was one, united apostolic church with a common outlook and a common set of practices faithfully portrayed in the New Testament. It is not, in fact, possible to construct a watertight theory of the church out of the New Testament materials and claim that this is a pattern to which contemporary churches should conform. Historically, this is what a wide range of radical Christian groups, including Friends, has tried to do with varying success. But the foundations of the argument have shifted over time, and a new approach is now necessary.

What we can say, in the light of what we now know, is that there was considerable variety within the early Christian community. Although there were certainly unorthodox or heretical opinions, and later on, sects, there was also a convergence of opinion which gradually developed into what can be called "orthodoxy." It is customary in some circles to see this as a negative development, but as Raymond Brown remarks, "…one can easily get the impression that all diversities were of equal value and that what emerged as orthodoxy was simply a historical accident, or the survival of the strongest rather than the survival of the fittest."[46] The position taken here is that if orthodoxy means the doctrinal formulations of the early period, this is acceptable to evangelical Quaker opinion as a leading of the Holy Spirit into the truth in keeping with the promises of Christ.

The church of the apostles, then, was not such a homogeneous entity as we might suppose, and we should not look at it as such. With the passage of time the church reached a consensus on matters of faith and practice, but we are not bound by every item in that consensus. With hindsight, it is perfectly possible to give general approval to what emerged, while reserving judgment on particular matters. If one is not obliged to believe that the church was perfect, one can give a more qualified and perhaps more convincing account of its nature. It is possible to accept the doctrine of the Trinity while rejecting the episcopacy that produced the figures who formulated that doctrine. If this is the case, "the church of the apostles" becomes a concept rather than an historical reality. The phrase will stand for those doctrines and values that we see as generally accepted by the early church but not necessarily expressed in the same way by later orthodoxy.

We only need to look round to see that the contemporary church exhibits the same diversity that was characteristic of the early church and that we face the same problem of discerning the voice of truth within a many-voiced chorus. Our situation is somewhat different, however. The early church was struggling to find its identity in the middle of myriad possibilities, whereas we are faced with the reconciling spirit of the ecumenical movement. We also have the New Testament and a considerable period of history to guide us. So there is no reason in principle why we should not be able to identify and articulate what is, or should be, common to all Christians.

Friends could always decline this task in a sectarian spirit, as they would have done at various times in the past, denying that there can be common ground with others because they do not share the correct understanding of the covenant and its requirements. In this view, only Friends truly grasp what the church of the apostles is. But a less-restricted approach would seek to come to terms with ·the reality of a denominational (and even a *post*-denominational) church by maintaining particular Friends principles of church order and government but accepting at the same time that they find expression in different forms elsewhere. The ecumenical movement is not monolithic, and cannot be, because unity is to be found in diversity, not beyond it. The reason is simple. We do not find common ground by relinquishing our distinctive features because if we all did that there would be no common ground at all, only ground belonging to others. But those distinctives must be used for the common good, and that means being able to recognize oneself in others.

Thus, the ecumenical movement invites Friends to engage in a dialogue with the wider Christian tradition. We cannot appreciate Friends understanding of the covenant and its implications unless we understand the much longer line of development to which it is historically related. A Quaker understanding of the Church must therefore contain a number of elements, including an assessment the New Testament Church, a theory of development accounting for the emergence of the Catholic tradition, and a basis for its reservations over the doctrinal and organizational changes that culminated in the Reformation. Like all evangelical churches, Friends need an assessment of what was achieved by the Reformation. In addition, we need to provide convincing reasons for our distinctive beliefs and practices.

> *We do not find common ground by relinquishing our distinctive features because if we all did that there would be no common ground at all, only ground belonging to others. But those distinctives must be used for the common good, and that means being able to recognize oneself in others.*

This does not mean that Friends have to have a distinctive position on every doctrine or historical movement. That would be ridiculous. But on the other hand, we do have a distinctive theology, and that is bound to affect the way we assess the overall significance of Christian doctrine and history. This illustrates the merit of denominationalism as a theory to explain the relationships between the different Protestant bodies. It is quite possible for one church to maintain a broad measure of agreement with others, yet insist upon its own distinctive views. The fact of the matter is that all churches have distinctives and get on with one another best when they regard their particular practices as adding to the common stock of what is essential but not reflected elsewhere. This attitude can be summed up neatly in the maxim that Friends are "of the Church and for the Church." [47]

The Church, then, is the body of Christ, the community of believers. We can recognize it precisely because it experiences the fullness of Christ. Friends have always made the claim that we are of this company, but our sectarian theology, if insisted on in every detail, would preclude inter-denominational fellowship because it would be raising an invidious standard by which others should be judged. This objection can be met by utilizing one of the most important features of covenantal life as Friends understand it, namely, that the spirit in which doctrines are held is as significant as the truth which believers find in them. For historical reasons, if no other, we should not expect to find the details of the Quaker understanding of the Church replicated elsewhere. But what we can expect to find is that the Spirit that inspires Friends inspires others also and that the church of the apostles exists wherever that spirit is found, regardless of history or formal affiliation.

> *But what we can expect to find is that the Spirit that inspires Friends inspires others also and that the church of the apostles exists wherever that spirit is found, regardless of history or formal affiliation.*

The Modern Church

So what might we say are the marks of the church of the apostles today? We must begin, plainly, with the fact that the Church exists, as William Temple remarked, primarily for the benefit of those who do not belong to it. The Church exists for the harvest, to proclaim the message of salvation and bring people into the Kingdom, and if it fails to do that, it will have lost its salt. This is a question of purpose. The Church is the indispensable vehicle by which the benefits of the covenant are conveyed to us. The Church teaches, supports and sustains, of course, but its primary purpose is to preach the good news—the New Testament is not the handbook of an inward-looking community. We can therefore say that the first and most obvious mark of the Church is that it is faithful to the Great Commission.

The early Church inherited the Old Testament and received the fulfillment of the promises and prophecies recorded there. With the passage of time, the Church gave birth to the New Testament and, under the guidance of the Holy Spirit, recognized the canon. Thus, the Church's witness is conditioned by its understanding of the purposes of God as revealed by Christ and recorded and interpreted in the scriptures. Although tradition, reason, and experience are helpful in interpreting the meaning of scripture, there is a boundary at which their usefulness expires. They are important adjuncts to the discernment of scriptural truth, but they are not the means whereby scripture itself is to be judged. The second mark of the Church is that it is true to the scriptures.

One of George Fox's most stringent tests for Christian commitment was that an individual or a group be willing to claim possession of the same power and spirit as the apostles were in.[48] The

Quaker tradition is very clear that the church does possess great power, not in the world's sense, the capacity to coerce, but in the religious sense, the power to convince and convert.[49] Scripture is clear that as the result of baptism we receive the power of the Holy Spirit, and thereby the gifts of love, wisdom, courage, endurance, sincerity, self-discipline, and all the personal qualities necessary for the imitation of Christ. Access to this power comes from our direct relationship with our redeemer, not on our own ability to understand and apply ethical or ritual principles. This is why grace supplants law in the new covenant. This power is the third mark of the church, because it comes from Christ, whose power is not of this world.

There is no doubt, moreover, that among the major sources of spiritual power for the Christian there are the experiences associated with baptism and communion. Entry to the kingdom of God requires conversion and rebirth, and baptism signals these realities. Membership of the kingdom requires participation in Christ's covenantal sacrifice, and without communion, this sacrifice will not effect our salvation. This is the point at which Friends appear to be at variance with the Church as a whole, but the difference is apparent rather than real. It is precisely because of the high value Friends place on baptism and communion that they decline to observe them outwardly. Indeed, an understanding of the true meaning of these rites is the fourth mark of the Church.

> *It is precisely because of the high value Friends place on baptism and communion that they decline to observe them outwardly.*

From the earliest times the Christian community has been organized. With growth comes the need to decide on methods of gover-
nance, and we can see the beginnings of this process in the New
Testament itself. Although Christianity has had its anarchists from
time to time, there is no reason to deny that some principle of church
order is essential. From the earliest period the Church possessed the
power of self-government, of arbitration, and of discipline over its
members. Possession of these powers, which are the fifth mark of
the church, derives, through the apostles, from Christ himself and
are witnessed to in scripture. Whether they can be inherited, require a hierarchy, or need the power of the state for support is another matter. There is one spirit only in which the church should be
governed: "You know that the rulers of the Gentiles lord it over
them, and their high officials exercise authority over them. Not so
with you. Instead, whoever wants to become great among you must
be your servant, and whoever wants to be first must be your slave—
just as just as the Son of Man did not come to be served, but to serve,
and to give his life as a ransom for many."[50]

There is one last feature of the church that cannot be ignored.
Christianity was born in persecution, and its founder prophesied
that this would always be its lot. In some parts of the world church
and state enjoy harmonious relationships, but in many other places
there is persecution. Indeed, even where the Church enjoys free
exercise of its faith, there is no guarantee that it will find the standards of secular life either tolerable or acceptable. The Church is
therefore always in danger and needs constant vigilance against forces
which might corrupt or destroy it. There are several such forces. The
most obvious outward force is the state, but there is also the challenge of cultural movements that uphold worldviews and moral prin-

ciples strongly at variance with the teachings of Jesus. It is apostasy to render under Caesar (or to Baal) the things that are God's.

Friends Distinctives and the Common Faith

There would be fairly wide agreement nowadays that these principles represent what the Church stands for. There would be differences of opinion on details, of course, but what I have said probably represents a reasonable consensus. Some might wish to augment the list with further principles, and there might be disagreement over questions of interpretation. I have given an account that reflects Friends' particular convictions, but they are variations on the general theme. Looking at these principles in general, however, we might say that Friends would bring to their interpretation two principles that reflect their particular understanding of the covenant. One is that though the canon of scripture may be closed, Christ continues to guide us in his offices, and we can therefore be the recipients of his continuing revelation. The second is that we will be able to discern this guidance properly if we submit to his leading and guidance in the proper manner. The covenant must be lived, corporately and individually, if it is to be a reality. So how can these principles be given effect?

Most importantly, as Friends experience tells us, by waiting for guidance so that we do not try to take the kingdom of God by force. The spiritual posture indicated by worship in silence and the spiritual experiences of opening, leading, concern, measure, and obedience to the light within is considered by Friends to be essential to the proper reception of Christian truth. This is crucial. Churches that claim to be part of the body of Christ must be able to give positive reasons for their independent existence.

> *The spiritual posture indicated by worship in silence and the spiritual experiences of opening, leading, concern, measure, and obedience to the light within is considered by Friends to be essential to the proper reception of Christian truth.*

Historically new churches and denominations arise as a corrective to developments within the wider body. Friends arose as a people at a time when there was an urgent need for a prophetic voice to protest against the internal corruption of the churches of their day. Their task, however, is not over. What we have called a "spiritual posture" is our only collective safeguard against idolatry, mistaking symbol for reality.[51] Historically, this has been the constant Friends witness.

Indeed, scripture contains sharp warnings about these dangers. Jesus himself was under no illusions that people would seek to avoid the challenge of his message by interpreting it to fit their own purposes, while appearing fully to accept his. Paul says the same to the elders of the church at Ephesus. There is a fairly extended passage in 2 Timothy where the Church is warned to be on its guard from those who hold the form of godliness but deny its power, and who are likely to (it seems) infiltrate and corrupt the Church.[52] So it does not follow that being within the covenant is to have insurance against challenge and danger. An echo deep from the past needs periodically to ring through the churches, "Woe to you who are at ease in Zion!"[53] The covenantal relationship will not maintain itself. Friends' corporate experience has led them to understand that the covenant relationship can break down and will do so whenever we neglect the process of corporate discernment. Waiting also requires vigilance.

We have to see the distinctive practices of Friends against this background, because they sustain the covenant community as well as express it. The place Friends make for silence in their worship is a testimony to their sense that they are guided by Christ and not by creeds. Gospel order, the sense of the meeting, the disuse of voting, and the avoidance of ordination are testimonies to the inward and immediate guidance of Christ, who governs the Church directly and not through surrogates chosen through imperfect human instruments. Friends do not compromise their devotion to peace, truthfulness, equality and simplicity, because these virtues arise out of the internal guidance of the Holy Spirit, not a dispassionate reflection on the human condition. To mitigate their demands in response to secular pressures would be to behave like the church at Ephesus with the same consequences.[54]   The distinctives and the covenant are one and the same.

Friends might reinforce this claim by asserting that the new covenant requires us to practice the inwardness that the prophecy of Jeremiah requires. If this prophecy forms a part of God's promises to us, we must look for its fulfillment in our own day and age. The prophecy is clearly about the new covenant, and if we are unwilling to accept that we are living within that covenant, we need to re-examine what we think of Christ, in view of his very clear assurance that we *are*. The law, then, is to be discovered within, and it is the embodiment of knowledge and truth, holy, righteous and good. It is not, however, the written law but another reality. Paul completes the prophecy when he writes; "Christ is the end of the law so that there may be righteousness for everyone who believes."[55]

The beliefs and practices that are distinctive to Friends, therefore, should not be seen just as the characteristics of Quakerism.

Rather, they are the touchstones of the Christian faith as understood by Friends. Friends' distinctives define not just our denominational principles but what we have to say to the world and the Church as reasons for the hope that is in us. Central to Quakerism is a vision of the new covenant in its fullness and an inward experience of Christ in his offices. The distinctives, from voteless decision-making and disuse of the ordinances to the principles of pacifism and simplicity of life, all flow from this experience. The new covenant is the fulfillment of all God's promises to us. It is a covenant of life in the spirit—of truth, love, peace, and victory over the forces of evil.[56] It is the new covenant, and nothing else, that makes us Friends.

> *Friends' distinctives define not just our denominational principles but what we have to say to the world and the Church as reasons for the hope that is in us.*

Notes

1   Philip Schaff, *The Creeds of Christendom* Vol. III, (New York: Harper,(1877), p. 677.
2   Eph. 3:11, Phil. 2:13, Heb. 6:17.
3   Charles A. Hodge, *Systematic Theology,* Vol. 1 (New York: Scribner's & Sons, 1871) p. 537.
4   Ibid. p. 540.
5   Schaff, p. 616.
6   The question of whether premillennial dispensationalism is an adequate alternative to covenant theology will be discussed in Chapter 9 below.
7   Gen. 9:8, 17:7, Deut. 5:2, 2 Chr. 13: 5.
8   See e.g. 2 Kings 22 *et seq.*
9   Hos. 2:18, Jer. 7ú?àP-4, Isa. 42:6, 49:8.
10 Mark 14:24, Matt. 26:28, Luke 22:20, 1 Cor. 11:25.
11 John 19:30.
12 Ezek. 36:26, Jer. 31: 33-34.
13 Hosea 8:13, Amos 5:21, Isa. 66:1-4.
14 2 Cor. 5:7, Heb. 11:3, Col. 1:5.
15 Ps. 50:5.
16 Heb. 10:19-22.
17 Heb. 6:20, 1 John 2:2.
18 Heb. 1:1-2, Matt. 13:57.
19 Rev. 19:16, John 18:33-40.
20 Rom. 8:3.
21 See John von Rohr, *The Covenant of Grace in Puritan Thought* (Atlanta, Ga.: Scholars Press, 1986).
22 William K.B.Stoever, *A Faire and Easie Way to Heaven,* (Indianapolis: Wesleyan Publishing House, 1978), p.10.
23 James Nayler, *A Word from the Lord, Sundry Books, Epistles and Papers,* London & Cincinnati (1829), p. 197. *See also,* Heb. 13:20-22.
24 George Fox, *Epistle XXI, Works,* Philadelphia (1831) New Foundation Fellowship Reprint, Vol.7, (1990), p. 203.
25 See Douglas Gwyn, *The Covenant Crucified* (Wallingford, Pa.: Pendle Hill Publications, 1995).
26 1 Cor. 1:23-25, 2 Cor. 13:3-4, Gal. 5:24, 6:14.
27 Rom.3:25, Eph. 5:2, Heb. 9:26, 1 John 2:2.
28 Heb. 6:1, Eph. 1:22.
29 John 5:27, 8:15: 2 Tim. 4:1, Exod. 20:3-6, John 14:15.
30 John 4:19, Luke 4:24, 7:39, Matt. 21:46.
31 Acts 3:22-23.

[32] Millard J. Erickson, *Christian Theology* (Ada, Mich.: Baker Book House, 1983), p.763.

[33] Joseph Pickvance, *A Reader's Companion to George Fox's Journal* (London: Quaker Home Service, 1989) p.59.

[34] See 1 Pet. 2:25, John 10:11, Isa. 9:6, Col. 2:10, John 13:14.

[35] 2 Thess. 2:13-17

[36] George Fox, *Epistle CXX, Works,* Philadelphia (1831), New Foundation Fellowship Reprint, (1990), Vol.7, p.68.

[37] Col. 2:10, Eph. 4:12-13, see Dietrich Bonhoeffer, *The Cost of Discipleship,* (London: SCM Press, 1953), p.15.

[38] George Fox, *Concerning the Kingdom of God, Works,* Philadelphia (1831), New Foundation Fellowship Reprint, (1990), Vol.7, p.485.

[39] Matt. 11:28-30.

[40] e.g. Matt. 22:36, Mark 12:19, Luke 12:13, John 13:13.

[41] Matt. 23:8-12.

[42] John 13: 12-15.

[43] George Fox, *Epistle 230, Works,* Philadelphia (1831), New Foundation Fellowship Reprint, (1990), Vol. 7, p. 68.

[44] Matt. 8:11-12.

[45] Robert Barclay, *The Anarchy of the Ranters* (1676), *Truth Triumphant* (London: T. Northcott, 1692).

[46] Raymond E. Brown, *The Churches the Apostles left Behind* (Mahwah, N.J.: Paulist Press, 1984), p.27.

[47] I owe this very helpful formulation to Rick Schoeff, pastor of Noblesville, Indiana, Friends Church.

[48] George Fox, *Journal,* (Nickalls), p. 419.

[49] Acts 4:33, 1 Cor. 4:9, 2 Cor. 6:3-10, Eph. 6:10.

[50] Matt. 10:25.

[51] 2 Cor. 3:15-18.

[52] Matt. 7:15, Acts 20:29, 2 Tim. 3:1-9.

[53] Amos 6:1.

[54] Rev. 2:1-7.

[55] Rom. 2:20, 7:12, 10:4.

[56] 2 Cor.3:6, Eph. 1:13-14, Dan. 9:4, Mal. 2:5, Jos. 6:6-21.

6

Worship in Spirit and in Truth

6

Worship in Spirit and in Truth

Over a hundred years ago, when successive waves of revivalism had invigorated church life on what was then the western frontier, the pastor and the programmed worship service entered the Religious Society of Friends. Neither was really welcome to a number of leading Friends at the time, but these developments have proved so successful that they are now the practice of most of the Quakers in the world. Having been with us for a third of the lifetime of Friends, they are here to stay. In one sense, they define the modern Friends Church.

Friends who meet for an hour of silence on Sunday morning with no pastor, no music, and no prepared sermon, sometimes ask what is distinctively Quaker about programmed worship. They regard it as an innovation that compromises the traditional testimonies of Quakerism. What critics tend to overlook, however, is that silence is still at the heart of the programmed meeting and that the tradition going back to the beginnings of Quakerism is still very much alive, but with us in a different form. Though it may be called open worship, expectant waiting, or communion after the manner of Friends, the words mean the same thing. There may be a programmed worship service, but it is built around the silence.

The fact of the matter is that neither branch of the Society of Friends worships as Friends did in the past. We live in a different kind of world, and nowadays we understand far more about the workings of the human mind and how our experiences affect our spiritual lives. In general, worship times are shorter, and we are not half as certain that there is a chasm between God and ourselves that we somehow have to leap over, or that God will not use our own personalities and imaginations to prompt us to give messages for other people. There has been a necessary, and quite proper, modification of the traditional form of worship in both branches of Friends.

What follows is an account of programmed Quaker worship intended to show, first, that it passes the test of continuity with the tradition; second, that it fulfills the scriptural and theological requirements for true Christian worship; and third, that as new covenant worship, it expresses the true meaning of the ordinances. Friends should not be defensive about the way they come before God. Their worship services retain the essential Quaker practice of waiting for divine guidance. This is not a concession to history or an obstacle to more adventurous forms of worship. It is a constant reminder to us that true worship is offered in spirit and in truth.[1] Friends are able to make this claim because they understand the importance of silence. It is the expression of a worshipful spirit and not its cause.

> *Friends should not be defensive about the way they come before God. Their worship services retain the essential Quaker practice of waiting for divine guidance.*

The Nature of Worship

The meaning of the word "worship" is fairly complex. It derives from the act of bowing or making obeisance in some way and is obviously connected with ritual, although we nowadays tend to think about it as an activity of the soul. In fact, both of these elements are essential to a full understanding of worship, because rituals express the collective faith of both the community and of individual believers within it. There are usually rules about what constitutes a valid ritual and what the proper attitude of the participant has to be. Needless to say, scripture has quite a lot to say about the subject. Among the components of worship are reverence, awe, gladness, and purity of heart.[2]

Without devotion, rituals are worthless. The Old Testament contains elaborate rules for sacrifice, but lays down equally important conditions for the spirit in which sacrifices are to be offered. The ritual of sacrifice is indispensable but must be performed in the correct spiritual condition. Mercy, devotion, righteousness, and justice are the prerequisites for successful sacrifice—"the sacrifice of the wicked is detestable."[3] Worship acceptable to God arises out of the covenantal relationship, so our devotion will have to be in accordance with its requirements. Although true worship may spring from our own hearts, it also has to be schooled and disciplined into the proper form. This is an unusual thought, since most people think that being spontaneous and conventional are polar opposites. In true worship, the two are in harmony. Let us see how this can be.

The Beginning of Wisdom

In a number of places, scripture says that the fear of the Lord is the beginning of wisdom.[4] This is also an unusual concept. We live in a generous age in which we assume that we can have an intimate knowledge of God, that God is gracious and companionable and would never judge people, let alone consign them to the outer darkness. We hear repeated themes of healing, restoration, and forgiveness but often without thought being given to the conditions on which such things become possible. Yet scripture is quite clear. The God who is revealed there has all these qualities, what we might regard as the negative as well as the positive ones; they have to be taken together. So how, then, can we combine them? How can fear lead to love and the expression of love through formal worship?

The answer lies in the nature of fear. Fear is not simply a matter of physical response to danger, which is part of our biological make-up—although we should not discount that part of who we are. There is also a particular kind of fear that has been experienced by any-body of a reflective disposition who has stood on the rim of the Grand Canyon or any other high and exposed place, like a cliff, a mountain, or other immense natural feature. We know, as we look into the abyss, that we are a foot, if not an inch, from death and that we could annihilate ourselves with one deliberate step. We have been brought up against our own limitations in a particularly sig-nificant way. If we exercise caution and stay within our limits, we will be safe. But if we ignore those limits, we run the risk of disaster.

The word for this experience is "awe," a combination of wonder and fear, which tells us that we are at some kind of limit we may not transgress without ultimate harm. Awe signifies the presence of the holy, spiritually as well as physically, and worship is our natural response to it. Scripture is quite clear that physical actions are inte-gral to worship. It mentions kneeling, bowing, and trembling[5] and also indicates the fundamental necessity of a pure heart and an up-right life.[6] Worship arises when we encounter the presence of God in our own limitations and are brought up against the fact of our own sin and mortality. We should fear the consequences of these things and rejoice that we are delivered from them.

Awe signifies the presence of the holy, spiritually as well as physically, and worship is our natural response to it.

Ritual in Worship

Worship, then, is a human creation under divine guidance and has certain fairly permanent forms, even in the case of Quaker silence. The purpose of ritual is to show us the boundaries and therefore the possibilities of our human condition, so corporate worship inevitably involves some sort of ritual. Its effectiveness, therefore, depends on its capacity to induce a sense of awe in us. We may not experience awe in every worship service. Our capacity for awe is dependent in part on subjective factors. Nevertheless, the principles on which our worship services are based should be to hold out the permanent possibility of experiencing awe. This is ultimately what worship services are for.

Different Christian traditions, of course, prepare us in different ways. Roman Catholic and Orthodox liturgies lead the worshiper toward the central act of communion at the altar, which is the focal point of the church building. In Protestant churches, the worship service is devoted to the preaching of the word, and the pulpit usually has pride of place. These are significantly different ways of reaching the heart of the worshiper. Yet what they have in common is a central event—the sermon or the communion—that embodies the whole range of a particular church's experience. The central event is what defines the worshipping community and conveys a specific understanding of what it means to be Christian through a particular tradition of faith, practice, and history.

By and large, Friends worship has a Protestant feel, but what distinguishes it is that the focus of the service is not the sermon, but the open worship—the period of silence that is sometimes very brief, but in some places takes up at least half the service. This period of silence is not an historical survival or a badge of peculiarity. It is not a watered-down version of the silent meeting practiced in other parts of the Society of Friends. However poorly Friends appreciate the fact, it is the embodiment of Friends understanding of covenantal Christianity. The hymns and scriptures that surround it have one purpose only: to lead the meeting into a direct encounter with God.

Worship and the Covenant

Originally, Friends worshipped in silence. Actually, it is more accurate to say that they worshiped on the basis of silence. The distinction is important because there is no particular merit in silence itself. Many things far removed from worship can be done without words. Silence itself can be lifeless, threatening, and tedious as well as helping us to experience the beauty of holiness. It can also cover a multitude of sins. If we wish to know why silence is important and distinctive to Quakers, we shall have to grasp the nature of its theological underpinning.

Silence is actually the outcome of Quakerism rather than what defines it, a misconception common in most branches of Friends. This misconception surfaces in the Friends Church as an ambivalence toward open worship. It is almost universally used, misunderstood, and neglected but continues for a variety of reasons. Individually many Friends find the open worship helpful and important, but corporately Friends are not very good at articulating its nature. In some places it is said that open worship should be done because it is an important part of the Quaker tradition. In others places there are meetings that would like to make a change but think that it would cause too much of a commotion to try. Then there are meetings that simply keep it because they cannot think of anything better to put in its place. This situation is quite unacceptable. We have open worship because it is theologically sound, spiritually helpful, conformable with our experience, and based on the word of God.

> *Individually many Friends find the open worship helpful and important, but corporately Friends are not very good at articulating its nature.*

The Importance of Open Worship

Open worship is the heart of Quakerism. It defines the way we approach God and reminds us of the kind of community we are. It is part of our spiritual inheritance and should be very precious to us. Nevertheless, it grew out of historical experience in times that are not ours. If we are to continue to practice it, we will need stronger reasons than just habit. There is, in fact, a strong combination of reasons to which we can turn. We need to look to scripture, which will encourage us to be faithful to what has been given to us and also show us how the qualities drawn out of us by silent waiting are those of the true worship of God.

Friends believe that personal experience of God is the only basis for worship. Thought may help, emotion may enrich, and desire may motivate. God may use surprising parts of our minds to speak to us, but we must not mistake thought, emotion, and desire as necessarily representing real experiences of God. Perhaps the best way to avoid mixing up our own inner voices and the voice of God is to quiet the inner voices so we can listen. The Psalmist says, "...a humble and a contrite heart, O Lord, thou wilt not despise."[7] These words suggest that there are two requirements for worship—contrition, an acknowledgement that we have fallen short of the glory of God, and humility, the surrender of our wills and lives to be disposed of by God as God wills. These things come at a personal cost. That is why worship has to be sacrificial.

> *God may use surprising parts of our minds to speak to us, but we must not mistake thought, emotion, and desire as necessarily representing real experiences of God.*

Private Worship

In the Sermon on the Mount we find Jesus repeating the same theme. "When you pray, go into your room and shut the door and pray to your Father who is in secret and your Father who sees in secret will reward you openly."[8] Partly, this is a warning against ostentatious piety, but there are also echoes here of the humility and repentance we have noticed above. Moreover, our own rooms are private places where we can be ourselves without having to put on a show for the world. Being alone with God we can say all the things we would probably find it difficult to say to any other human being. We need that depth, and silence protects us in it. The silence of the open worship is a corporate statement of this truth, because Friends bring the inner room into the Church, and the Church—at the most solemn point in its worship—directs us to the inner room.

Such hearts are what God desires, because they are teachable.

We read, "...behold, thou desires truth in the inward being; therefore teach me wisdom in my secret heart."[9] These are interesting words. They mean that whenever we are willing to recognize the truth of God we will receive the gift of wisdom. They also imply that the place where we recognize the truth of God is not in the mind, but in the heart. We use this word by analogy to mean the very life in us, in a way that goes beyond any particular dimension of our personality. The worship of the heart is beyond words. But the heart is the deepest part of us, and God speaks to us there in the most intimate way. Open worship reminds us that what we say has to come from our hearts, not just our minds. That is what the Psalm is telling us.

> *The worship of the heart is beyond words.*
> *But the heart is the deepest part of us, and God*
> *speaks to us there in the most intimate way.*

In using the language of silence, Friends sometimes lose sight of the fact that it is not so much silence as the spiritual quality of stillness that Friends have traditionally sought to cultivate. In the stillness of the heart before God we can see the reality to which these texts have been pointing. Friends are not alone in this, of course, for there have been other movements in Christian history that have made the same discovery. The reason is that the stillness spoken of in scripture is waiting to be discovered by anybody who seeks it. "Be still, and know that I am God"[10] is the advice we are given. The desire to find stillness is a sign of the openness to God's leading, which we should expect to experience in our open worship as a church community and which can be a sure guide to our everyday life.

Friends attitude to stillness is more than a meditation on the Psalms, however. It relates to the covenantal understanding of the nature of the Church that we have already discussed and that, we have argued, provides a theological justification for the separate and independent existence of the Friends Church. If Friends faith and practice reflects the nature of the new covenant, we will expect our worship to do so also. We saw in Chapter 5 that the key to our understanding of the covenant is in the words of Jeremiah and that under this relationship—the one instituted by Christ—the law will be written on the hearts of God's people, and all, from the least to the greatest, will have the knowledge of God. What we have just seen are the ways in which scripture prefigures the new covenant for us and in which open worship is the visible sign of its presence.

True worship, therefore, is essentially inward. This does not mean that Friends have to deny the importance of public worship. It simply means that Christians need a standing reminder that ceremonies and rituals depend for their power on the spiritual condition of the participants. We can have communion with the power behind the universe in the quiet of our own hearts before ever we set foot in the Temple. "For this is what the high and lofty One says—he who lives forever, whose name is holy: 'I live in a high and holy place, but also with him who is contrite and lowly in spirit, to revive the spirit of the lowly and to revive the heart of the contrite.'"[11] Perhaps paradoxically, Friends have always claimed that devout inward worship also has a power to inspire and uphold the whole community of those gathered in God's name.

Open worship, then, is about bringing to God a humble and a contrite heart that is God-dependent because it has nowhere else to turn. No music, beauty, or eloquence is allowed to give form to this devotion, lest the activity be mistaken for what it should be facilitating. Although these other things may have a place in the worship service, we shall only be able to keep them in their place if we understand why we have them. Early Friends rejected them as dangerous and dispensed with them entirely. It is not necessary to go that far, provided that worship services are properly ordered by the open worship and that the principles behind the open worship are clearly understood.

> *We can have communion with the power behind the universe in the quiet of our own hearts before ever we set foot in the Temple.*

Silence is the most powerful sign of inward dependence on God. Words, from whatever source, are human and are inevitably adulterated by our worldly ways. Silence, on the other hand, is a reflection of purity. Also, silence is a sign of our condition. In worship it means that we wait, expectantly and patiently, for what God has to say to us.

The Psalms hint at this reality in two places. First, the Psalmist says, "Surely you desire truth in the inner parts; you teach me wisdom in the inmost place. Cleanse me with hyssop, and I will be clean; wash me, and I will be whiter than snow." The choice of the word "inner" is significant. There are no rituals or burnt offerings in the inmost places.[12] On the second occasion the Psalmist says, "Find rest, O my soul, in God alone; my hope comes from him: With their mouths they bless, but in their hearts they curse... Find rest, O my soul, in God alone; my hope comes from him."[13] In this context the Revised Standard Version uses the phrase, "...my soul waits in silence." The exact word is immaterial. The passage draws its strength from the contrast between the deceit of words in outward expressions of faith, and the reality of inward dependence on the power of God.

I have already suggested that the basis of our worship is silent awe at the power and majesty of God and that the response of fear and denial in the face of this experience is what gives rise to idolatry. We read, "Of what value is an idol, since a man has carved it? Or an image that teaches lies? For he who makes it trusts in his own creation; he makes idols that cannot speak. Woe to him who says to wood, 'Come to life!' Or to lifeless stone, 'Wake up!' Can it give guidance? It is covered with gold and silver; there is no breath in it. But the Lord is in his holy temple; let all the earth be silent before him."[14] A messianic prophecy from late in the Old Testament says the same: "'Shout and be glad, O Daughter of Zion. For I am coming, and I will live among you,' declares the Lord. 'Many nations will be joined with the Lord in that day and will become my people. I will live among you and you will know that the Lord Almighty has sent me to you. The Lord will inherit Judah as his portion in the holy land and will again choose Jerusalem.' Be still before the Lord, all mankind, because he has roused himself from his holy dwelling."[15]

Emerging from Stillness

Historically, therefore, Friends have found their identity as a community of faith in the words of scripture, "Be still before the Lord and wait patiently for him."[16] The early Friends were noted for their insistence that this was the beginning of Christian worship, although originally there was no barrier to singing in their meetings, and they well knew that preaching, teaching, testimony, and prayer were also of great importance. Silence is not intended to exclude but to strengthen, and that is why the programmed worship service has the potential to equal the silent meeting in power. Both are based on stillness and waiting, but some will argue that the newer form can express more of the worship we feel in our hearts than the former. The most striking example of this is the place the program makes for music, the greatest of the arts.

Finally, a critic might say that this exposition of the principles of open worship leads to the conclusion that Quakerism is a faith of withdrawal and that the silence of open worship is a way of escaping from the challenges of living the Christian life in the tough reality of the world. But the image Isaiah gives us is that of action coming out of contemplation, retirement and stillness giving birth to empowerment. This is also part of our identity as Friends. "Do you not know? Have you not heard? The Lord is the everlasting God, the Creator of the ends of the earth. He will not grow tired or weary, and his understanding no one can fathom. He gives strength to the weary and increases the power of the weak. Even youths grow tired and weary, and young men stumble and fall; but those who hope in the Lord will renew their strength. They will soar on wings like eagles; they will run and not grow weary, they will walk and not be faint." "Be silent before me, you islands! Let the nations renew their strength! Let them come forward and speak; let us meet together at the place of judgment."[17]

> *The image Isaiah gives us is that of action coming out of contemplation, retirement and stillness giving birth to empowerment.*

Friends Worship Today

The importance of open worship within a programmed service can therefore be substantiated from scripture. It is certainly part of Friends tradition, but that is not its justification. It is practiced because Friends in the past correctly understood the principles of worship as set out in the Bible. If the principles of Quaker worship are referred to the underlying theology that supports them, they will be seen to take their place with the other distinctive features of the Quaker way of life as part of a larger whole. It is naïve to see open worship as having no more significance than an option or a matter of convenience, or, for that matter, to isolate it from its doctrinal foundations and make it the foundation or *sine qua non* of Quakerism.

Open worship is a survival of the older, longer meeting for worship, which was held in silence and punctuated by spoken ministry. This pattern still continues among conservative and liberal Friends, but it fell out of use among evangelical Friends at the end of the nineteenth century. The older form was criticized as having become a dead form in itself, which in many places it doubtless had. It was attended by a series of conventions and expectations that were experienced as quenching the spirit and that failed to express the range of emotions and convictions many people believed were essential to the religious life.

Friends had got themselves into a curious bind here. On one hand, there was the principle that ministry had to be spontaneous, on the other, the requirement that it had to be spirit-led. These principles were both taken with such seriousness that a kind of paralysis seemed to have occurred. At any rate, many Friends found their worship inhibited by excessive solemnity and the exuberance of the holiness movement must have felt like latter-day rain. Perhaps we could recapture some of that enthusiasm if we threw over the program entirely and came to meeting prepared to sing, praise, testify, preach, and search the scriptures as each of us is led and forget about conventions or the clock. Then we would have the best of all worlds— the unprogrammed programmed meeting.

> *Perhaps we could recapture some of that enthusiasm if we threw over the program entirely and came to meeting prepared to sing, praise, testify, preach, and search the scriptures as each of us is led and forget about conventions or the clock. Then we would have the best of all worlds— the unprogrammed programmed meeting.*

It is interesting that the traditional form of worship has been preserved in the liberal branch of Quakerism. Evangelicals may raise questions about whether what now goes on in unprogrammed meetings has any similarity to what took place in former times. They will take note of the lack of corporate commitment to Jesus Christ and inquire how this could have come about. One of the reasons may be that, outside the Conservative yearly meetings, the unprogrammed meeting is unbalanced. Without words, music, or any other formal way of anchoring the worship in the Christian revelation there is no obstacle to the entry of ideas and concepts that are fundamentally inimical to the faith. Open worship in a programmed service, however—coupled with the principles outlined above—preserves the significance and the theological integrity of the silence.

But, a critic might say, what about the reverse argument? Do Evangelical Friends themselves really take the open worship seriously? The question is a proper one and is not easily disposed of. In the absence of a clear understanding of why Friends worship as they do, there is nothing to stop Friends churches from simply imitating others or inventing whatever kind of worship seems best to them. That is why principle matters and why Friends need to appreciate clearly that worship depends on doctrine. There is little doubt that open worship is seriously defective in many places, and a concerted effort would be necessary to restore it to its rightful place. It is unlikely that this will happen without a thorough re-evaluation of the faith and practice of evangelical Quakerism and a consequent appreciation of why open worship is essential to our faith.

> *In the absence of a clear understanding of why Friends worship as they do, there is nothing to stop Friends churches from simply imitating others or inventing whatever kind of worship seems best to them.*

This does not require a wholesale change in the way Friends program their worship service, however. Friends churches use most of the musical and other techniques common in contemporary evangelicalism, and, judiciously chosen, these things can be very useful. But there is a tendency, in the age of the sound bite, for worship to become entertainment. This is an insidious development and represents a real challenge to many pastors and their meetings, because it raises the question of how far they are to go in adapting to the religious idiom of the times. If we are not instinctively hostile to such developments, we have to remember that they are a means to an end and not the end in itself. If we see our worship as something God-given, rather than something where market principles apply, we need the security of knowing what we are doing before we adopt proposals that have far-reaching consequences.

A Friendly Defense of Traditional Practices

To defend a denominational practice in an ecumenical age might seem to be ungracious, indeed contrary to the real feeling of fellowship evangelicals have across the boundaries of particular communions. Nevertheless, we do not have to agree with people to be well disposed toward them. Although it is easy to visit the churches of another denomination and accept the hospitality that is offered, it does not follow that one needs to relinquish one's own convictions about the nature and significance of worship. Respect for others must be balanced by respect for oneself. Friend's distinctive doctrine of worship needs no apology whatever. Friends believe that it is the truth.

> *Respect for others must be balanced by respect for oneself. Friends' distinctive doctrine of worship needs no apology whatever. Friends believe that it is the truth.*

There might also seem to be an inconsistency between endorsing modern styles of worship and simultaneously calling for a renewal of open worship based on stillness and silence. Admittedly, there is a fairly sharp contrast between these things, and this perceived inconsistency led to the development of the conservative movement within the evangelical Quaker household. Nevertheless, if silent worship is seen as a sign of Friends understanding of the gospel and its theological rationale is widely understood, there is no reason why it should not lend significance to the more outward manifestations of worship in Friends churches rather than the reverse.

The sting is in the *if.* Part of the American evangelical tradition is the conviction that churches need periodic renewal. It is not possible for Christians simply to coast along. We need a path to walk on and periodic reminders of where we are going. A church is more than a succession of Sunday services, and it is not worth much if it cannot show people an enduring way of life. Accordingly, open worship will flourish where congregations and meetings understand both the reasons why it is there and the way of life that supports it. Once again it is necessary to emphasize that refusal to recognize that doctrine, worship, and conduct are all of a piece is like building a denomination on sand.

A Place for Open Worship in Programmed Services

The essence of the open worship is that it is the fulfillment of the programmed part of the service and provides a space in which worshippers can process what is happening to them. This is an important matter that does not often receive the proper consideration. We need time to reflect, particularly on the things of God. Moreover, reflection often stimulates response. Because Friends have always believed that God can speak to us through anyone, not just the pastor, open worship is the time when the whole congregation is assembled to hear what the spirit is saying to the church. Consequently, when there is an expectant sense in the meeting that God might call upon any member of the congregation to speak, open worship can become the seedbed, and an important training ground for the ministry.

> *Because Friends have always believed that God can speak to us through anyone, not just the pastor, open worship is the time when the whole congregation is assembled to hear what the spirit is saying to the church.*

There are times when our worship of God is clothed in light, song, and splendor. That is as it should be. It has been said that music can take us to heights that the written word cannot reach. But there are also times when we are wordless in prayer, and perhaps imageless, and the Holy Spirit prays for us with sighs too deep for words. What we have seen of the teaching of the Psalms and the nature of the new covenant shows us that this is the true nature of the worship Christians should offer. What we do with our music and preaching should be to prepare our congregations for this experience.

For open worship to thrive, it needs to be recognized for what it is—the worship of the new covenant. Friends should learn to understand it as such. It is inward, moral, and sacrificial, and it is the sign of the unity of the Church, which is Christ's body.[18] Individualistic forms of Christianity cannot rise to these heights. In worship Christians come before God as one. The Church will bear the marks of the passion because its members carry their cross daily. It will share the imperishable glory of Christ's resurrection because it has already passed from death to life.[19] It offers its worship on behalf of the world because its spiritual unity with Christ means that it possesses a measure of his priesthood.[20]

Inevitably, this sort of language raises the question of the ordinances. Historically, Friends have not observed the outward ceremonies familiar in other denominations but have always insisted on the necessity of the inward experience they symbolize. There are one or two yearly meetings that permit the use of water, bread, and wine, but this practice is comparatively rare. Although there does not seem to be a widespread demand for the ordinances, there does not seem to be a widespread understanding of the traditional position either. Perhaps there should be. There are occasions on which Friends are asked what their position is, and those asking are entitled to a reasoned and scriptural answer.[21]

It seems quite clear that Jesus instructed the Church to baptize and celebrate the supper. At the last supper he said, "Do this in memory of me."[22] His last instructions were that his disciples should "...go and make disciples of all nations, baptizing them in the name of the Father and of the Son and of the Holy Spirit."[23] However, these texts are not without their critical difficulties. If we assume, for example, that the Trinitarian formula in the Great Commission is a later interpolation, what we have is a text representing the convictions of the Church as to its history rather than a prime historical source. This may or may not affect the authority of the passage, but it does open the door to the kind of argument early Friends used: that the later rituals were justified by reference to these texts rather than being the direct consequence of them.

Friends have traditionally maintained that Christ utilized the prevailing practices of the fellowship meal and the ritual bath to explain the nature of the new relationship he came to establish and that these remained part of the practice of the first Jewish Christians, though vested with a different significance. Unlike circumcision, which gradually ceased to be a part of the life of the new Christian community, baptism and the supper acquired the status of permanent rituals, so that what was originally a feature of the Church in transition became permanently established. Historically, the development of the ceremonies went hand in hand with that of the monarchical episcopate, and the original meaning became lost.

This represents a theological critique of later Church history derived from Friends reading of the New Testament. It rests on the judgment that the New Testament supports the inward/outward distinction in full, and that in spite of Christ's use of the forms; it was never part of Christ's intention to institute permanent outward ceremonies of any kind. Certain ceremonies continued during apostolic times, though they were transitional in nature and were ultimately intended to lapse as the full, inward, spiritual implications of the new covenant were established. Modern Friends are faced with the consequences of these claims. If they are true, how should Friends regard other churches that observe the ordinances and on what grounds are they now to maintain their testimony?

The Ordinances

It is important to be clear exactly what Friends say and have said about the ordinances. Plainly, Friends reject the belief that there are certain ceremonies that convey a specific kind of grace if they are validly performed. Friends also reject the belief that Christ ordained two specific ceremonies, participation in which is essential to salvation. However, rejection of a ceremony is not a rejection of the spiritual reality that it claims to embody. Friends have always strenuously asserted the need to be baptized and to feed on the spiritual body and blood of Christ. What they deny is that ceremonial observance is necessary to bring about these ends.[24] Let us see how two leading Friends, writing in different historical circumstances, have made this point and then ask what Friends can say today.

> *Friends have always strenuously asserted the need to be baptized and to feed on the spiritual body and blood of Christ. What they deny is that ceremonial observance is necessary to bring about these ends.*

Isaac Penington uses a straightforward covenantal argument.[25] He rests his case on the claim that the true Church is an expression of the new covenant; that the new covenant is an inward reality characterized by power rather than form; that this inward reality is demanding, and historically many have found themselves unable to meet its demands; and that the result is the development of a sham Church that has the form of godliness and not the power. He points to a number of New Testament references that show Jesus, Peter, and Paul warning the Church that it is in danger of succumbing to intellectual and moral corruption, and claims that this corruption took place soon after the death of the Apostles.[26]

Penington presents us with a contrast between what was intended and what occurred, between what *is*, and what, by God's will, *should be*. His judgment on the Church is that its history reveals a record of corporate ostentation, greed, lust for power, cruelty, and oppression. He locates the decline of true Christianity in the development of the Church's institutional life, because of the ease with which participation the ceremonial aspects of religion can be mistaken for genuine personal devotion. This situation cannot be remedied from within. Only an entirely new start, the restoration of the true Church by an act of God, can restore the purity of the Christian faith.[27] Clearly, on Penington's analysis, Friends cannot recognize, participate in, or themselves observe any outward ceremony. Because the true Church does not have them, Friends may not. Hence, any yearly meeting that permits the ordinances takes itself outside the true faith. We might call this the uncompromising position.

Joseph John Gurney, who plays defense to Penington's offense, adopts a more moderate position.[28] He writes at a time when many Friends were coming to feel the need for a denominational, rather than a sectarian, understanding of their faith. Gurney bases Friends testimony squarely on scripture, with the matter-of-fact implication that in fair-minded denominational controversies, the Friends view will be found correct. He takes the passages used to justify the ordinances and finds in them evidence of the forms of worship in use under the Old Covenant. He argues that these are merely a pattern or indication of the substance and the reality of worship that will come in the New Covenant, the new relationship with God inaugurated by Jesus.[29] So much is common to all Christians that without these beliefs the faith could not have differentiated itself from Judaism, historically, if for no other reason.

He then sets out to show two things about baptism and the supper. In common with most Christians outside the Catholic tradition, he argues that what is necessary for entry into the Church is not participation in a ceremony, but the experience of conversion.[30] Spiritual food, or communion, is available to all who gather with their fellows to remember the sacrifice and redemption offered by

Christic.[31] This establishes the symbolic nature of the ceremonies with reference to the spiritual realities they represent and is a rejection of the Catholic system. He then goes on to argue that all forms are to be abolished by the work of Christ and that it is by him alone that we can come to God. He concludes that forms in themselves have no spiritual value so cannot be obligatory.

It is necessary, therefore, to show that the elements of water, wine, bread, and the ceremonies of which they are a part fall into the category of "forms." Gurney's rationale is a scriptural argument in which he seeks to demonstrate that each had a peculiar origin and temporary function, so that, on the evidence of scripture alone, observation of them cannot be binding on Christians. One needs to follow the cumulative force of his argument to understand its strength, but at the same time it depends on a number of controversial points like the nature of the last supper, whether baptism was ever effected by the laying on of hands, or whether the ceremonies that developed into the ordinances did so through doctrinal necessity or from some other historical cause.

We might call this the moderate position, because it maintains the truth of Friends' claim that participation in the ordinance is unnecessary for salvation but does not carry the implication that other churches fall into error when they do observe the ordinances. The moderate position sees the outward ordinances as *adiaphora*, ceremonies neither commanded nor forbidden by the word of God in scripture and open to each church to observe as it sees fit. Historically, the moderate position has prevailed among Friends but may now be under challenge once more. Its weakness is that it respects the position of other churches but denies Friends themselves the liberty to do what other churches do.

It is outflanked by what was once called the tolerationist position among Friends, which says that there may be circumstances in which it is permissible for Friends churches to baptize and observe the supper. There are pastors who take this view; both Eastern Region and Southwest Yearly meetings have amended their disciplines to permit it officially. It has to be said that there does not seem to be any great demand for the ordinances, so Friends practice has not significantly altered. But some pastors find it very difficult to refuse a request for baptism when one is honestly and sincerely made. The tolerationist position certainly has the advantage of allowing spiritual liberty, but fails to appreciate that Friends testimony on the ordinances is related to a number of wider questions involving the nature of the Church and is not so easily detached from them.

Taking the Long View

In thinking about Friends and their unusual attitude to the ordinances, it is necessary to maintain an historical perspective and to remind ourselves that in church history it is necessary to take the long view and think in terms of centuries, millennia even—not just the last decade or two. The Church is an historical entity living in response to its surroundings. Periodically it makes compromises either with the state or the prevailing culture. As time passes, these compromises can be seen to be inimical to the gospel and false to the Church's true inspiration. They come to be regarded as corruptions. The history of the Church in Soviet Russia is only now being written, and in China, Sudan, Indonesia, Iran and many other parts of the world, the choice between collaboration and martyrdom is a real one.

In the past, circumstances like this have led to compromises with the world and then to great movements for the reform of the Church. Usually, these movements couch their critique in scriptural terms. They also make historical claims, because it is necessary to advance some reason as to why the corruptions of the Church could emerge in the first place. Inevitably this gives rise to theories about the dynamics of Christian history, quite apart from the general scriptural principles underlying the theory of the Church. What is usually said is that practice has departed from principle and must be returned to it. Always the standard applied is that of the New Testament Church as described in scripture.

No evangelical can escape this reality. The evangelical faith depends vitally upon a rejection of the doctrines and practices of late medieval Catholicism. The courtesies of an ecumenical age should not be allowed to obscure the real theological differences that exist between the evangelical Protestant worldview in all its complexity and that of the Roman and Orthodox churches. Those who live under the American Constitution, which preserves an official separation between church and state, have no very great reason to reflect on these matters. Nevertheless, they are part of the reality within which evangelicals live. To dismiss Friends testimony about the ordinances because it seems somehow outdated is historically ill informed.

Friends are not alone in generalizing from historical experience to establish a theory of the Church, for this aspect of their doctrine has much in common with that of the sixteenth-century European Anabaptists from whom (among others) the modern Mennonites are descended. Racked, burned, and drowned for their faith, the Anabaptists asked themselves how the Church of Christ could commit such atrocities and naturally answered that it could not. They concluded that the Church had suffered a corruption serious enough to be compared to the Fall when Christianity was adopted as the official religion of the Roman Empire following the death of the Emperor Constantine in 337 AD.

Reaching a similar conclusion to the one Friends arrived at later, they concluded that the New Testament provides no precedent for hierarchy, formality, or ceremonial display within the Church. Nor can it be interpreted to justify warfare, infant baptism, or the physical enforcement of belief, and it gives no authority whatever for the political oversight of the Church by the state. Hence, no church that practices or accommodates itself to these things can have continuity with the Church of the apostles. The sixteenth-century Anabaptists therefore came out of what they believed to be the false church, and they paid the price.[32]

We should look at the Friends attitude to the ordinances against this background. Though we are distant in time from these events, we are close enough to be able to recognize that we can still hear their echoes. The Anabaptist Fall theory and the Quaker Apostasy theory both provide answers to the problem of how the condition of the sixteenth-century Church could have arisen by suggesting that it is the culmination of a long-term process. What distinguishes the Quaker answer to the problem is that it sees the existence of outward sacraments and the restriction of access to them as the means by which the corruption of the Church was facilitated. Since this cannot have been within the intentions of Christ, the scriptures must be interpreted in terms of inward spiritual sacraments and not outwardly observable ones.

It has to be said that these theories may have made sense in the sixteenth and seventeenth century, but today they are more difficult to sustain in their pure form. It is hard to date the Fall or the Apostasy in a convincing way or to state the principle on which an institution could be apostate yet nevertheless harbor and, apparently, nourish those of the true faith within it. It is not clear whether apostasy resides in institutions or in people or how we can distinguish apostates from such figures as Boniface, Benedict, or Francis of Assisi. Moreover, much of the experience of Eastern Orthodoxy has been persecution at the hands of Muslims, and these churches have for centuries not occupied the dominant position required by the theory. The Quaker version, if we take the brief account given in Fox's sermon on Firbank Fell[33] or the more considered exposition of Isaac Penington already noticed, probably proves too much. It amounts to saying that Christianity fell stillborn from the womb, which is hardly credible in this day and age.

Preserving Friends Testimony

We have, therefore, to make a balanced judgment and say that the uncompromising position is based on a particular view of history that is difficult to sustain in detail but is convincing in general. It is not necessary to go all the way with Isaac Penington to recognize the truth of his main thesis, which is that the Church is not kept automatically pure, but has experienced periods of deep corruption. What has happened once may happen again. There are places in the modern world where the Church has chosen martyrdom when faced with the power of the state and places where it has compromised with worldly power. The historical argument for preserving the Friends testimony is that an inward religion without institutional forms provides no handle for a corrupting power to grasp. To serve as a standing reminder of this truth may be a significant part of the vocation of Friends, and this is one reason why the testimony should be maintained.

> *The historical argument for preserving the Friends testimony is that an inward religion without institutional forms provides no handle for a corrupting power to grasp.*

The moderate position, provided it is not uncoupled from this historical analysis, meets a number of both evangelical and Quaker criteria without the drawbacks of the uncompromising position. It arises out of scripture and involves a developed theory of the covenant, but it also permits Friends to insist that their distinctives are justified and also to accept that others with equal *bona fides*, may understand the covenant differently. The moderate position does not require a specific historical theory but does make allowances for the circumstances that such theories purport to explain. Instead of apostasy and restitution, it can be accommodated by the theory that church history is best interpreted in terms of stagnation and renewal. The moderate position illustrates the hybrid nature of evangelical Quakerism. It accepts a reformation understanding of the dynamics of church history with a gathered church understanding of how those dynamics are constituted.

It can be seen, therefore, that Friends have solid historical and theological reasons for their testimony on the ordinances. This is the answer to the tolerationist position. On the surface, giving liberty to meetings to make their own decisions looks attractive. But such a course would raise a number of significant issues that go well beyond the local meeting. First, it would mark a departure from what Friends have always said about a major matter of discipleship and church order. Second, if such departures are contemplated, they should be based on theological principles and not the simple desire for freedom of action in the matter. Third, the testimony on ordinances, reasserted by the Richmond Declaration, is the consensus view of Friends and should be observed until that consensus alters. Finally, it is not as easy as it looks to overcome the biblical and historical basis of the doctrine. The testimony on the ordinances is not a matter of personal conviction; it is Friends' settled corporate doctrine.

But leaving theology and historical circumstances aside, there is another, more fundamental reason for Friends testimony about the ordinances. We have already suggested that central to Friends worship is the period of silence at the heart of the meeting. Certainly it is traditional, and we should not be reluctant to use it on that account. But it is traditional because we have always seen it as the true worship of the covenant and fundamental to our faith. Christ wishes us to approach him in a humble, contrite, self-sacrificing spirit, but also as a fellowship of his disciples.[34] As we come together in a body, the true shepherd meets us as his flock, feeds us, and gives us to drink. The practice of silence goes to the heart of our relationship with God and can properly be seen as communion. It is essential, it is unique, and it is inseparable from what it means to be a Friend.

NOTES

1 John 4:24.
2 Heb. 12:28, Ps. 100:2, 2 Tim. 2:22.
3 Hos. 6:6, Prov. 21:3, 27; Isa. 1.
4 Eg. Prov. 9:10, Ps.111:10, Job 28:28.
5 Ps. 95:6, 95:9, 96:9.
6 Ps. 24: 1-4, Ps. 11:7, John 4:23.
7 Ps. 51:17.
8 Matt. 6:6.
9 Ps. 51:6.
10 Ps. 46:10.
11 Isa. 57:15.
12 Ps. 51:6.
13 Ps. 62:1,4-5.
14 Hab.2:18-20.
15 Zech. 2:10-13.
16 Ps. 37:7.
17 Isa. 40:28-41:1.
18 Col. 1:18.
19 John 11:25-26.
20 1 Pet. 2:9.
21 See the discussion in Wilmer A. Cooper, *A Living Faith* (Richmond, Ind.: Friends United Press, 1990), Ch. 7.
22 Luke 22:9, 1 Cor. 11:23.
23 Matt. 28:19.
24 Rom. 6:3-4, John 6:53-58.
25 Isaac Penington, (1616-1673) *The Way of Life and Death made Manifest* (1667) *Works*, Vol. 1(Philadelphia, 1863).
26 Matt. 24:11,24, 2 Tim.3:1-4, 2 Pet. 2:1-2.
27 Rev. 14:6-12.
28 Joseph John Gurney, (1788-1847) *Observations on the Religious Peculiarities of the Society of Friends* London, (1827) Ch. 4.
29 Heb. 9:9-10.
30 Titus 3:3-7, Heb. 10:19-22, Matt. 3:11-12, Luke 3:16, Mark 1:7-8.
31 1 Cor. 11:20-33 read as a whole. Why is Luke 22:19 followed and not John 13:15?
32 For a general discussion see Franklin H. Littell, *The Origins of Sectarian Protestantism,* (New York: Macmillan, 1964).
33 George Fox, *Journal* (Nickalls) p.109.
34 1 Cor. 10: 1-4.

7

Discipleship and Faith

7

Discipleship and Faith

Like many other people, I was brought up with a fairly simple form of faith. At home and at Sunday school, I received the same consistent message. I was to believe in Jesus, go to church, say my prayers, and witness to my faith whenever there was the need. I was also taught that above everything else, Jesus wanted me to be good. If I was not going to be good, there was not much point in being a Christian. Simple though these precepts may be, I have never once doubted their wisdom. They seem to me to be a pretty fair summary of what the Bible says.

Actually *being* good is another matter, however. Most of us are fairly virtuous as a rule, but there are times when we face significant challenges to our moral integrity. We may be called upon to do something we do not want to do and doubt whether we have the inner resources to meet the challenge. We may face a conflict of loyalties where someone will be hurt, whatever action we take. We may find ourselves in an entirely new situation where there are no guidelines and it is exceedingly difficult to see where the right path lies. In times like this we face the challenge of deciding what goodness requires of us.

Friends have always placed great emphasis on the moral life, but have never theorized about it or developed a formal moral theology. One might suppose that their moral advice comes on a case-by-case basis, often as a negative reaction to others' standards. This would be mistaken. In what follows, we shall discuss the general nature of moral discernment and then argue that Friends covenantal doctrines give rise to a particular kind of ethical theory on which much of the traditional vocabulary is based. This vocabulary, we will argue, reflects an understanding of both conscience and virtue as necessary expressions of the light of Christ within.

Moral Discernment

The moral life is that part of our experience that has to do with our obligations, those things we feel required to do out of our own free will—even if they might not be in our own interest or if we might wish to do something quite different. Very often we find no difficulty in doing what is right, because our upbringing and education ensure that most of our actions are quite habitual. There are also occasions when we have to make choices about what to do. These are the times when our own conscious or unconscious motives come into play or we need to calculate the results of any decisions we might make. Our character and reputation depend to an important degree on the choices we make and on what kind of moral principles we choose to act.

Moral discernment is the art of bringing harmony and stability to our moral lives so that they are more than just a series of arbitrary and possibly inconsistent decisions. Christians will wish to live in accordance with the precepts of the faith, which urge us to devote ourselves to doing good and promise that those who are persistent in the endeavor will be rewarded with eternal life. The test of our love for Jesus is not what we say, but whether we keep his commandments. These commandments are twofold, as is generally known. We are to love God unconditionally and love our neighbors as ourselves. [1]

> *If our moral lives are not to be simply a series*
> *of arbitrary and possibly inconsistent decisions,*
> *we need to reflect upon them and give them*
> *some kind of order.*

As a statement of principle, this sounds quite clear. Nevertheless, before we can begin to act on Jesus' words we have to reflect on the nature of love, gain some awareness of the different senses in which the word can be used, and understand how it is connected with other realities, like duty and goodness. Love can be spontaneous but also disciplined and thoughtful. It can be an inward disposition or a pattern of action. It can give us great blessings and at the same time great pain. It is neither easy nor simple. Love, in other words, is not self-explanatory. Our understanding of it cannot be separated from our understanding of God.

In these circumstances, moral discernment is inevitably a religious process and part of the wider spiritual life of the Christian believer. Discernment becomes visible in the form of individual decisions, but these decisions reflect a continuing process that includes personal reflection on moral realities and what we might call pursuit of the good. Thus, right action is the outcome of practice and experience, personal devotion to God's purposes, and divine help. Moral uprightness is a dimension of the spiritual life, not an autonomous religious faculty.

This is borne out by another way in which the word "moral" is used. Sometimes the sense of the word extends beyond specific acts of moral discernment to the character of the person making them. There are reasons for this. Moral leadership, for example, cannot be exercised by just anybody. The real thing comes from someone with understanding and fixity of purpose and an ability to weigh complex issues. The decisions of such people can be seen as the outcome of their personal qualities and ways of life rather than just the ability to make specific decisions on particular occasions.

If Christianity is to make claims about what is right and wrong, then, its teaching will need to go beyond just providing rules for making decisions. This is not to say that rules are unimportant, but to emphasize the point that the scope of ethical inquiry does not stop at a discussion of what is or is not good. It also extends into the character of moral agency and what influences are likely to produce individual virtue. Inevitably, therefore, there is a public, indeed political, aspect to ethics. Because we live in society, moral questions usually arise out of our relations with other people. What we do will be the outcome of who we are.

> *If Christianity is to make claims about what is right and wrong, then, its teaching will need to go beyond just providing rules for making decisions.*

Christians differ in matters of ethics, as they do in doctrine. There is no generally agreed path to virtuous living, and this is due, to some extent, to the complexity of social life and the diversity of human nature. Nevertheless, a number of Christian traditions have distinctive ways of giving moral guidance, and Friends have a place in this group. As we have seen, the ethical expectations we have of people will depend partly on what we make of their character and partly on what we believe are the general limitations of human nature. This is why ethical distinctiveness tends to arise out of theological distinctives. Our understanding of human nature arises out of our understanding of the ways of God.

232

Friends traditionally regarded our personal and corporate behavior as an expression of our covenantal relationship with God. Central to this relationship is the guidance that comes to us through the light within, which both leads us into the truth and is the agent of moral discernment. Specific items in the Quaker moral vocabulary—bearing the cross, bearing testimony, being under concern, receiving openings, having one's measure, and being led—all come from this understanding. It is surprising, to say the least, that such an upright and moral people as Friends have never produced a moral theology. The reason lies in Friends inclination to see the making of moral decisions as an opportunity for discernment rather than moral reasoning in the normal sense. They are therefore less occupied than one might think with the application of abstract moral principles or judging the desirability of the outcomes of certain courses of action. Let us see how this works by drawing some preliminary distinctions.

The Moral Sense

The moral sense is the set of more-or-less automatic assumptions about the world and our relations with it that provide rule of thumb, or even unconscious guidance, about how we should behave and how our values should be translated into action. In family life, at work, in public places, as citizens, church members, or tennis players—in all kinds of circumstances—our moral sense is at work governing our behavior and making us who we are. Although based on conscience, the moral sense is intimately connected with our reasoning powers and often operates unconsciously. We usually steer our course toward right and away from wrong without deliberating over every action we take or attitude we adopt.

In most matters our attitudes are clear, and we spend no time considering what we think because we know. Old principles provide clear and acceptable answers to new questions, whether positive or negative. When we are faced with the need to decide what we think about something or what to do, we often decide without reference to the conscience, because the moral sense is sufficient. We simply apply whatever evidence or reason we possess and arrive at a conclusion. We usually make an intuitive leap of some kind. This does not mean, of itself, that we are being irrational or unreasonable in making moral judgments, just that the reasons that bring about our conclusions originate in our own choices or intuitions and not the power of our logic. It is the quality of our choices and intuitions that provide the quality of our moral sense.

These moral conclusions derive in part from non-ethical considerations, because the moral sense, while primarily concerned with right and wrong, also makes judgments about the general nature of the world we live in. Many fundamental questions about the nature and significance of human life are not in themselves moral questions, but there is immense moral significance in the answers we give to them. For example, the nature of God, the historical existence of Jesus Christ, and the question of whether he is the Savior are not primarily moral propositions. But immense moral consequences flow from a decision to accept them. There is inevitably a cognitive, or intellectual, component in the moral sense.

> *Many fundamental questions about the nature*
> *and significance of human life are not in*
> *themselves moral questions, but there is immense*
> *moral significance in the answers we give to them.*

This conclusion holds for believers and unbelievers alike, for there is no formal difference between the moral sense of Christians and other morally upright people. Both make ethical and non-ethical judgments based on fundamental convictions that are built up over time by the continuing process of inference in which we are all naturally engaged. This is how human beings in general acquire the framework within which their moral judgments are made. When new questions arise, we tend to answer them by referring to what we already know or what we have previously committed ourselves to.

That is not the end of the matter, though. Although our moral sense reflects certain truths that we regard as unquestionable, we also know the experience of moral uncertainty and ambivalence. The moral sense operates over time, often in an imperceptible manner, and therefore tends to be underestimated. We realize, rather than learn, the guidance that comes from the moral sense. However, the promptings of the conscience are never unconscious. They are always moral and usually accompanied by initial doubt and discomfort. Doubt and discomfort are dissolved if we obey the conscience, but if we ignore or repress what it is telling us, we know that there will be damage to our self-respect. Having a bad conscience is to be in this situation.

Conscience

Conscience is the faculty by which we know right from wrong, but it is not quite the same thing as the moral sense. We do not need to make a judgment about what things actually are right or wrong to recognize that the conscience is a source of involuntary feeling which gives us mental pain if we act contrary to its dictates. The conscience produces feelings of guilt and is an agent of moral improvement, because we know what feelings await us if we offend it. Conscience can also be a positive influence, providing an endorsement for our conduct on those occasions when we have done what is right. It is hard to see how we can be happy if we do not live in harmony with our conscience.

> *Conscience can also be a positive influence, providing an endorsement for our conduct on those occasions when we have done what is right.*

In terms of experience, therefore, the conscience is an immediate guide, operating when the moral sense reaches its limits. Conscience is a court of appeal rather than a court of first instance, but that status itself, and the fact that it places consequences on our disobedience, means that it is the superior faculty. Conscience is the governor of the moral sense and the faculty that oversees its operation. But that is not all. Evidence of the operation of conscience is also discernible in the framework of assumptions that I have argued form the basis of the moral sense. If we look at conscience solely as an arbiter in any given case, we will lose sight of its continuing influence endorsing the guidance of the moral sense. It provides the link between *is* and *ought,* not by confusing the logical status of ethical and factual propositions but by influencing the way in which they are held.

Hence, conscience is God's means of making us human, because it determines our basic experience of the world through its influence on our moral sense and the rationality that sense necessarily employs. Indeed, scripture clearly envisages conscience as a guide to life, which we inherit with our common humanity and which it is our highest duty to obey. The nature and functioning of conscience, therefore, goes well beyond correcting us when we go wrong. Rather it is, as Friends tradition claims, the primary mode of revelation and the faculty in which we come closest to God. We tend to forget that it commends as well as corrects and endorses the good as well as telling us when we go wrong.

The light within, while present in the conscience, is not *itself* the conscience, because it is not a human faculty. We experience it in the conscience because the conscience is the most fundamental part of our being, and that is where we should expect to encounter God. The gospel calls for repentance; the instrument of repentance is the conscience; and the voice that awakens the conscience is Christ himself. The light of Christ within is neither innate nor a mystical capacity human beings are born with. On the contrary, the light is that of God within us, and our proper attitude to it is obedience to its guidance and recognition of what it teaches.

> *The gospel calls for repentance; the instrument of repentance is the conscience; and the voice that awakens the conscience is Christ himself.*

Religious belief, however, is not essential to a person possessing a conscience. The universality of conscience is an example of the common grace God extends to all creatures, regardless of their attitude toward him, whereby they may discern the natural laws by which he has provided order and stability in the world. Clearly, morality is more than religious morality. There are many people who conscientiously try to do their duty, although for various reasons they may not have accepted Christ. However, if their reasoning faculties are at work reflecting on experience and being informed by conscience, they will be in the position of the upright pagans to whom the early Church appealed. The existence and experience of conscience is a necessary preliminary to conversion, and it is the medium though which our hearts are prepared to receive the gift of salvation itself.

The Light Within

As we saw in an earlier chapter, Friends believe the Bible to teach that every person possesses a measure of divine light, the presence of Jesus Christ the light of the world, working within their conscience to move them away from evil toward the good, and striving continually to bring them to an awareness of their condition and a desire for salvation. The conscience is a human characteristic, but the light within is another name for the presence of Christ himself. The light within is not like an energy supply that we can turn on and off or an entity that will answer our questions if we frame them properly. The light within uses our experience of the world and our innate capacity to reflect on it and encourages us to accept guidance as we constantly try to discern the truth and work out what to do. Moral and intellectual discernment is a process in which there is a place for human faculties, reason, and authority as well as the direct illumination of the light within. The light is in the conscience, but it is not the conscience itself.

> *The light within uses our experience of the world and our innate capacity to reflect on it and encourages us to accept guidance as we constantly try to discern the truth and work out what to do.*

This presents a major difficulty. Quaker writers have generally claimed that because we can have direct access to the will of God through the light within, other means of trying to ascertain it will be uncertain, second-hand, and risky. What guidance we receive from our experience of the world will be of human, not divine, origin and will be ultimately dependent on the senses for its transmission to us. It will have all the defects of unaided human knowledge, being incomplete, limited in vision, and tainted with the residual effects of sin. If the evidence of the senses is open to doubt, the senses themselves cannot be a source of sound religious knowledge. The only way to a true knowledge of God is by means of direct inspiration.

In his short philosophical treatise *The Possibility and Necessity of Inward and Immediate Revelation*,[2] Robert Barclay provided a rational justification for this suspicion by drawing a fundamental distinction between natural truths, which come to us through the operation of the senses, and supernatural truths, which are revealed directly to us by God without the mediation of the senses. This is commonly thought to be the principle of dualism that underlies all Quaker faith and practice. But Barclay's formulation makes it very difficult to resist the claims of those who say they have been led to a certain course of action by divine illumination, because inward knowledge must always be more secure than the fruits of reason and the senses. A moment's thought will show that any tests for the genuineness of such claims must fail because they belong to the same category of outward knowledge that Barclay was attacking. Barclay in fact bequeathed to Friends a highly unstable metaphysics.

There is reason to question whether Barclay's analysis is a fundamental expression of Friends principles or just one way in which they can be expressed. It has been argued that he has elevated a practical distinction made for evangelical purposes into an immutable principle and has drawn legitimate distinctions much too sharply. Early Friends wished to emphasize the fundamental difference between notional or formal Christianity and "a transforming and creative personal acquaintance with and relation to, Christ in the Spirit."[3] What Barclay succeeded in doing was to confuse what he saw as two different kinds of truth with two modes of receiving one and the same truth. The fact that God is good is something we can be convinced of either by what our parents have told us or our own inward experience. What we know is in each case the same.

Nevertheless, it is possible to retain the substance of Barclay's position without accepting every detail of it. The human mind possesses a moral sense that develops over time and is influenced by our reflections on our experience and the great questions of human existence. It is possible to see the conscience entering continuously into this process rather than exerting an influence from a separate standpoint. It is as if conscience operates as a compass guiding our thoughts even when we are unaware of it and as an arbiter when we need its direct intervention. It is a vehicle of the light within, but will also open the doors of our mind to allow the outward light to shine in. There is one light, and it comes to us in more than one way.

The heart must be prepared to listen, though. The voice of God comes to us as a still small voice, and we need to be still in our own hearts to hear it. This is the importance of inward retirement and corporate waiting for guidance. By putting the devices and desires of our own hearts on one side, we are better able to hear what the voice of God is saying to us. The light speaks to us through the whole range of our human capacities but primarily through the conscience, because this is the point at which the presence of God is most real.

Hence, the conscience, as the locus of the light within, is the faculty that will be the foundation of all the others. It is primary and definitive, and whatever we do will be conditioned by what it requires.

We have now reached the point at which we can claim that the inward light in the conscience is the wellspring of moral knowledge and that obedience to what the light requires constitutes right action. If this is so, we have broken down the absolute barrier between moral and other kinds of understanding. It follows that neither the search for a principle on which to act nor a calculation of the consequences of an act can be a sufficient basis for right action. They may each lead to an understanding of what God requires, but the movement from understanding to commitment, from possibility to probability, to certainty and action, requires God's active intervention to indicate what his desires are. The light enables us to come to the point of understanding.

So what is our part in the process of discernment? Are we passive recipients, as the Quaker tradition held? Or do we have a more active part in the acquisition of spiritual knowledge and the making of moral judgments? That we have a part in this in process is the teaching of scripture. At the Last Supper, Jesus tells his disciples that he would no longer call them servants but instead would call them friends, because servants (unlike friends) do not know what their master is doing. He says he has made known to them everything he has received from his Father. The condition is that the disciples should keep God's commandments and love one another.[4]

This process is a variant of the commandment to love God and one's neighbor given elsewhere in the gospels.[5] The conditions under which we will be able to discern the voice of God will be those in which we set aside, as far as it is in our power, the sound of our own voices, whether they be our personal inclinations, our favorite imagery, the authorities we choose to obey, or the intellectual influences we espouse. However, these things usually represent the fruits of the moral sense. There is an apparent conflict between what we have said about the gradual accumulation of moral knowledge and the need to set aside our personal preferences in the process of discerning the truth.

The conflict can be resolved if we remember that the conscience is working, so to speak, at the subconscious as well as the conscious level. If we are faced with an important decision and want to discern what Christ wishes us to do, we are unlikely to overcome our own preferences unless we are open to the possibility that we should, and even better, already have had, experience in doing so. If we are open in this way, however, our minds will have been prepared by our experience over time for the demands that will be made upon them at any particular moment. At the point of decision, these streams converge; the light within is able to give its guidance, and we are able to respond. We must be open to whatever pride or self-centeredness we still have, but at the same time we need to realize that using our faculties properly is not the same thing as denying them.

Character and Virtue

This is not easy, but it comes with practice, and the traditional institutions of Friends were designed to enable us to live in this fashion. Through its vocabulary and customary practices, Quakerism tries to provide a model of the Christian life that emphasizes obedience to God and constant vigilance for the promptings of the light within. Historically, perhaps, it has concentrated on inward obedience to

God in such a manner that the outward forms of obedience have been neglected. One does not find the word "virtue" used much among Friends, partly because of a reluctance to be prescriptive in ways that might drown out the voice of the light within. Nevertheless, a religious body must be able to give guidance to its members on a moral and upright life and the qualities requisite to live it.[6]

These qualities can all be understood in a variety of ways, but they need to be collectively defined and cultivated before they can become models for the religious life of a community. To find out exactly what constitutes a virtue, one has to have regard for the historical and cultural circumstances of which it is an expression, because the meanings of moral terms change over time. In Christianity, the virtues represent the way of life to which the believer is called, and they also represent the patterns according to which character is formed. Virtues are, therefore, the means of initiation into a particular moral tradition, whether it is the Roman confessional or the Quaker understanding of divine leading. To understand virtues we must pay attention to the whole corpus of practice that constitutes a religious tradition.

This is a complicated matter and inevitably draws us into a consideration not just of individual virtues, but also of the self-understanding that causes a particular group to maintain its identity, thereby giving rise to the moral expectations it has of its adherents. This is a dynamic and historical process in which a number of elements combine. Partly it is a question of positives: What does this group stand for, and what are those joining it called upon to commit themselves to? Partly it is a matter of negatives: What alternatives are ruled out by the positive claims the group makes? The decisions a group makes on these matters will reflect its origins and history and require the definition of the kinds of change that would make it different from what it has historically been or what its members originally committed themselves to, or were brought up to accept.

Religious groups like Friends reflect the circumstances of their times, of course, but they also exemplify traditions.[7] In the normal sense, tradition is the handing on of statements, beliefs, rules, and customs from generation to generation, and the word often has the connotation of the way things are done. In this sense, the word has a folkloric character and represents heritage rather than history. However, tradition takes on an altogether more powerful meaning if we define it as "an argument extended through time in which certain fundamental agreements are defined and redefined in terms of two kinds of conflict: those with critics and enemies external to the tradition and those internal, interpretive debates through which the meaning and rationale of the fundamental agreements come to be expressed, and by whose progress a tradition is constituted."[8]

In this sense, Quaker ethics can be seen as a moral tradition of a particular kind. The ethical requirements of Christianity are that we love God and love our neighbor. Converted, we must pursue love, joy, peace, longsuffering, gentleness, goodness, faith, meekness, and temperance. These are spiritual gifts, but they also become virtues we must practice and develop. Friends distinctives arise out of an engagement with that part of the wider tradition that was seen to give these moral qualities a lesser priority than doctrinal conformity. It is crucial to understand, however, that Friends do believe in the truth of their doctrines. Notwithstanding that, Friends at their best have always tried to school their members into an understanding and inward espousal of doctrine through the conviction of the light rather than by imposing sanctions upon disbelief and disobedience.

Friends at their best have always tried to school their members into an understanding and inward espousal of doctrine through the conviction of the light rather than by imposing sanctions upon disbelief and disobedience. At the same time, there is a need to maintain a corporate understanding of what obedience means, because the light within guides the community, as well as the individual. In the foregoing discussion, I rejected duty and outcome as moral guides, useful and helpful though they are, because they do not carry within themselves the reasons why they should be obeyed. I argued that obedience to divine leading, however, does. This places great responsibility on individual Friends, who have to take charge of their own moral lives and not simply do what they are told. But there is no reason *not* to do as we are told, provided that we understand why we are told and accept the truth of what it being enjoined upon us. What is important is the process. If we are unquestioningly obedient, we may be ignoring what the light is telling us. If we question everything, the same applies. But if we accept the truth of what we are told because we are willing to accept guidance and have reasons for our trust, we will be acting as true moral agents.

> *Friends at their best have always tried to school their members into an understanding and inward espousal of doctrine through the conviction of the light rather than by imposing sanctions upon disbelief and disobedience.*

Friends name for this delicate balance between individual and corporate discernment has always been called "gospel order," and Friends have a variety of ways of maintaining it. Many of the institutions of Quakerism exemplify gospel order and also school Friends into the way it should be practiced. It would take far too long to catalogue them here, but it should be clear that the practice of virtue is at the root of gospel order. There is a reciprocal relationship between the functioning of Quaker institutions and the kind of person who possesses the qualities necessary to those functions. Let us take just two of those institutions and see how they operate as a school of virtue.

Keeping Spiritual Journals

First, there is the spiritual journal, the characteristic and unique literary genre that fits the virtue-ethics approach to Quakerism exactly. George Fox began his *Journal* with the words, "That all may know the ways of God with me..." His intention was not to write an autobiography, but an account of what God had done in his life and with his life. What emerges from the narrative is an account of one man's faith lived in and tested by the world. It is a portrait of his virtues, though not intended to be. Strength of purpose, tenderness, courage, patience, and endurance shine though the book. One has to say that this is not the whole picture. Fox was also pugnacious, touchy, uncompromising, censorious, and conceited. We certainly get a portrait of him, in Oliver Cromwell's words, "warts and all."

But that is the merit of the genre. Many other Friends, possibly as many as three hundred in the century following Fox's death, produced similar accounts of their lives.[9] What is significant in all these journals is the sense that the author is under the protection of Almighty God and is called to witness to the truth of the gospel as understood by Friends in all kinds of circumstances. To live according to a book of rules would have been impossible. To come safely through the troubles, toils, and snares of an Elizabeth Ashridge or an Oliver Smith one needed trust in the light within to give guidance when it was needed most. The virtues of these diarists were the fruits of their moral sense under divine guidance, developed and strengthened over time.

It is significant that the journals continue to have a strong influence on the formation of the Quaker character. Certain journals, like those of George Fox and John Woolman, have never been out of print, and at times of uncertainty Friends turn back to them and a significant number are reissued. There was a noticeable increase in interest in the middle of the nineteenth century, and a glance at any contemporary list of Friends publications will reveal what looks like a similar trend. The journals record lives lived by the light, and this is probably the secret of their appeal. They are about ordinary people who became extraordinary because they were willing to let God live in them, and then to tell us, by implication, how we can do the same.

Conducting Church Business

The second, and perhaps the clearest example of the schooling of moral sensibility among Friends is the process of conducting church business without voting. Friends sit in worship and are presented with the matter to be decided, usually quite routine, but sometimes of considerable significance. Various members of the group rise and give their opinions about the matter in hand, but not in a spirit of debate. Instead, there is a spirit of reconciliation and willingness to listen to what others say. Due weight is given to every contribution, but what is happening is an attempt to discern what God wants, not to recruit opinion for what any particular Friend wants. The clerk at the table is the servant of the meeting and records the sense of the meeting, or what it appears God has led the meeting to decide.

There is scriptural precedent for this way of reaching decisions. Acts 15 gives an account of the Jerusalem conference that was called upon to make the momentous decision as to whether gentile Christians were to be obliged to observe the Jewish law. We read that when the Pharisees stated the problem, much debate followed. Peter then gave a powerful speech, but we read (the context seems to indicate that this was the mood of the gathering), "and all of the assembly kept silence." Finally James summarized what he took their conclusion to be. The chapter records the decision and the proposals for action that flow from it, and Paul and Silas and a party of others are sent off to Antioch with a letter of record or "minute."

This letter of record is significant for two reasons. First, it says, "...it has seemed good to us, having come to one accord..." and then a little later, "For it has seemed good to the Holy Spirit and to us..." A two-way harmony is revealed here. First, a group of individuals with different points of view finds itself of one mind. Second, these individuals discover that they have been led into unity in the Holy Spirit. This, needless to say, is the basis of Friends decision-making procedures. The "sense of the meeting" is a clear expression of unity in the understanding that what has been done has received the blessing of the Holy Spirit.

To do this clearly requires us to be, as George Fox always insisted, "in the same power and spirit that the apostles were in." To read this chapter of Acts for historical interest rather than for a blueprint of how the church should take its decisions today is to be out of the covenant and out of the life. Consider the demands the business method makes. First, those who participate must have turned to the light, have been converted, and have a deep and lasting relationship with Jesus Christ. Second, they must have taken up the cross and must have engaged in an inward turning away from self-interest to devote themselves to God and to serve the interests of others. Third, the business method requires waiting with patience and confidence for the will of God to be revealed instead of rushing to judgment on the basis on one's own principles or convictions.

What we have here, then, are the spiritual conditions for moral discernment and an indispensable element in Friends ethical theory. The business meeting requires that those present set aside their own wisdom and look for the wisdom from above. As James says, this wisdom is pure, peaceable, gentle, readily accessible, full of mercy and goodness, and neither partial nor deceitful.[10] It is quite plain that only those who can recognize these qualities can know the wisdom of which the apostle speaks, and only those who practice these things in their own lives can acquire this wisdom for themselves.

Tradition and Testimony

Perhaps the clearest illustration of Friends' simultaneous promotion of virtue and reliance on personal moral responsibility lies in the area of testimony, a venerable word that has changed its connotation over the years. Originally it was an expression that emphasized the covenantal and sectarian theology that animated early Quakerism. In yearly meeting epistles in the late-seventeenth and early-eighteenth centuries, Friends are urged to maintain "all branches of our Christian testimony"—to provide sound arguments and practical ethical examples for the Quaker interpretation of Christianity by showing in considerable detail how precisely it differed from what was usually assumed to be orthodoxy.

With the passage of time, the theological testimonies like the rejection of ordination, insistence on the purely spiritual nature of baptism and the supper, the real nature of the new covenant, and the alleged apostasy of the other churches faded into the background as the theological agenda changed. What remained constant, though, were the ethical principles, or virtues, which were held to be characteristic, and therefore emblematic of the new covenant. These were respect for life and the rejection of warfare in all circumstances and emergencies; telling the strict truth at all times without reservation, particularly when it is not in one's own interests so to do; maintaining a pure and simple style of living void of all superfluities, including those of speech and dress, to the greater glory of God; and regarding and treating every other human being with strict equality, because they are as much the children of a loving God as we believe ourselves to be.

Friends place great stress on these ethical testimonies today, because they play exactly the same role that they did when they took a different form. They provide a guide to the corruptions of popular culture, the biases of the information media, the excesses of politics, the dangers of wealth, and what Pope John-Paul II called "the culture of death." They call us to a very different style of life by virtue of which it is possible to live modestly in a world of vanity, generously in an acquisitive society, honestly in the company of those who are concerned more with image than virtue, and peaceably in a nation and a world characterized by systematic violence.

The decision to live in this way, which is, and is intended to be, counter-cultural, requires a number of personal qualities. When one is in a minority in society and is regarded with contempt, ridicule, or occasional violence, one needs courage; to maintain a witness, one needs endurance also. To make a testimony it is necessary to understand what one is doing. Early Friends took the Bible literally. One could not take part in violence and claim to be a disciple of the prince of peace. One could not varnish or subvert the truth if one followed him who is the way, the truth and the life; one could not devote oneself to earthly treasures when the Son of Man had no where to lay his head.[11]

The scriptural justification for the testimonies is so strong that it is incomprehensible that there are those who consider that they, being part of Friends distinctives, should be played down as irrelevant or disturbing. One does not just have to look at the specific texts that make these points but also the whole thrust of Jesus' teaching. The argument for maintaining the testimonies has cumulative force. They are taught in scripture. All Christians ought to observe them (they are not obligatory on Friends only). They derive their cogency from their status as moral principles deriving from the covenant (which makes them of equal status with the Ten Commandments). They represent the Christian virtues in their purest form.

This whole argument rests on the principle that what gives us moral certainty is the light within, influencing our continuing moral judgment and entering our lives specifically in the voice of conscience. This is an organic, growing process. With the passage of time we acquire deeper insight, and our conduct inevitably changes. The wisdom of Friends practice is to articulate what our testimony is as a community, but then to allow each sincere Friend to decide in what ways that testimony is to be given. The testimonies encourage us to practice the freedom of the gospel. There are times when Friends have descended into legalism, to be sure, but these periods are exceptions. Properly understood, the testimonies are expressions of obedience to a God whose service is perfect freedom.

> *The wisdom of Friends practice is to articulate*
> *what our testimony is as a community, but then to*
> *allow each sincere Friend to decide in what ways*
> *that testimony is to be given.*

More is involved in the testimonies than an attachment to the heritage, then. Arguments from tradition may have some value, but ultimately they rest on an emotional attachment to the past. That is not a sufficient justification for a religious practice. No true child of the Reformation could entertain such reasoning for one moment. Evangelical Friends naturally ask what scripture has to say about these things, and too often in recent years they have not had the kind of guidance they should have received. The testimonies about truth, simplicity, and peace can each be justified by proof texts that are hard, if not impossible, to get around. All Christians should take them at face value. But it is also essential to understand how these texts build up into a consistent worldview that has a strong claim on our allegiance, because it is the historic basis for our separate existence as a church. What is involved in the testimonies is no less than a vision of Christianity and a vision of what the Christian life, in all its fullness, is.

In fact, there is wide agreement across the Quaker world as to what the testimonies are and what they require. The principles behind them have also been adopted widely in the contemporary Church, so they are not as distinctive of Friends as they once were. That is no reason for us to weaken in our devotion to them. Other Christians have made a place for ethical principles that have been nurtured by Friends, but they show no signs of being equally open to our theological testimonies. They may pursue peace and simplicity, but church hierarchies remain. The testimonies cannot be divided. They come together because they are the necessary outcome of our understanding of church and the basis of our corporate, not just our individual, morality. They make us a people, and without them we are nothing.

To summarize, moral discernment reflects the quality of the spiritual life, and character and experience—rather than discursive thought—are the basis of sound morals. The kind of character Friends tradition seeks to build up derives from the specifically Quaker conception of how the individual Christian life is developed within the Christian community. That life is one authenticated by God, not by the community. The community, however, has an important role in showing the individual how to seek God and needs to remember that its own advice and divine guidance is not the same thing.

Friends have developed a particular vocabulary and way of speaking about the interior life that reveals something of the processes of character formation. We have already seen how the light within is the instrument of conversion and the means to reform and refine the life of the believer into fuller conformity with the will of God. Friends' particular spirituality is seen in this process of sanctification, though the tradition takes exception to this way of putting it.

We have seen how silent waiting is central to this process and is, therefore, something evangelical Friends need to reclaim. The silence of open worship is the school in which the soul learns to distinguish between its own wishes and concerns and those of God by deliberately setting aside the self. In a self-obsessed age this is difficult to do, but our whole analysis of the Christian religion insists that it is essential. The times call for the witness of churches who put God at the center.

God speaks softly to us and in his own time. One of the hardest temptations to overcome is the temptation to religious enthusiasm, to lose sight of the fact that spiritual growth is organic and requires a range of experiences to be properly balanced and ordered. There is something in us that is spiritually impatient, and we always wish to run before we can walk. God slows us down, and Friends have always realized that this lack of patience can lead us to misinterpret what God wishes for us. Throughout scripture we see the importance of waiting for God, for the moment, for the right time. The silent waiting of the open worship should be an expression of the attitude of waiting we should carry with us all the time.

The degree to which we will be able to do this rests partly on our willingness to bear the cross, for this is the beginning of discipleship and moral discernment. The cross, spiritually speaking, represents the reality we bring to our own condition, which causes us to realize the state we are in and the strength of our self-centeredness. This is not a counsel of despair. We are assured of a victory, but it is not cheap. We are required to tread in Christ's footsteps if we really wish to follow him. The victory over self represents release from bondage. This is when the voice of God is most audible, when we are strengthened to do his will and when the battle with sin is won.

Friends and Wesleyan Methodists belong to a spiritual tradition that teaches very clearly that we can have the victory in this struggle and that perfection is a real possibility for quite ordinary people. Friends' particular spiritual practices build into a discipline of the soul and lead inevitably to this point. It was an early Quaker complaint that Puritan ministers "pleaded for sin," which indeed they did, and Friends saw this attitude as extremely harmful. It was biblically wrong; it was discouraging because it said we could never prevail. It was spiritually deadly, because it meant that the excuse that goodness was beyond us lay ready at hand for any imposter or apostate who wished to be known as a Christian but who would not accept the cross.

Against this, Friends, and later the Methodists, raised up a different standard. As we shall shortly see, they have their differences, but on the main point they are united. If all the Christian faith can do is provide insurance against ultimate destruction with no assurance that we will ever overcome our sins, it is a recipe for despair and not for hope. That cannot be the intention of Jesus Christ. "Everyone who believes that Jesus is the Christ is born of God, and everyone who loves the father loves his child as well. This is how we know that we love the children of God: by loving God and carrying out his commands. This is love for God: to obey his commands. And his commands are not burdensome, for everyone born of God overcomes the world."[12]

NOTES

1. John 14:21, 15:10, Matt. 5:6, Luke 10:27-8.
2. Written in 1676 and published a decade later.
3. Maurice Creasey, "'Inward'and 'Outward,' A Study in Early Quaker Language," *Journal of the Friends Historical Society,* London, Supplement No. 30 (1961).
4. John 15:7-15.
5. Mark 12:29-31, Matt. 22:37-40, Luke 10:27.
6. 2 Pet. 1:1-11.
7. Those familiar with the work of Alasdair MacIntyre will recognize the general approach to the question of moral obligation taken here.
8. Alasdair MacIntyre, *After Virtue* (Notre Dame, Ind.: Notre Dame University Press, 1978), p.86.
9. See Luella M.Wright, *The Literary Life of the Early Friends, 1650-1725,* (New York: Columbia Univeristy Press, 1932) and Howard Brinton, *Quaker Journals* (Wallingford, Pa.: Pendle Hill, 1972).
10. James 3:13-18.
11. Matt. 5:38-48, 1 Cor.13:6, Luke 12:13-31.
12. 1 John 5:1-4.

8

Righteousness
and Holiness

8

Righteousness and Holiness

The sight of our neighbor tending a bonfire has little importance beyond adding to the cozy atmosphere of an autumn evening. But a man standing in front of a burning bush that is not being consumed is a different matter. When Moses was told he was standing on holy ground, he knew it, but our neighbor, though he might love his garden, would scarcely call it holy. There is a recognizable boundary between our experience of transcendence and our experience of the ordinary, and language marks it very clearly. The word "holy" is perhaps the most significant of these markers. The step from the ordinary to the extraordinary is a short one, but we know when we have taken it.

The early Friends taught clearly that Christians are called to holiness, and in this chapter we will consider what this doctrine means. It certainly has its difficulties, and it is not often preached today. Early Friends condemned Puritan preachers for "pleading for sin" and asserted boldly that we are saved from sin and not in our sins. They did not compromise with human weakness but called people to work out their salvation with fear and trembling.[1] What else should *Quakers* do? Those who denied the possibility of perfect holiness thereby denied that the victory over sin is possible. In the seventeenth century, this was the "miserable salvation" of which Edward Burrough spoke.

Historically, the preaching of holiness has not been confined to Friends. It was a significant component in the theology of John Wesley during the eighteenth century, and was central to the nineteenth-century revivals that created the Friends Church. After the Civil War, many Friends meetings adopted holiness doctrines and enjoyed considerable growth as a consequence. But increasing numbers put pressure on the traditional unprogrammed system of ministry and pastoral care, and the pastoral system and the programmed worship service were the result. The character of the Friends Church therefore bears a strong family resemblance to the Wesleyan holiness movement, and there are historical and theological reasons why that should be so. It is important for us to examine these reasons.

Friends are not Methodists in spite of the similarities between the two churches, and we need to appreciate why. Friends and Methodists approach one another significantly in their attitudes to conversion as the beginning of the Christian life, and holiness as its logical conclusion. But proximity is not identity, and we shall see that there are also significant differences between the way the revival understood perfection and the pattern of discipleship traditionally followed by Friends. Equally, we should not forget that Wesleyan holiness principles are still to be found among Friends and that there are three avowedly holiness yearly meetings.[2]

The holiness revival was (and is) a healthy counterweight to Quaker scholasticism, but it should be remembered that holiness doctrine is capable of assuming several different forms. The Quaker doctrine of perfection is not the same as Wesley's doctrine of entire sanctification and cannot be made so. On the other hand, the two doctrines have common features and common implications, and we are entitled to claim them as variants of a common theme. Friends doctrine is the older of the two, and there is no reason to defer to the Wesleyan version of the doctrine if a good scriptural justification can be given for our own.

What Is Holiness?

In scripture, the meaning of the word "holy" is fairly clear. It indicates a frontier of some kind between the contingency of human experience and the absoluteness of God. Three pairs of opposites illustrate this contrast. God is supernatural, and we are natural. God is incorporeal, but our existence is embodied. God is being itself, while we do not exist apart from the divine will. The sign that we are at this frontier is the feeling that we are in the presence of something that is simultaneously terrifying and alluring.[3] The quintessential encounter with the holy was that of Moses at the burning bush.

Statements about the holy inevitably rest on some degree of inference. What Moses saw was not God, but the sign of God's presence. Actually to see God would be to go beyond the limit of human understanding, which is by definition impossible. "And the Lord said, 'I will cause all my goodness to pass in front of you, and I will proclaim my name, the Lord, in your presence. I will have mercy on whom I will have mercy, and I will have compassion on whom I will have compassion. But,' he said, 'you cannot see my face, for no one may see me and live.'"[4] What brings the holiness of God within our grasp are its manifestations: the power, glory and moral righteousness of which scripture is the witness and which Christians know in the course of their earthly lives.

> *What brings the holiness of God within our grasp are its manifestations: the power, glory and moral righteousness of which scripture is the witness and which Christians know in the course of their earthly lives.*

The Old Testament reflects the conviction that those who have seen this glory, and are moved by it, enter a new and fundamentally different relationship with God. They become members of the covenant community and are set apart by their participation in God's power and righteousness. This new relationship finds expression in worship and liturgical practices, and, by extension, in the ceremonies, seasons, and regulations for daily life that are part and parcel of the covenant. Holiness is not inherent in the practices, though they signify its presence. Holiness is given by God within the confines of the covenant relationship and is maintained by ritual observance and moral uprightness. Holiness is what makes the covenant community distinctive. Holiness, the ritual, and the community go together.

> *Holiness is what makes the covenant community distinctive. Holiness, the ritual, and the community go together.*

In the New Testament, these conceptions are given a different focus by a body claiming to be the beneficiary of a *new* covenant. Although the Church originated in the life and work of Jesus Christ, it also claimed continuity with the religious community into which he was born, and much of its faith and practice depends on this. The Church, as Paul portrays it, is a wild olive shoot grafted into a stock,[5] which becomes holy because its root is holy. We must therefore expect to find both continuity and innovation in the distinctively Christian understanding of holiness.

The most significant principle of the old covenant to be carried forward into the new is that covenantal holiness depends on the believer's relationship with God established through sacrifice. Under the old dispensation, continual oblations were offered in the Temple, but in the new dispensation they are no longer required. The Letter to the Hebrews presents the death of Christ as the final sacrifice of the old covenant. It carries such an immense power that it is a final, full, and complete sacrifice for all future human sin wherever and however committed, and it renders the temple system superfluous.

Since membership of the new covenant is established by virtue of Christ's sacrifice, we might have expected the new covenant to generate its own ceremonies and religious authorities to parallel the old, giving outward expression to the realities of the new dispensation. However, Hebrews states explicitly that the rituals were "only a matter of food and drink and various ceremonial washings—external regulations applying until the time of the new order."[6] The author draws a very clear distinction between inward and outward realities. The benefits of the new covenant extend to those who accept the priesthood of Christ by faith alone. In this context, therefore, holiness is an *inward* quality attaching to those who have been redeemed and reborn as a consequence of Christ's all-sufficient sacrifice.

To be a Christian is to partake of this quality because one has accepted Christ. In the New Testament, the first Christians were called saints. We use the Latin root of the word, but in Greek it simply means "the holy ones."[7] This is a better translation and clearly reflects the distinction between the two dispensations. Formerly, one became holy through one's membership of the covenant community and by carrying out the obligations it imposed. In the Church, however, holiness does not come from observance and status but by reception of the Holy Spirit, which is the inspiration—the life—of both individual Christians and the Church. The Spirit is the bearer of holiness.

Friends, broadly speaking, follow the traditional understanding of sanctification, though they complete it with a doctrine of perfection. We can put the position like this. What sanctifies us is the truth.[8] When we have accepted Christ, that is to say, accepted his sacrifice on our behalf, we begin to change. Unless there is an instantaneous change in our nature, there will be a period of time in which we gradually grow toward what God wishes us to be. By spiritual struggle we gain the victory over the old self, which is still in us, but continually being weakened. We sin, but we sin progressively less.[9] Unless Christians are rendered perfect by their conversion, which experience tells us conclusively is not the case, there must inevitably be such a process in the course of their spiritual development, however long or short it may be.

Sanctification, or the development of personal holiness, is that "by which one's moral condition is brought into conformity with one's legal status before God. It is a continuation of what was begun in regeneration, when newness of life was conferred upon and instilled within the believer. In particular, sanctification is the Holy Spirit's applying to the life of the believer, the work done by Jesus Christ."[10] This definition emphasizes the gradual nature of sanctification, and therefore fails to reflect the Wesleyan claim that, as we shall see, became immensely important in the development of American evangelical Christianity. This is the doctrine that we are promised the possibility of sinless perfection as one of the gifts of the Holy Spirit.

John Wesley and the Holiness Movement

Holiness was a constant, significant, and controversial theme in the writings of John Wesley (1703-91). It appears in the writings of other theologians, many of whose works Wesley studied, but his own doctrine is distinctive. He articulated it on more than one occasion, clarifying it and seeking to protect it from the over-zealous. It reached the peak of its influence with the foundation of a number of explicitly holiness churches in the United States at the end of the nineteenth and the beginning of the twentieth century.[11]

Wesley taught that it was possible for human beings to be completely holy, or as he put it, entirely sanctified. He uses the term "Christian perfection" to describe this state. He did not like to divorce the two terms in the expression because he regarded the one as dependent on the other. Non-Christian perfection is not possible. He was quite satisfied that this was the condition to which scripture was calling us.[12] At the same time, he was aware that the world now tends to think of perfection as meaning flawless, or measuring up to some abstract standard, but this was no part of his doctrine. He was quite clear that we are prone to ignorance, mistake, and weakness, but that these things are no obstacles to being perfect in the biblical sense of fulfilling all the potentialities with which we are blessed.

Perfection is an ever-present possibility that we should seek. It is the natural condition for Christians and not the prerogative of those with a special calling or who place themselves under a particular discipline. Perfection is a divine gift, the fruit of grace, and cannot be procured by means of particular devotions or disciplines. Although forced to acknowledge that perfection *may* be the culmination of a process, Wesley is far more concerned to preach entire sanctification given in an instant though the agency of the Holy Spirit. This gift represents a complete cleansing from original sin and in this sense can be seen as the ultimate purpose of the Christian life. Like justification, it is a matter of faith, and not works. Such are the bare bones of his teaching. We need to flesh them out a little, because his ideas were developed in America and taken in certain directions he might not have wanted them to go.

> *Perfection is an ever-present possibility that we should seek. It is the natural condition for Christians and not the prerogative of those with a special calling or who place themselves under a particular discipline.*

The obstacle to holiness is, of course, sin, the natural moral and spiritual character of human beings that separates them from God. Sin is expressed in a deep-seated tendency to disobedience, lawlessness, selfishness, and particular words, attitudes, decisions, and courses of conduct by which these innate tendencies are revealed. We are thus sinful at two levels: by committing individual acts contrary to God's will and having a nature that continually prompts us to do so. This produces actions and patterns of behavior that are offensive to God and self-destructive. So to be brought out of this condition, made holy, and become children of the covenant, we must be released from the power of both kinds of sin. This is the nature of entire sanctification.

Regeneration and Sanctification

The process begins with regeneration, the new birth of the soul in the justified sinner who accepts Christ. It is customary in the churches to regard justification as the act of God in forgiving the new Christian from sins already committed. Sanctification is the process whereby the regenerate soul is led into a greater obedience and likeness to God. "In the moment we are justified, the seed of every virtue is then instantaneously sown in the soil. From that time the believer gradually dies to sin and grows in grace. Yet sin remains in him, yea the seed of all sin, till he is sanctified throughout in spirit, soul and body."[13] Entire sanctification is the logical end of this process, whether or not it occurs in any given case.

It is important to note that entire sanctification, which is often called the second blessing or the second work of grace, must be sharply distinguished from the process of gradual sanctification, which is the normal experience of the committed Christian life. Wesley taught that entire sanctification is a work of grace alone, and its sole condition is personal faith. A leading holiness theologian describes it in the following terms: "This second work of grace is obtained by faith, is subsequent to regeneration, is occasioned by the baptism of the Holy Spirit, and constitutes a cleansing away of Adamic depravity and the empowerment for witnessing and for the holy life."[14]

Early Friends and the Second Blessing

Friends with misgivings about this way of putting it might reflect on early Quaker experience. George Fox describes the experience of coming up in spirit through the flaming sword, so that he knew nothing but pureness, innocency, and righteousness, so that he had reached "the state of Adam which he was in before he fell." He generalizes from his own experience in these words, "And the

Lord showed me that such as were faithful to him in the power and light of Christ should come up into that state in which Adam was in before he fell...."[15] Some see this as a record of a mystical experience, but in Wesleyan terms it looks suspiciously like Fox receiving the second blessing, and then preaching it. Without release from Adamic depravity, it does not mean much.

Fox is not an isolated example. In a number of extracts cited in his study of early Friends writings, Arthur Roberts shows the extent to which such conceptions, now associated with Wesleyanism, were integral to early Quakerism. He concludes, (inter alia) "The early Quakers considered heart holiness as the end and purpose of Christ's coming...they were people of tender conscience, ever seeking to make ethics of holiness confirm and follow the experience of holiness...(they) found these concepts of holiness effective for evangelism, for worship, and for all social relationships. Pacifism, honesty in business, simplicity, and truthfulness frames the exquisite beauty of heart purity."[16]

One could go further. Earlier, we portrayed convincement as a particular seventeenth-century conversion experience too culturally conditioned to be replicated beyond the circumstances of the times. Theologically, however, one of the main drawbacks of thinking of it as a variant of conversion is that those who underwent it were already Christians. Whatever they may have said themselves about the validity of their previous conversions, they certainly knew Christ, and it is precisely because of that conviction that they sought a more powerful and intimate experience of him. If this is the case, the periods of travail can be recognized as highly dramatized accounts of the process of sanctification as normally understood.

Moreover, if we continue to look at these accounts with a different frame of reference, the final stage of convincement begins to look uncannily like the experience of entire sanctification and can easily be placed in a Wesleyan setting. Early Friends believed that one was justified to the extent one was sanctified. On this dangerous assumption—if the final stage of convincement is entire sanctification—they seem very much like the uncompromising Wesleyans who look for sanctification on the heels of salvation and do not consider conversion genuine if it does not quickly issue in the second work of grace. This would be considered a heretical suggestion in many places, but the inference is hard to resist.

By the late nineteenth century, Wesley's teaching had become enshrined in the holiness movement, an extraordinary phenomenon that could, perhaps, only have developed in the United States. In 1812, The Doctrinal Tracts, which contained John Wesley's writings on perfection, were removed from the Methodist Discipline for extraneous reasons, and a generation grew up not knowing the doctrine. By 1900, however, the doctrine had been revived, preached, developed, and established with such effect that by schism and secession a whole range of specifically Wesleyan holiness churches had come into existence. This cleared the ground for the emergence of Pentecostalism, now the dominant form of Protestant Christianity in the world.

Origins of the Holiness Revival

The Holiness Revival was the product of many influences, of which two are particularly significant. First there was the rural camp meeting, often conducted by Methodist circuit riders, who emphasized the intense and sudden crisis experience of conversion, the urgency of immediate decision, and, whatever the doctrinal irregularities, the call for individual choice and commitment. The second stream was the urban revival movement associated with Sarah Lankford and Phoebe Palmer, which set the pattern of the Tuesday Meetings, interdenominational prayer meetings, often presided over by women and held during the working week, which were held in a large number of northern industrial cities.

Women played a crucial role in the development of the holiness movement through their writing, preaching, and organizing abilities. Because the evangelical churches generally place a lower value on sacramental observance than preaching and the various forms of sanctification, there are fewer theological obstacles to a full range of women's ministry among them. Before the overlay of fundamentalism, holiness believers were quite open to women in the pulpit.[17] It has been suggested, moreover, that the holiness movement represents a recovery of the mystical heritage of the Church, based as it is, on a doctrine of union with Christ. "Wesley's theology of holiness and concern for spiritual formation and social ministry was deeply rooted in the monastic and mystical tradition of Catholicism. Early Quakers drank from the same deep well of spirituality."[18]

Periodicals and personalities were very important in the development of holiness doctrine, and many preachers and writers were active in this process. As Melvin H. Dieter writes, "Those who look for the differences between original Wesleyanism and the tone and teaching of the American holiness movement will probably discover that there were not radical differences in theology and belief, but, rather, they will find subtle differences of emphasis that derive from the application of all that was America in the nineteenth century to the promotion and practices of the Wesleyan emphasis."[19] It can be argued though, while noting the general cultural influences noted here, that the differences of emphasis were so marked that what emerged was something rather different from what Wesley might have envisaged.

Wesley's Doctrine Developed

At issue were a number of developments of the doctrine of entire sanctification. Whatever the intentions of the leaders, certain ideas emerged that extended the doctrine in unforeseen ways. For example, if the second work of grace came to those wholly consecrated in body, soul, and spirit, even without any outward evidence, it was possible to lay claim to the gift, or even to teach (as Phoebe Palmer denied she did) "Believe that you have it and you have it."[20] Moreover, emphasis on the second work of grace downgraded the significance of the first (that is, conversion), and some people began to teach that until entire sanctification one's salvation was incomplete. Indeed, the doctrine tended to produce the view that there are two classes of Christians—those blessed with entire sanctification and those merely saved. The feeling also grew that if one received the second blessing, but did not testify to it, the blessing itself might be lost.

The holiness community required certain standards of conduct, for moral purity is obviously a concomitant of spiritual purity. However, what emerged were simply the ethics of an individualistic Puritanism. Dress and speech codes were developed similar to the way the early Quakers developed and then defended their way of life by emphasizing their separateness. But the holiness code did not reflect the broader themes which characterized early Quakerism— emphasis on the inward cross, conversion of life (the process of sanctification), divine leading, corporate discernment, and a social and political witness, which has significantly assisted in the amelioration of an imperfect world.

This was not the case in Wesley's homeland, though. In England, Methodism is credited with having produced a class of influential and self-confident artisans whose worldview prevented them from succumbing to the ideas of the French Revolution. Later, this same class of religiously aware and socially conscious individuals took a leading part in the development of friendly societies, building societies, children's homes, retail cooperatives, trade unions and, indeed, the Labor Party itself. In the United States, however, Wesley's holiness disciples were fatally unable to provide their nation with an enduring moral vision.

The Rise of Gurneyite Quakerism

Quaker settlers followed the frontier, as did so many others. Stronger in Indiana and Ohio than in Tennessee and Kentucky, they were nevertheless pioneering people coming mainly from Virginia, the Carolinas, and New York, as well as the Quaker heartland in the Delaware Valley. In the first half of the nineteenth century they were largely of the Orthodox party[21] and therefore evangelical in theology. Their meetings and discipline were outwardly traditional, but there was gathering unease. In the first half of the century Friends had divided into three antagonistic factions, and the gradual emergence from Quietist isolation meant that each group had to find new ways of relating to the wider society.

By 1850, rising prosperity, improved communications, new business opportunities, and increased leisure meant that Friends enjoyed a much wider range of choice than economic circumstances had ever provided before. The order and routine of the traditional way

of life became increasingly divergent from society at large. The changing pattern of the lives of Friends can be seen as a response to these
changed circumstances. Friends began to read a much wider range
of tracts, books, and periodicals and took great interest in the provision of Bible study and First Day (or Sunday) Schools in their meetings. They were active in politics at the grass-roots level (as Whigs,
and later, Republicans) and served in the territorial and then state
legislatures.[22]

Friends worked harmoniously with members of other denominations on a range of mutually important matters. At that time the
evangelical movement was strongly animated by the belief that the
rising trend of social improvement presaged the return of Christ to a
world ready and prepared to receive him. The anti-slavery movement was one of the major evangelical concerns with its varied range
of objectives and methods. Temperance was seen as the necessary
basis for all good social and family life. Friends, because of their own
historical experience, took an important part in the movement for
prison reform. If we look for the channels through which evangelical ideas flowed, these are the most important. Friends read evangelical materials and they engaged in the wider evangelical campaign for personal improvement and social reform.

The figure exemplifying these trends most distinctly is Elisha
Bates (1780-1861) of Mount Pleasant, Ohio. One of the most influential (and neglected) figures of the period, Bates was a teacher, an
entrepreneur, an editor, a polemicist, and a supporter of many righteous causes. Rather than developing an ideology of improvement
and looking to the government to implement it, he believed in individual social action taken in collaboration with others of like mind.
He therefore supported voluntary societies of all kinds. In his jour-

nalism and public advocacy he used moral and Christian arguments designed to appeal to a wide public, rather than ones which might appeal more directly to Friends on their own terms.

Bates' outlook was results oriented. He valued interdenominational cooperation for social reform so highly that the logic of his position entailed a revision of the sectarian features of Quaker church organization. He was moving toward the same position as Joseph John Gurney at much the same time and for much the same reasons. For both of them, the practical expression of Christianity was more important than maintaining distinctive practices and doctrines. Bates marks the beginning of the process whereby Orthodox Friends would develop from a sect into a denomination.

As Donald Good writes, "The potential problem of losing sight of the positive meaning of one's heritage in the milieu of evangelical fervor and in the cooperative expression of the denominational view of the church was a real danger for many 'orthodox' Quakers in the nineteenth century. Their difficulty in avoiding this danger and the accommodation to prevailing modes of Revivalism which accompanied it in the post Civil War years has contributed to the present confusion among a large segment of American Friends concerning who they are and where their roots are found."[23] Bates was ultimately disowned, and joined the Methodists, but Joseph John Gurney gave serious thought to these questions, and it is at least arguable that if his ideas had been more widely appreciated, the 'confusion' Donald Good identifies would have been avoided.

Gurney and Bates both mark a change from a sectarian to a denominational understanding of the Friends Church. They envisaged a general body of Christian truth to which all churches subscribed, which could form the basis of Christian unity. At the same time they recognized that individual churches might have distinct emphases, indeed, doctrines, which were not part of the common core, or that churches might have internal differences, like that between the Old and New School Presbyterians and Congregationalists in the years leading up to the Civil War. On this analysis, Friends were in the same position as everybody else. Everyone accepted the authority of scripture, the triune God, and the atonement. But the Presbyterians taught the decrees and election, the Methodists taught assurance and entire sanctification, and the Quakers taught the peculiarities, which became the distinctives.

> *Gurney and Bates both mark a change from a sectarian to a denominational understanding of the Friends Church. They envisaged a general body of Christian truth to which all churches subscribed, which could form the basis of Christian unity.*

In this way it became possible for Christians across the divisions to make common cause, because the divisions were not seen as fundamental. It is suggested by Donald Good that the period before the Civil War was characterized by a growth in denominational self-confidence encouraged by the First Amendment to the Constitution, which precluded the establishment of a state church on the European pattern. In this light the movement of the Quakers toward some form of evangelical orthodoxy represents a growth toward maturity. There was no longer a need for the sectarian defensiveness, which brought Quakerism into being and preserved it through its years of persecution in another country and in another time.

Those Friends who sought to promote this rapprochement between tradition and new ways identified themselves as Gurneyites,
following both what they knew and what they supposed were the
attitudes of the English Friend. Following his emphasis on the outward atonement and the authority of the scriptures, they placed less
emphasis than before on the writings of early Friends and the immediate guidance of the light within. With the passage of time the
ministry became increasingly preoccupied with the need for personal conversion and the promotion of the experience. It is hard to
see how evangelical Friends could have taken any other course, and
take it, they did.

This had the advantage of lessening denominational differences,
but it began a process of change that took them where they did not
want to go. They encouraged Bible study at the expense of the tradition, they encouraged all kinds of study and prayer groups that were
unprecedented, and they got the rule against marrying outside the
faith rescinded. They began the first modern Friends missions and,
by means of queries and personal influence, sought to open up the
ministry in meeting to a wider range of voices. They considered conventions like the sing-song style of delivering ministry to be dead
forms. They lost a sense of how silence was integral to both worship
and Friends way of life, and thus were the progenitors of the "fast
meeting."[24]

The Gurneyites had initial success in their attempt to stem the
decline in membership caused by the rigidities of the Discipline. Although they were innovators, they also sought to preserve the identity, practices, and traditions of Friends and did not go outside the
familiar structures and ways of doing things. However, the widespread compromise with the peace testimony during the Civil War

and divided opinions about the propriety of seeking the conversion of emancipated slaves, together with internal disputes of various kinds, produced an air of uncertainty in the Gurneyite ranks. Education and renewal through the traditional device of the regular general meeting were seen as the solutions.

What the Gurneyite Friends could not have known was that they were on a converging course with the rapidly developing holiness movement and had created the institutions and the climate of opinion hospitable to it. First, they had accepted the doctrinal innovations of Gurney and Bates and emphasized their similarities with non-Quaker evangelicals. What they had not perhaps grasped is that the evangelical movement is a changing entity, and the more closely tied to it they were, the less control they would have of their own destiny. Second, the new practices they encouraged widened still further the channels through which evangelical ideas could flow into the Society of Friends. Third, the new general meetings provided a forum for the expression of views by the ordinary Friend. The Gurneyite leaders were educated, better off, and from urban backgrounds. Friends, by and large, were not.

> *What the Gurneyite Friends could not have known was that they were on a converging course with the rapidly developing holiness movement and had created the institutions and the climate of opinion hospitable to it.*

The Holiness Revival

Because they were primarily evangelistic, holiness services were characterized by strong emotional appeals for conversion. Preachers

277

held out the possibility of the second blessing and, in some circles, the test of a conversion came to be the speed with which the second blessing followed conversion. They used the altar call and the mourner's bench, innovations associated with Charles Finney. Hymns and sermons were essential as was the time of testimony, another of the tests of a true second blessing. All these things derive from the frontier camp meeting and have put an indelible mark on American evangelicalism in general.[25]

The movement was primarily a Methodist phenomenon, as we have seen, but was spread by preachers, many of whom were not officially sanctioned by the Methodist church, and supported and strengthened by a range of independent publishers and periodicals. In 1867 the National Camp Meeting Association for the Promotion of Holiness was set up, followed by a network of local and state holiness associations at state and sectional levels. These bodies were independent of denominational control, and as it turned out, possessed an internal dynamic that altered the character of the denominations to which most of their supporters, including Friends, belonged.

Friends and the Holiness Revival

As we begin to look more closely at the influence of the holiness movement on Friends, we need to appreciate this general picture. The movement failed to capture control of any of the major denominations, so its para-church activities increased, dividing the loyalties of Friends, Methodists, Baptists, and anyone else with both holiness convictions and denominational loyalties. As a consequence, some remained where they were and some came out from among the unbelievers into the new holiness denominations.[26] Among

Friends, those who remained formed a group too large to be ignored, but too few to give ultimate identity to the denomination. The character of the contemporary Friends Church is profoundly influenced by this unstable state of affairs.

Holiness teachings entered Friends meetings in a number of ways. First, there were leading Friends like David Updegraff and Dougan Clark, one a Minister in Ohio Yearly Meeting, the other a professor at Earlham, who both received the second blessing and preached holiness doctrines. Then there were other prominent ministers like Esther and Nathan Frame who came into the Society of Friends from Methodist backgrounds and were already familiar with the doctrine. Many Friends at that time, particularly younger ones, attended revival meetings in other churches. Through them the demand grew, and was satisfied, for revival services to be organized by Friends. It has been estimated that by 1875 the revival was widespread in the Orthodox yearly meetings.

A number of factors facilitated this growth. The foundation of it was doubtless continuing dissatisfaction with the tradition and the dead forms it seemed to offer. This may well have been a generational matter, for there are records of Friends registering their astonishment and pleasure at the ease with which non-Quaker friends both spoke of God and prayed spontaneously without the long waiting Friends were familiar with. Plainly it met a deep need, and it is possible to reflect that the tradition had moved so far from the original verve and intensity of the Quaker experience that it really was as dead as its critics alleged.

The spontaneity of the holiness revival contrasted sharply with the quiet and measured devotion of the Friends tradition. The revival was dependent on an emphatic and dramatic style of preaching, so ministers began to accumulate authority at the expense of elders—an interesting and possibly unique reversal of the usual principle of the routinization of charisma. Untraditional though it was, there was precedent in Quaker history—the enthusiasm, the burning devotion to Christ, the desire to win souls, the piety and devotion, and, yes, for those who knew their Barclay and their Penn, *the doctrine of perfection.*

> *Plainly the holiness movement met a deep need, and it is possible to reflect that the tradition had moved so far from the original verve and intensity of the Quaker experience that it really was as dead as its critics alleged.*

Nevertheless, one should not underestimate the strength of resistance to these trends. In a period of ten short years, 1881-1891, the holiness movement was checked and contained by a series of moves that gave the Friends Church its present character. First, when a number of influential Friends accepted baptism, there was an open challenge to one of Friends cardinal doctrines. Seeing the way the wind was blowing and realizing at the same time that the new programmed meetings also marked a radical departure from Friends traditional principles, Indiana Yearly Meeting convened the Richmond Conference of 1887, which issued the Declaration that now appears in the Disciplines of all but one of the evangelical yearly meetings in North America.[27] All the Orthodox yearly meetings in the world were represented, including London and Ireland, but not all endorsed the Declaration.

The Richmond Declaration of Faith

The Richmond Declaration has not had a good press. It is regarded as a sectarian document by non-evangelical Friends and is said not to have the spirit of early Quakerism, because it says nothing about the inward light. It was accused of amounting to a creed and being authoritarian as well as sectarian. It was certainly a partisan document and was designed to state Friends attitudes to a certain range of topics. It is certainly unbalanced because it begins like a comprehensive doctrinal statement and then does not follow through. But it says what had to be said about worship, ministry, and the ordinances at this precise juncture and cannot really be read without some awareness of the strength of the holiness movement, and therefore, Wesleyan principles at the time. Its great strength is that it marks a line in the sand: This is as far as Friends can go in an evangelical direction without ceasing to be Friends.

> *The Richmond Declaration's great strength is that it marks a line in the sand: This is as far as Friends can go in an evangelical direction without ceasing to be Friends.*

After the Richmond Conference there was a strong sense that there should be much stronger links between yearly meetings, and in 1892 at Indianapolis, the idea was seriously canvassed to set up some sort of federal, delegated body. In 1902, the Five Years Meeting came into existence to provide a forum of discussion for matters of mutual interest: the more efficient promotion of Friends concerns like evangelism and missions; peace work, what was then called the condition and welfare of Negroes; religious education; and, if possible, the promulgation of a uniform discipline for the yearly meetings that belonged to the Gurneyite tradition. Although a uniform discipline never came into existence, common interests meant that there was in fact considerable similarity across the yearly meetings, and for the future, a fertile ground of controversy and acrimony was removed from the path of Friends.

The Rise of the Pastoral System

Two consequences of the holiness revival that should also be noted are the rise of the pastoral system and a number of conservative secessions. The number of Friends newly converted as a result of the revivals intensified the need for preaching and spiritual nurture, and the custom grew of liberating Friends through modest payments to undertake this work. An illustration of this is the situation in Indiana Yearly Meeting in the 1888-89 church year, when there were meetings with several recorded ministers in the congregation, and others—amounting to about a fifth of the total—that had none. The yearly meeting was already providing assistance, and at this date there were twenty-six ministers engaged in regular pastoral work and a total of fifty-eight ministers receiving aid from the Committee on the Ministry.[28]

As these developments took place, there was a change in the character of Friends meetings. The need to maintain preaching and pastoral care was pressing, but many Friends perceived a shift of power from elders to ministers and a need to maintain the older evangelical faith among Friends in the face of inroads made by Wesleyan holiness teaching. A second consequence of the revivals was that secessionary bodies were set up at Plainfield in Western Yearly Meeting and in other places, though only one has survived—

Iowa Yearly Meeting (Conservative). That these divisions happened at all indicates the strength of feeling the revivals provoked and, perhaps, that opposition to them was more widespread than has hitherto been appreciated.

The Consequences of the Revival

As the century drew to its close, the holiness movement took new directions. First, several new, explicitly holiness denominations came into being. The Church of God, Anderson emerged as a separate entity in 1880, the Pilgrim Holiness Church in 1887 and the Church of the Nazarene in 1908. Former Friends ministers like Seth Rees, Harry Hayes, and Susan Fitkin were active in each of them. Second, the consequences of entire sanctification were seen more clearly, and a new vision of a spirit-led church emerged as Pentecostalism. In 1902 a Friends pastor, A.J. Tomlinson, was called to a small group of Pentecostal churches in rural Tennessee which is now the Church of God (Cleveland) with three million members worldwide. Third, there was a strong reaction to modernism in the Bible-believing churches, which coalesced round the fundamentalist movement.[29]

It is about this time that the name "Friends Church" comes into use, but the word seems to express a desire for a denominational identity rather than being based on a precise theology that provides a theoretical basis for that church. It is probably fair to say that American evangelical Friends at this point in their history reflected a variety of influences, none of which was powerful enough to stamp its identity on them to the exclusion of the others. Holiness sentiments were strong in many places, but weaker in others, and at the turn of the century the fundamentalist movement began to exert its own spell on evangelical Friends. It is hard to measure the relative strengths of the diverse influences at work, but it looks as if the process of becoming a denomination was incomplete because of a fundamental and hidden division of principle of varying proportions in the different yearly meetings that make up the Friends Church. It is quite possible that this is the main historical reason for the ambivalence toward the distinctives that I am arguing here is the primary obstacle to a renewal of the Friends Church.

For most of the century, the Five Years Meeting, (since 1960, Friends United Meeting) was the center of theological controversy. Since its foundation, as we saw earlier, five yearly meetings have resigned from it. The points at issue were different in each case, but what unites the seceding yearly meetings is that they have a stricter conception of what evangelical Friends should stand for than the federal body. A number of Friends in those yearly meetings, recognizing that they had a strong community of interest with many who remained, and wishing to have continuing fellowship with them, founded the Association of Evangelical Friends in 1956 as a body of Friends concerned for the renewal of the Friends Church, but without corporate affiliation to any organization or yearly meeting

The Statement of Faith of the Association of Evangelical Friends included the following clause: "We believe in holiness of heart and life through the instantaneous baptism with the Holy Spirit subsequent to the new birth and to His continual presence and ministry in the sanctified heart." The wording is deliberately cautious. In response to a letter questioning these words, the President of the Association, Gerald Dillon, wrote, "Since the terms, 'carnal nature,' 'second definite work,' 'entire sanctification,' and 'eradication' are of the Wesleyan, rather than Quaker, flavor, since they are so easily misunderstood by both friend and enemy, and since any one of them requires so much space to carefully define what is and what is not meant we thought it advisable for a short and brief statement to use other terminology."[30] Gerald Dillon went on to base Friends holiness teaching firmly in the Richmond Declaration.

Dillon's statement marks a watershed. It brings together a loyalty to the Richmond Declaration, the cornerstone of any structure to be called the Friends Church, and, at the same time, a sympathy for the holiness movement to which so many Friends were, and continue to be, affiliated. It may be construed as negative in tone because of its reluctance to use the buzzwords of Wesleyanism, but it implies that these words point to a reality to which we should be devoted for more reason than theological affiliation. It also shows that the practice of the Association of Evangelical Friends lived up to its intentions. Holiness is not the whole of evangelical Quakerism, but is an essential component of the faith.

> *Holiness is not the whole of evangelical Quakerism, but is an essential component of the faith.*

Of course, it would be strange if four yearly meetings with very strong similarities were to remain isolated from one another. As, one by one, they left the Five Years Meeting, they found a community of interest with Ohio (Damascus) Yearly Meeting,[31] which had been isolated by the Richmond Declaration and never joined the united body. Inevitably, a body parallel to Friends United Meeting was formed. In 1965 the Evangelical Friends Alliance came into existence, and in 1991 it was augmented by yearly meetings from all parts of the world and took the name, Evangelical Friends International. The name is accurate in that it is, undoubtedly, an evangelical body, though as we have seen, the whole body of evangelical Friends is much wider than this particular affiliation.

So at present the body of evangelical Friends in North America is distributed between two bodies that derive from particular historical circumstances. Though the loyalties of evangelical Friends are at present divided, both branches are actively engaged in mission, relief work, education, and other activities. Some Friends believe that this division is an impediment to more effective witness, and that evangelical Friends would perform their task better if they were all under one organizational umbrella, as we saw earlier. Certainly this point of view should not be dismissed out-of-hand, because it arises from a serious concern for a revival of the Friends Church. On the other hand, each of the branches has its own strengths, as well as its own particular challenges, and it may be that a better course is to recognize the historical similarity between the groups and work more closely together through the internal renewal of each branch, and explore together the question of what it means to be the Friends Church in the twenty-first century.

This book began by raising the possibility that the general decline in the fortunes of many evangelical yearly meetings in North America is due to corporate ambivalence over identity. I have argued in this chapter that the problem arises because of the unresolved tensions that the partial adoption of Wesleyan holiness principles bequeathed to Friends about a century ago. So the time is now right for a re-examination of the theological basis for the separate existence of a Friends Church. If this were to be done as a cooperative venture between Friends of the different affiliations, it might be a better way of recovering our identity than a contentious and possibly fruitless quest for organizational unity. It might also show the continuing vitality among us of ideas of purity and Christian perfection.

The Possibility of Perfection

Although each tradition has its different emphases, Friends and Wesleyans both insist on the possibility of perfection in this life. There is considerable common ground between them, and if each is to remain true to its inspiration, it will have to continue to maintain what is a highly controversial doctrine in modern times. The complexity of modern life raises all kinds of unprecedented moral challenges, which we are often able to deal with constructively because of our greatly enhanced understanding of the processes of the human mind. Both traditions have a common interest, before any question of divergent doctrine arises, in maintaining the possibility of perfection.

To claim that perfection is impossible is to argue that we may not rise above our own natures and that the vision of perfection is an illusion. This seems to be the lesson of history, which says that perfectionist sects and communities attempting to build perfect human communities always founder on the imperfectibility of human nature. It is also the lesson of the human sciences. In the twenty-first century, we know that the mind is always colored by deep-seated influences deriving either from heredity or psychological or social processes beyond our conscious control.

It is scarcely a novel discovery that people find themselves unable to rise above their sins, and the twenty-first century may discover its own characteristic excuses for avoiding obedience to the difficult standards God requires. In the *Apology*, Robert Barclay begins his discussion of perfection with God and not contemporary sensibilities, arguing from scripture and reason against those who claim that perfection is impossible.[32] His purpose is to show first, that those who claim that we neither can, nor ever will, be free of sin in this life are wrong on both scriptural and logical grounds and second, that the texts on which they rely do not prove what they claim. The thrust of his argument throughout is that a lot of people make excuses for not doing what scripture tells them they ought to be doing. This is not Christianity.

Barclay reasons that it is the nature of God to abhor evil and that God's love is conditional on our forsaking sin.[33] If Christians are to be partakers of the divine nature, it is inconceivable that they should continue in sin, the two conditions being completely incompatible.[34] It is even less conceivable that God, denying the possibility to any of his creatures to please him, should arbitrarily exempt some from his wrath and exact the penalty from others. That would be putting God in the same position as those who were unrighteous but knew better than to give their children stones instead of bread. Indeed, if God were going to tolerate sin, says Barclay, it is hard to see the purpose of Christ's sacrifice or the purpose of his ministry.[35]

Nor is Barclay satisfied by the texts usually cited to justify the doctrine that we can never overcome the power of sin in this life. For example, he points out that when John says that we deceive ourselves if we say we have no sin, the force of the word 'we' is to identify everyone and thus to indicate the human condition in general. The sentence should be read with the one following, which clearly states that when we confess our sins we will be cleansed from all unrighteousness.[36] He deals similarly with the extended passage in Romans 7:11-25 where Paul is generally thought to be describing his present spiritual condition, saying that he does the evil he does not wish to do. Not so, argues Barclay. Both passages use the figure of speech where general statements are made that are understood not to include the speaker. Clearly, Paul cannot assert that he is in bondage to sin and at one and the same time say that the law of the spirit of life in Christ Jesus had freed him from the law of sin and death.[37]

We have to remember that Barclay is writing fifty years before Wesley began his ministry and seventy-five years before the publication of *Thoughts Concerning Christian Perfection*. He is also writing a polemic rather than a pastoral exposition, so it is not easy to compare the thinking of the two men. But for Friends purposes we must try to reach some estimate. The first thing to be said is that Barclay is putting up a long and sophisticated argument against the doctrine of imputed righteousness. We have argued above that when this doctrine is combined with perfectionism, it loses many of the features Barclay found objectionable. Nevertheless, perfection in Barclay's mind is the outcome of the process of sanctification understood in the usual sense, rather than the experience of an instantaneous second blessing such as the holiness movement at its zenith taught people to seek and to expect. Are these doctrines alternatives, or can we accept them both?

The doctrine has neither the explosive nor divisive force that it once did and can be discussed more dispassionately today. There are Friends who hold the nineteenth-century holiness movement's understanding of perfection as the second blessing and still seek it and preach it. There are others who have a more nuanced understanding of what perfection requires.[38] Then there are those who effectively take a reformed position and deny that the victory over sin is possible in this life. There are others who consider that the early Quaker approach to perfection as illustrated by Penn, Barclay, and Penington preserves all the features emphasized by Wesley, but combine this with a much more realistic estimate of what perfection is, and the nature of the soul who is to seek it.

> *The doctrine of imputed righteousness has neither the explosive nor divisive force that it once did and can be discussed more dispassionately today.*

So what can we say? How can we chart the differences and the similarities? To begin with, if the descriptions we have of the mature convincement experience are anything like the truth, there is a possibility that it was the same thing as the experience of entire sanctification. On that basis, the two traditions are, at least, twins. They are not identical twins, though. In Barclay, there is very little sense of the hyper-enthusiasm that characterized the earliest period of Quakerism and the holiness movement at its height. Friends lost their enthusiasm early and developed a different kind of perfectionism. The possibility of entire sanctification was a necessary corollary of their doctrine, but they did not stress it. Instead they preferred the daily growth in grace.

So Robert Barclay and John Wesley offer slightly different routes to perfection, and these pathways are embedded in the preaching, practice, and conceptions of church order characteristic of Friends and Wesleyans, respectively. Though perfection may not be talked about very much in the contemporary Friends Church, it is easy to see that it is as much a consequence of Friends foundational covenant theology as other more obvious aspects. The two traditions, then, unite in the assertion that perfection (Friends) or entire holiness (Wesleyan) is a real possibility in this life, but draw contrasting implications from the fact, and offer different accounts of how such perfection can be attained.

The holiness movement took up Wesley's emphasis. Wesley was ready to accept that the process of sanctification in the usual sense was a possibility, but he was uncomfortable with the thought that it could be the main route to perfection. A doctrine of gradualness could easily result in a less than full-hearted endeavor to seek the second work of grace. Moreover it ran the risk of turning into a doctrine of works righteousness. Instead, he preached the second work of grace, almost to the exclusion of the usual doctrine of sanctification, in order to emphasize the power of God and the response of faith, thus protecting the doctrine against Pelagianism. As it turned out, the doctrine created as many problems as it solved. We will never know how many people have deserted holiness churches with a deep sense of failure, or how many claims to entire sanctification really are genuine. As we have seen, Methodism as a whole was never easy with the doctrine.

Friends followed Barclay and took a different route. Perfection was equally the outcome of their doctrine. As with Wesley, it was seen as a gift available only to the saved, and was granted by the Holy Spirit. Friends also had to guard against allegations of works-righteousness in their doctrine. In its developed form, Quakerism came to require constant spiritual vigilance and moral endeavor. However, the beauty we see with hindsight was a stark contrast to the deadness many young people felt in the traditional silent meetings before the advent of the holiness movement. Perhaps it was the fear of enthusiasm, but very few Friends, if any, ever claimed to have reached the condition of perfection their doctrine said was available.

With hindsight it appears that each of the traditions suffered from a fatal drawback that limits its usefulness for today. By insisting that the perfection that comes through the second work of grace must be instantaneous and a matter of pure faith, the holiness tradition is open to the criticism that it is inconsistent. If, prevenient grace assisting, we are able to turn from our wickedness and live, it is not going too far to see grace as the vehicle for the process of gradual sanctification that allows for the moral and spiritual self-discipline preferred by the Friends tradition. The Friends tradition on the other hand, which places its major emphasis on the *process* of sanctification, travels hopefully rather than pressing on enthusiastically to the destination. There are spiritual dangers attendant on each of these doctrines of Christian perfection. Gradual sanctification can open the door to spiritual sloth, and entire sanctification runs the risk of spiritual pride. But sloth and pride do not of themselves invalidate the doctrine. So what should be preached in Friends churches?

> *The Friends tradition on the other hand, which places its major emphasis on the process of sanctification, travels hopefully rather than pressing on enthusiastically to the destination.*

Although it had a great influence on the Friends Church, history and tradition argue against a general revival of holiness doctrine among Friends. The doctrine, while influential, was never a majority persuasion. It was not strong enough to divide Friends as it divided other denominations, although to be truthful the conservative separations of the 1880s were a direct result of the influx of holiness ideas. The Methodist church, however, suffered major divisions as a consequence of which there are now a number of holiness churches to which any Friend seeking a faith community based on the doctrine of entire sanctification can go. This is not to say that holiness congregations are out of place among Friends, but that our collective sense is against the doctrine. A major revival would involve a reworking of the entire corpus of Friends belief and practice contrary to the wishes of probably the great majority of Friends.

Perfection matters, however, and we need to remedy its present neglect. The process of gradual sanctification toward a fulfilled (perfect) life is both a great challenge and the medium of a great vision. There are reasons to think that a revival of this vision is more than overdue. As we saw above, the therapeutic model of spiritual endeavor is something millions are familiar with, and the idiom of challenge, change, and renewal is highly contemporary. And so is a strong public interest in the spiritual life. This is no more, in Christian terms, than taking the process of sanctification seriously. If this process is truly Christian, it will find expression in the good works, which are inseparable from the fulfilled or perfect life. Ultimately, it is this that inclines Friends tradition to favor the doctrine of gradual rather than instantaneous and entire sanctification.

> *Perfection matters, however, and we need to remedy its present neglect. The process of gradual sanctification toward a fulfilled (perfect) life is both a great challenge and the medium of a great vision.*

Nevertheless, let us end with what is common. When John Wesley was asked, "But what good works are those, the practice of which you affirm to be necessary for sanctification?" he replied, "First, all works of piety such as public prayer, family prayer and praying in our closet, receiving the Supper of the Lord, searching the Scriptures, by hearing, reading, meditating, and using such a measure of fasting or abstinence as our bodily health allows... Secondly, all works of mercy, whether they relate to the bodies or souls of men, such as feeding the hungry, clothing the naked, entertaining the stranger, visiting those that are in prison, or sick, or variously afflicted, such as endeavoring to instruct the ignorant, to awaken the stupid sinner, to quicken the lukewarm, to confirm the wavering, to comfort the feeble-minded, to succor the tempted, or contribute in any manner to the saving of souls from death. This is the way wherein God hath appointed his children to wait for complete salvation."[39]

NOTES

1 Phil. 2:12.
2 Central YM (Indiana, USA), Bolivia (Amigos Santidad) and Guatemala Santidad.
3 See Rudolf Otto *The Idea of the Holy* (1923) (London: Oxford University Press, 1958).
4 Exod. 33:19-20.
5 Rom. 11:17.
6 Heb. 9:10.
7 Eph. 5:26-7; 1 Pet. 2:5, 9; Rom. 12:6; Gal. 5:22; 1 Cor. 14:33.
8 John 17:16-22.
9 Rom. 6:6, Eph. 4:22, Col. 3:10.
10 Millard J. Erickson, *Christian Theology*, (Ada, Mich.: Baker Books, 1983), p.968.
11 e.g. The Church of the Nazarene, The Church of God (Anderson), The Church of God (Cleveland), the Pilgrim Holiness Church, and the Christian and Missionary Alliance. Also the Salvation Army.
12 Matt. 5:48, 2 Cor. 13:9.
13 John Wesley, *Doctrinal Summary, Second Annual Conference* (1745) Outler, p.152.
14 Kenneth J.Grider, *A Wesleyan-Holiness Theology*, (Kansas City, Mo.: Beacon Hill Press, 1994), p. 367.
15 George Fox, *Journal*, Nickalls, p. 27.
16 Arthur O. Roberts, *Concepts of Perfection in the History of the Quaker Movement*, B.D. Thesis, Nazarene Theological Seminary, (1951).
17 Rebecca Laird, *Ordained Women in the Church of the Nazarene* (Kansas City, Mo.: Nazarene Publishing House, 1993).
18 Carole Spencer, "The American Holiness Movement: Why Did It Captivate Nineteenth-Century Quakers?" *Quaker Religious Thought*, Vol. 28, No. 4., January 1998.
19 Melvin H. Dieter, *The Holiness Revival of the Nineteenth Century* (Lanham, Md.: Scarecrow Press, 1980), p. 136.
20 John Leland Peters, *Christian Perfection and American Methodism* (Nashville, Tenn.: Abingdon Press 1975), p.112.
21 In general, the term 'Orthodox' is applied to the evangelical branch of Friends prior to the period of the Gurneyite-Wilburite separations, 1845-54.
22 See Thomas Hamm, *The Transformation of American Quakerism* (Bloomington, Ind.: Indiana University Press, 1988) Chapter II,"The Breakdown of the Older Vision, 1800-1850" *et seq.*

23 Donald Good, "Elisha Bates, American Quaker Evangelical in the Early Nineteenth Century," Ph.D. diss., University of Iowa, 1967, p. 80.

24 See Hamm, pp. 49-52. It is not generally appreciated that until the mid-nineteenth century spoken ministry was delivered in a "sing-song" or chanted tone. It can still occasionally be heard in Ohio Yearly Meeting.

25 Charles A. Johnson, *The Frontier Camp Meeting* (Dallas, Tex.: Southern Methodist University Press, 1955).

26 2Cor. 6:15-17.

27 Ohio (Damascus) YM, now Evangelical Friends Church Eastern Region was the ghost at the feast.

28 Lawrence E. Barker, *Development of the Pastoral Pattern in Indiana Yearly Meeting of the Religious Society of Friends*, M.A. Thesis, Earlham School of Religion, 1963, pp.72-6.

29 See Ernest E. Sandeen, *The Roots of Fundamentalism*, (Chicago: University of Chicago Press, 1970).

30 Arthur Roberts, *The Association of Evangelical Friends* (Newberg, Ore.: Barclay Press, 1975), p.21.

31 Now Evangelical Friends Church, Eastern Region.

32 Barclay, *Apology*, Proposition VIII.

33 Rom. 1:14.

34 2 Peter 1:4, 1 Cor. 6:17, Isa. 59:2, 2 Cor 6:14.

35 Matt. 7: 8-11, Titus 2:14, 1 John 3:5,8.

36 1 John 1:6-10.

37 Romans 8:2.

38 See Everett C.Cattell, *The Spirit of Holiness* (Grand Rapids, MI: William B. Eerdmans Publishers, 1963).

39 A.C. Outler, (ed.), *John Wesley, A Representative Collection of His Writings* (New York: Oxford University Press, 1964), p. 280.

9

The Day of Judgment

9

The Day of Judgment

The second coming of Christ hovers over the Church as a dream, a hope, an expectation, and a shimmering vision of glory to come. High up in the apses of Byzantine churches the mosaics pick out the features of Christos Pantocrator, the king in glory. The design is frequently accompanied with the letters alpha and omega to signify his presence at the beginning and the end of time.[1] It takes little imagination to see the same image appearing in the noonday sky and to see the peoples of the earth assembled before Christ, some with trepidation, some with remorse, and many with inexpressible joy. That Christ will come again is the clear teaching of scripture.

It is also the teaching of scripture that there will be a thousand-year period in which the saints will rule the earth with Christ. The meaning of this prophecy has always been a matter of debate, but it is impossible to form an adequate view of the end times unless one comes to some conclusions about it. In this chapter we shall try to grasp this nettle. Although I shall adopt one particular position, I will also try to show that of the variety of viewpoints it is possible to take, some are more compatible with a covenantal Quakerism than others.

That does not exhaust the significance of the topic, though. The second coming represents God's second decisive entry into human history, and the course of events in which we are even now involved is part of the process leading up to it. Different views of the nature of the millennium provide different estimates of the nature of history, and therefore the possibilities open to the human race. Unless we are to turn our backs on our collective experience, we will need to take account of politics from the Christian point of view as an extension of the ethics of the kingdom and perhaps the millennium. We shall discuss Jesus' teaching about the second coming, the dispensations, the millennium, and what a Christian view of politics requires.

The Kingdom of God

The reality called the kingdom of God or the kingdom of heaven is central to the message Jesus preached and to the life he led. The gospels are not a systematic account of the kingdom, however. They are not treatises. They contain much material that does not appear on the surface to have kingdom characteristics. Nevertheless, the form and substance of what they record is determined by this central concept. The kingdom of God is not a place. "Kingdom" in this context, while it may also indicate a realm or territory, carries the primary implication of sovereignty. The kingdom of God exists wherever God is obeyed.[2]

Scripture can tell us much about the kingdom, but we have to be prepared for some uncertainty when we seek to unravel the mystery of what it tells us. We are dealing with mystery in the strictest sense of the word and with a reality that is ultimately beyond our comprehension. We can know something of it, but not all. If curiosity is not tempered with reverence, we shall find what we want to find rather than recognizing the truth that is already there for us to see. "The knowledge of the secrets of the kingdom of God has been given to you, but to others I speak in parables, so that, 'though seeing, they may not see; though hearing, they may not understand.'" Nobody really knows the real meaning of this saying, but we shall take it as a warning against literalism in matters of the spirit.[3]

In both his preaching and teaching, Jesus draws a sharp contrast between the requirements of the kingdom and the rules of conventional morality, and a rapid inward transformation is required to move from one to the other. The first step is to realize the spiritual condition one is in, to grasp that one is being offered the chance of escape, and to seize the chance. A merchant finds a pearl, a widow relinquishes her last coin, a tower builder makes a calculation, and a man builds on a rock. The second step is to live with what one has done, because the kingdom into which we have been called is not present in its fullness, and its citizens have made a bargain that can bring hardship and persecution. Servants have to wait for their master's return, and the wise virgins have to safeguard their oil.[4]

Life in the kingdom is markedly different from life outside it. The point is made in the parable of the great feast. Those who are originally invited all find reason to decline the invitation, but those who do come are the poor, the crippled, the blind, and the lame.[5] They enjoy the plenty that is denied them in the normal course of life, and the king gives it to them for no reason except his own bountiful impulse. The implications of this story are clear. The guests will return to their usual station in life, but they will have received a foretaste of the joy and fellowship that is to come. The feast is given because of the king's generosity. The guests receive what they could never ever have hoped for. The essence of the kingdom is the giving and receiving of grace.

*The essence of the kingdom is the giving and
receiving of grace.*

The nature of Jesus' teaching about the kingdom has been a
matter of vigorous debate in the last century or so. We have just
considered the spiritual message of the gospels, but it is also important to consider the critical questions which have been raised and
which have a direct bearing on the Christian doctrine of the last
things. We need to know the relationship of Jesus to the kingdom,
whether he taught the kingdom as a present or a future reality, and
what we are to make of his dramatic prophecies of the last judgment
and the end of the world.

The historical-critical method of the nineteenth century was not
greatly concerned with eschatology, the doctrine of the last things,
as one might have expected in an age of optimism. The liberal
worldview accommodated the moral challenge of Jesus' preaching
to its own prior conception of human progress. Jesus' portrayal of
the last judgment and end of time was viewed as a symbolic husk
surrounding the rich kernel of universal truth constituted by his
self-sacrificing life combined with the ethical precepts of the Sermon on the Mount. It was a noble conception and entirely faithful
to the challenge of moral transformation made by Jesus. Its weakness was that it discounted that part of the gospel narrative that
gave context and reason for that challenge. It was unwilling to take
the last judgment seriously.

The early years of the twentieth century saw a reaction to this
outlook. One of the earliest synoptic texts reads, "And he said to
them, 'I tell you the truth, some who are standing here will not taste
death before they see the kingdom of God come with power.'"[6] The

plain meaning of this verse is that the coming of the kingdom is a future event, and that it will take place in the lifetime of Jesus' hearers. The urgency in his preaching arose because the end was near and there was very little time to prepare for it. Considerations of this sort allowed Albert Schweitzer (1875-1965) to argue that Jesus' teaching was entirely apocalyptic and proclaimed the kingdom of God as an imminent, not a present reality.[7] Hence, the moral order portrayed by the parables and the Sermon on the Mount is not of timeless significance. It is an interim ethic designed solely for the time remaining till the judgment.

In due course, a contrary interpretation appeared. On another occasion, having been asked by the Pharisees when the kingdom of God would come, Jesus replied, "The kingdom of God does not come with your careful observation, nor will people say, 'Here it is' or 'There it is,' because the kingdom of God is within (or, among) you."[8] The implication here is that that the kingdom is not a future event or state, but a present reality. Now if this is the case, the scriptural references emphasized by Schweitzer have to be reassessed. This passage clearly indicates that the kingdom has begun and is encountered whenever someone responds to Jesus' proclamation of the kingdom. In these circumstances, the ethics of Jesus take on a more enduring significance.

This way of understanding the kingdom preserves the note of crisis absent from the older interpretations, but it opens the way to a figurative understanding of the second coming and the judgment. The rule of God is present because Jesus is present, and his prophecies can be understood as symbolic formulations of a present reality. "It appears that while Jesus employed the traditional symbolism of apocalypse to indicate the "other worldly" or absolute character of the Kingdom of God, he used parables to enforce and illustrate the idea that the Kingdom of God had come upon men there and then. The inconceivable had happened: history had become the vehicle of the eternal; the absolute was clothed in flesh and blood. Admittedly, it was a "mystery" to be understood by those who have eyes to see and ears to hear, by those to whom it is revealed 'not by flesh and blood but by my Father in Heaven.'"[9]

There is a tension in scripture between the texts suggesting that the kingdom has come and those that indicate that the fullness of the kingdom is future and will only come with the return of Christ and the last judgment. So in interpreting Jesus' words, we appear to have two possibilities before us—a figurative interpretation, which regards the second coming as symbolic, and a realistic one, which sees it as an event in space-time. The problem with the symbolic explanation is that if we adopt it, we are caught in a logical trap. We can only understand a symbol if we know what is being symbolized. This would give us an understanding independent of the symbol, which therefore limits its scope as a vehicle of revelation. Whatever the kingdom of God stands for, that entity is more than an element in a symbolic system derived from the historical and cultural particularity of New Testament times.

> *There is a tension in scripture between the texts suggesting that the kingdom has come and those that indicate that the fullness of the kingdom is future and will only come with the return of Christ and the last judgment.*

One way to resolve the difficulty over the kingdom as a present and a future reality is to think whether it may be present in different ways at different points in time.[10] There is no objection to this in principle, because all manifestations of the kingdom have the rule of God and the presence of Christ in common. There must be an ultimate event in the history of the world, and that will be the coming of the kingdom in its fullness. Until then, there is a partial manifestation of the kingdom in those who are Christ's. "...Jesus went into Galilee, proclaiming the good news of God. 'The time has come,' he said. 'The kingdom of God is near. Repent and believe the good news!'"[11] This is the age in which we still live. The kingdom that entered the world in the person of Christ is therefore a divine reality in the past, the present, and the future.

> *The kingdom that entered the world in the person of Christ is therefore a divine reality in the past, the present, and the future.*

The Millennium

We have been looking at the teaching of Jesus in the synoptic gospels, but we must now turn to the rest of the New Testament, where there are fourteen other references to the kingdom.[12] These reflect tensions we have already noted, so they add no new element of interpretation. When we reach the last book in the Bible, however, we find that what we have just concluded about Jesus' teaching must be integrated with a very different kind of evidence. In the book of Revelation there is what appears to be a detailed account of how the world will come to an end and the circumstances surrounding the second coming of Christ. It has to be said that this account stands in the middle of a highly symbolic book. None of these details were given by Jesus when, it may be presumed, he was in a position to do so.

The relevant passage is as follows. "I saw thrones on which were seated those who had been given authority to judge. And I saw the souls of those who had been beheaded because of their testimony for Jesus and because of the word of God. They had not worshiped the beast or his image and had not received his mark on their foreheads or their hands. They came to life and reigned with Christ a thousand years. (The rest of the dead did not come to life until the thousand years were ended.) This is the first resurrection. Blessed and holy are those who have part in the first resurrection. The second death has no power over them, but they will be priests of God and of Christ and will reign with him for a thousand years."[13]

So this is the picture that emerges. At the return of Christ, the first resurrection of the faithful martyrs will occur. They will then rule with Christ for a thousand years together with the saints then alive (though the passage does not say so). The general resurrection will then take place. At this point Satan will be released from his prison, there will be a widespread rebellion against the rule of Christ and the saints, and only then, when the rebellion has been defeated, will the final judgment take place. The millennium is therefore a part of a longer sequence of events representing the closing stages of human history. It is not figurative or symbolic because the second coming will be personal, physical (that is, in space-time), visible, sudden, glorious, and triumphant.[14]

There is a sharp contrast, however, between the account of the last judgment given in Revelation and what is said in the gospel of Matthew. The latter document records the words of Jesus, rather than the details of a vision granted to one of his apostles. This leads some to give greater weight to what is said there. In Matthew, there is a speedy conclusion to the history of the world. The second coming is followed immediately by the judgment and the entry of the saved and the unsaved into their final states. There is one resurrection and no capture and release of Satan. Nor is there a suggestion of a millennium or any other interim period. What is done is done, and done quickly. Now if we are to regard Revelation as inspired scripture and binding on us, we must find some way of reconciling these two authorities. If there is to be a millennium, when will it come, what will it be like, and will it precede or follow the last judgment?

Differing Views on the Millenium

The earliest Christians were premillennialists. They took the view that the second coming would precede the millennium, and that therefore the first resurrection would unite the living and the dead in Christ prior to the events leading up to the final defeat of Satan and the end of the world. In many churches today, premillenialism is combined with dispensationalism to produce a detailed theory of the end-times, but there is no necessary connection between premillennial and dispensationalist belief. It is apparent that the nature of the millennium will be determined by this crucial question of whether it will occur before or after the second coming. Premillennialists stress that Jesus envisaged a period of severe trial before the second coming and that gradualist interpretations, which see the world being spiritually prepared for the physical return of Christ, discount these very clear teachings.[15]

However, postmillennialists draw different conclusions from scripture and perhaps cast their net more widely. While accepting the texts that teach there will be apostasy and tribulation before the second coming, they place these events against the background of a gradual amelioration of the human condition under the inspiration of the Holy Spirit. The millennium is therefore the period in which the world is made ready for the Second Coming and obviously precedes it. The Old Testament clearly envisages that God will ultimately rule over a harmonious and obedient world,[16] and it is unlikely that the Great Commission will fail. Moreover, concentration on the tribulation and the survival of the elect raises questions about the purpose of the First Coming. It regards the Church as an institution providing refuge from the wrath to come, rather than proclaiming the message and the way of life by which God intends to transform the world.

> *The Old Testament clearly envisages that God will ultimately rule over a harmonious and obedient world, and it is unlikely that the Great Commission will fail.*

A third stance, amillennialism, is derived from the teaching of St. Augustine, who regarded the millenium as the period during which the martyrs reign with Christ in heaven. It is begun by the resurrection of Christ, when Satan is deprived of his power and doomed to ultimate destruction and those who accept Christ receive their first, *spiritual* resurrection. It ends with the Second Coming, when all who have died are *physically* resurrected and undergo the last judgment, following which the world comes to an end.[17] So the millennium is a spiritual rather than a physical reality that begins with the earthly work of Christ and extends throughout the present period of time that we might call the Church age.[18] While there is not, strictly speaking, an earthly millennium in this view, the church age certainly has a religious dynamic. It serves the purpose of preparing the world for the judgment and, along with the other theories, takes for granted the ultimate rule of the saints in heaven.

Deciding between these competing views is not easy. In the early years of the nineteenth century, postmillennialism was the evangelical creed *par excellence* and exerted a profound influence on the social expectations of the period. It was also strong in the Middle Ages and in Pietism and Puritanism, numbering Philip Spener, Jonathan Edwards, and the Wesley brothers among its adherents. Premillennialism was strong in early Christianity, however, and was espoused by such figures as Justin Martyr, Irenaeus, and Tertullian. Many important contemporary evangelicals like Oscar Cullman, George Eldon Ladd, and G.R. Beasley-Murray are premillennialists.[19] Premillennial belief was widespread at the beginning of the seventeenth century and provided a significant addition to the theological armory of Anabaptists and radical Puritans.

The Millenium and Quaker Thought

Given this background, it is interesting that millennial speculation has never been a prominent feature of Quaker thought. Most evangelical Friends Disciplines include George Fox's *Letter to the Governor of Barbados* and the *Richmond Declaration*, but the former makes no mention of the judgment, nor the latter of the millennium. So we need to ask why this should be. In part this neglect arises from the historical circumstances in which Quakerism developed. But at the same time it has a lot to do with Friends insistence that the substance of religion is practice and not theory, particularly in cases where all the evidence is available and Christians take different views of it. Let us then see how we can relate each of the three general theories of the millennium to what early Friends had to say.

The predominant theory of their time was premillennialism, and some of the features of their thought fit this position quite well. As we have seen, Isaac Penington and others take the apostasy of the Church with great seriousness and see a continuous decline since the time of the apostles. There is certainly no sense of postmillennial social improvement here, and tribulation was the everyday experience of many of those who became Friends. Because of the highly extravagant apocalyptic language Friends were prone to use, they were plausibly but falsely associated with the Fifth Monarchy Men, a well-organized politico-religious group who, in 1660, sought to inaugurate the millennium by armed force.

Although it might seem that early Friends held a premillennial belief of *some* sort, we need to bear in mind that their use of scripture language was symbolic rather than exegetical, directed always at bringing their hearers to repentance and very seldom, if ever, having reference to the overall time scheme in which salvation history unfolds. Fox indeed scoffs at those who "looked for Christ's coming in an outward form and manner…and…did prepare themselves when it thundered and rained and thought Christ was coming to set up his kingdom."[20] Although they say very little about the millennium or the end-times, some of the things Friends do say can be interpreted to mean that they believed the second coming was actually in process of arrival as a spiritual reality facing every single person.[21]

Although they say very little about the millennium or the end-times, some of the things Friends do say can be interpreted to mean that they believed the second coming was actually in process of arrival as a spiritual reality facing every single person.

In George Fox's preaching, as we have seen, there is a powerful sense of the apostasy of the Church and a new work being undertaken by God in his times. He argues that Christ had set up his kingdom during his earthly reign, but at the same time, the kingdom was not of this world.[22] His watchword, "Christ is come to teach his people himself" carries implications in two directions. One is that it is the contemporary manifestation of what Christ has been doing since the beginning. The other is that, at the same time, something new is here. It is not hard to see how this could produce the claim that the second coming was spiritually in progress, and to see the intense efforts by early Friends to "Let all nations hear the word by sound or writing…"[23] as a preliminary to Christ's imminent and final victory.

On the face of it, however, Friends original, spiritual doctrine of the second coming is questionable, because Jesus taught that this would be an event that will be witnessed by everyone in the world. "All the nations will be gathered before him, and he will separate the people one from another as a shepherd separates the sheep from the goats."[24] This statement is quite unambiguous. It claims that the judgment will be public and that everybody will come to it simultaneously. It is very hard to explain why it should be glossed to mean that the judgment would come to us separately and independently.

Yet this seems to be what early Friends said, and it distinguishes their position from classical premillennialism, or postmillennialism, for that matter. They did not theorize, so we have no real notion of how they conceived the end of the world. If we leave on one side the spiritual interpretation of the second coming, we see a Quaker mission uprooting tares and gathering wheat in seventeenth-century England. There is a possibility that the profound experiences of Christ, which early Friends identified as the second coming, might have been misunderstood. The amillennial perspective will deal with early Friends claims by saying that they evidence a widespread occurrence of the *first* resurrection, an event which merits the descriptions Friends gave of it and leaves with them the challenge of accounting for the clear message of scripture that the second coming will be an open and public event like the Olympic games or a day at the beach.

However that may be, we are certainly looking at another example of early Friends theological originality. We can perhaps illustrate it by considering the nature of time and the medium in which events occur. Time, as the New Testament writers understood it, was linear, proceeding from the creation of the world to its end. However, within this sequence there are certain points that are more significant than others. Greek distinguishes *aion* from *kairos*, the passing of time and the point of time, particularly some climax or other that indicates an event of particular importance.[25] In the New Testament, time moves directly through the age, proceeding toward the end. However, the end is not necessarily the most significant event. What gives meaning to time within Christianity is the cross and not the second coming. Without the first, the second would be unnecessary.

The reason, as Oscar Cullman puts it, is that the decisive battle in a war can be fought long before the end of hostilities, but will ultimately be seen to have determined the outcome. By analogy, the story of salvation arises out of the work of Christ in offering himself as a sufficient sacrifice for human sin in a particular time and place. All the elements of the end-times must be understood to draw their significance from this state of affairs and not to have a determinative influence on the meaning of human life or salvation history. Certainly they have great importance, but they are part of a wider drama, the nature of which has to be clearly understood.

Thus, there is past, future, and eternal significance in everything that happens. Part of the practice of Christianity is to understand this truth and yet not allow it to distort the meaning of the faith. In the parable of the last judgment, those welcomed into the kingdom are those who fed, clothed, and nursed Christ and visited him in prison. Not recalling this, they asked when they had done so. Christ's reply is engraved on the Christian conscience. "I tell you the truth, whatever you did for one of the least of these brothers of mine, you did for me." Surviving the Last Judgment, then, depends on what we do in this life. Our fate is decided by what we do now. It is stretching the meaning of words only a little to say that those who are saved anticipate the Judgment. Necessarily, they do it individually and in isolation.

> *Thus, there is past, future, and eternal significance in everything that happens. Part of the practice of Christianity is to understand this truth and yet not allow it to distort the meaning of the faith.*

Perhaps what we can say about early Friends doctrine of the last things is similar to what we said about convincement. The teaching of early Friends reflected not so much a different pattern of experience from everybody else (though they said it did) but an intensity of experience of a very marked character that other people denied was necessary or possible. Yet that level of devotion is exactly what we know in our bones that Jesus Christ is worthy of. We might shy away from our spiritual forbears because we are afraid of the standards they set us. They called their mission "the Lamb's War," and they saw those standards—what we know as the distinctives—as the spiritual weapons with which the victory of the Lamb would be accomplished.[26] This is why there is an unavoidable millennial dimension to any account of Friends faith and practice.

Early Friends were right to place immense significance on the present reality. If we want to make any claim to be their children, we must also. The gospel they preached does full justice to the ethical standards Jesus requires of us and is based on an understanding of time in the fullest New Testament sense. On the other hand, it is hard to deny that early Friends underplayed or misunderstood the Last Judgment as the general culmination of history, and we are not bound to follow them in this respect. Rather, we might conclude that taking all things into account, what they had to say could best be accommodated under the aegis of amillennialism.

Premillennial Dispensationalism

If some variant of the amillennial perspective best accounts for our tradition, we inevitably have to set our face against premillennial dispensationalism as our explanation for the end times. That is bound to follow from the adoption of an alternative point of view. But there are also substantive objections to be offered against dispensationalism. Dispensationalism in its modern form developed out of the teaching of J.N.Darby (1800-82) in the mid-nineteenth century and received strong impetus from the later prophetic movement that was one of the sources of fundamentalism. Dispensational views are one of the defining features of fundamentalism, and a number of Friends accept them.

The basic principle of dispensationalism is that the Bible teaches a single system of truth and should be interpreted literally wherever possible. There is a place for symbolic or figurative methods of interpretation but only when use of them is unavoidable. Consequently, we can expect prophecies to be fulfilled in every detail, with no allowance being made for imaginative expression or deliberate exaggeration. It is often overlooked that there are unfulfilled prophecies in both the Old and New Testaments so we may legitimately look for the fulfilment of all these prophecies at the end-times or in the period between now and then. Hence, the study of prophecy should rank very high on the list of Christian theological priorities.

Dispensationalism distinguishes seven distinct periods, or dispensations in scripture. A dispensation, according to the *Scofield Reference Bible*, is "...a period of time during which man is tested in respect of obedience to some specific revelation of the will of God." In each dispensation there is a new revelation of God's will and a new governing relationship between God and his human creation. There is ultimately human failure, however, and this is followed by a new revelation and a new dispensation. There are a number of variant schemes, but they are of the same general type.[27] According to this scheme we are now in the dispensation of grace, which began with the descent of the Holy Spirit and will continue until the

second coming and the beginning of the dispensation of the millennium.

Certain consequences are drawn from this, of which the most
well known is probably the distinction between Israel and the
Church. This distinction rests on the claim that in each dispensation
God makes promises to identifiable groups, some of which have been
fulfilled and some of which remain to be fulfilled. If there are promises (or prophecies) that remain outstanding, we can expect them to
be fulfilled now or in the future in the interests of those to whom
they were originally made. Because Israel exists and is still capable
of receiving the fulfillment of God's promises, it must follow that
the Jews, as well as the Church, will have a place in the messianic
kingdom to be instituted at the millennium. The prophecies and
promises of each dispensation must be fulfilled in the terms in which
they were given.

While accepting the elegance of dispensational doctrine, a number of objections can be made to it. We can certainly agree that at
various points in scripture there have been new beginnings and those
suggested by dispensationalism merit considerable reflection. But
we are not obliged to accept that there are specific dispensations
succeeding one another or that there are fundamental changes in
God's attitude toward us from one dispensation to another. That
would imply that there are different standards of salvation at different times. However that may be, dispensationalism does provide a
firm basis for progressive revelation in its ability to show the gradual
unfolding of divine truth.

There is one point, however, where dispensational and covenantal theories of salvation history diverge sharply. In the period between the Fall and the saving work of Christ, dispensationalism dis-

tinguishes five distinct periods: pre-Fall, Adam to Noah, Noah to Abraham, Abraham to Moses, and Moses to Christ. Each is complete in itself with its own governing relationship, and this explains, in part, why it is necessary to separate the promises to Israel and the promises made to the Church. But this makes the distinction between law and grace too rigid. In the words of the Westminster Confession, "there are not...two covenants of grace different in substance but one and the same covenant of grace under various dispensations *(sic)* of the Old and New Testaments."[28]

Concentration on prophecy, then, has the effect of producing a kind of Christianity in which the emphasis is less on what has been done than on what is to come. Speculative questions as to the nature of the tribulation, the rapture, and the millennium move to the forefront in determining where the Christian's energies and attention should be directed—at the expense, it can be argued, of more immediate and pressing concerns. A balance has to be struck between the end-times as the necessary dénouement of the drama of salvation and the atonement wrought by Christ as the event that determines the nature of that later event. Premillennialism strikes that balance at a point to which the wider evangelical movement and the Friends tradition does not require us to move.

Millennial beliefs have been very significant in the history of Anglo-American evangelicalism in the past three hundred years, and it is important to bear in mind that they have always provided the main theological justification for Christian involvement in public life. Historically it seems that prevailing views of the end-times are correlated with the prevailing secular mood. In periods of stability or improvement, postmillennialism comes to the fore. Where there is social unrest and pessimism over the future, premillennial beliefs are dominant. The course of the revivals, which gave birth to the Friends Church, exhibits both of these patterns. Let us examine them in turn before asking whether a new rationale is now called for.

The Postmillenial Revival

The rise of capitalism in Britain and the United States has had immense consequences for both social and religious life. There have been great economic benefits in the process, but they have come at a price. The early and middle phases of the industrial revolution were characterized by poverty, population movement, and changing expectations of the workforce, resulting in social unrest and political instability. Quakerism and evangelicalism both developed in the North Atlantic community during this period and have been deeply influenced by the social conditions in which they arose. We cannot explain either phenomenon adequately unless we take account of these far-reaching changes.

In the early years of the nineteenth century, British evangelicals were drawn into social action of various kinds as a consequence of their mission work.[29] Folk who could not read had no access to scripture, so evangelicals set up Sunday Schools, and later, independent day schools for the poor before the age of universal elementary education. The poor and unchurched lived in the inner cities, so evangelical philanthropy set up housing and relief schemes, and distributed coal. Lord Shaftesbury (1801-85) was the model evangelical reformer. He ended the scandal of child chimney sweeps and led the campaign to limit the hours of work in factories. The statue of Eros in London's Piccadilly Circus is the nation's homage to him.

Converts were often exposed to strong temptations to relapse, and to counteract these influences, British evangelicals began a long campaign to reform public morals. The family was seen as the institution most in need of protection, particularly from the evils of alcohol. Evangelicals had the same preoccupations then as they do now. They struggled against the coarseness of the environment in which their converts lived, carrying on sustained campaigns against blasphemy, gambling, prostitution, and lewd and depraved public entertainments. It is customary in some quarters to sneer at their naiveté, but they revolutionized the nation.

The major evangelical cause was the campaign against slavery. In 1783, London Friends set up a committee to promote the abolition of the slave trade. It was widened to include non-Friends in 1787, and this brought into one body the Quakers, who had an efficient national communications network, and Anglican evangelicals like Zachary Macaulay and William Wilberforce, who had political pull and were engaged on a long and arduous Parliamentary campaign to outlaw slavery. In 1807, the slave trade was ended in the British dominions, and in 1833, slavery itself was abolished.

In the United States a similar pattern was emerging, though social conditions were very different. The impetus given to social reform by the Second Great Awakening was immense, and the most striking feature of it, as in Britain, was the association between revivalist evangelical Christianity and the abolitionist and, later, antislavery political position.[30] The roll call of the leading evangelicals is strongly correlated with the roll call of leading abolitionists, with Charles G. Finney perhaps being the most striking name on each list.[31] The link between these two political and religious orientations is not coincidental, and in due course we shall see why.

Similar social concerns show up on the American frontier and

319

in the slums of Manchester. Drink and loose morals are a threat to the stability of the family everywhere, particularly to the well-being of children, and it went without saying that the convert at a camp-meeting in America, or an inner city mission in England was going to have to lead a very different style of life. Visiting speakers gave encouragement through a wide range of bodies and activities, like Bible and Tract Societies, Sunday School and Temperance Unions, magazines, periodicals, and lectures. One could witness to the genuineness of one's new faith by getting involved in the organizations that promoted the values and practices one had adopted. One renounced secret societies like the freemasons, observed the Sabbath and gave money and time to organizations devoted to what was known in England as the "bettering" of the condition of the poor.

Both the United States and the United Kingdom enjoyed a proliferation of these grassroots organizations dedicated to religious and social work. Of New York City in the period immediately before the Civil War, Timothy L. Smith writes, "The experience of evangelicals in co-operative benevolent and missionary enterprises was rapidly awakening a new sense of responsibility for those whom a soulless industrial system had thrown upon the refuse heap of the city's slums...Local units of the Home Missionary and Tract Societies performed similar roles, moving rapidly from simple evangelism to the establishment of mission churches and Sunday schools, job placement, resettlement of destitute children and youths, and the distribution of clothing, food and money to the poor."[32]

In the early nineteenth century, the evangelical revival was an optimistic, benevolent and outward-looking social movement with both religious and political significance. "At first, Protestants' efforts to cultivate and sustain a Christian republic developed through voluntary organizations outside the arena of party politics. But as the young nation moved from a more restricted, deferential form of republicanism towards a discernibly modern mass democracy, the worlds of evangelicalism and politics found themselves bound together in a process of cultural symbiosis."[33]

Conversion inevitably involves radical changes in the individual. Among the precious gifts bestowed on those who are bought at the price of the Savior's blood are self-respect and personal independence. A reformed drunkard or an illiterate who has learned to read has been liberated from bondage. Quite obviously, the possibilities that open up before such persons are in stark contrast to their earlier condition. Conversion can therefore produce radical changes in how one sees one's place in the world, and indeed, the nature of the world itself. This view of human potential had important consequences. If perfection is more than a theoretical possibility, there is a real prospect of a civil society free from the kinds of moral and spiritual corruption against which the evangelical movement so strenuously struggled. Social involvement leading to political action is therefore the logical outcome of conversion.

Though in retrospect the link between the revivals and politics has been questioned, many thoughtful religious people at the time were clear about their significance. The success of the revivals and the undoubted improvements taking place in society came to be seen as more than the accidents of history; to the instructed Christian they were harbingers of the second coming. This proved to be a theological position perfectly conformable to the spirit of the age. It was democratic, optimistic, and full of the sense of manifest destiny. It is not surprising that in this period we find a reaffirmation of the belief that America is a nation specially blessed and given a special role in the advancement of God's kingdom on earth.[34] The Christianity of the Second Great Awakening was overwhelmingly postmillennial.

The Premillennial Revival

After the Civil War, however, it was a different matter. The devastation and shock of the conflict echoed through the subsequent decades, and its cost has to be reckoned in more than economic terms. A sober, indeed pessimistic, mood developed in many quarters. This was the period of an accelerated exodus to the towns, a greatly accelerated rate of non-Anglo-Saxon immigration, cultural dislocation caused by rapid economic change and the concomitant desire for the older, more familiar ways. A gap of income, education, and expectations opened up between a rising middle class and the urban and rural poor. Social as well as religious factors began to draw the children of the revivals apart from the mainstream of national life.

A changing intellectual climate helped. *The Origin of Species* appeared in 1859, but made no immediate impact, partly because the concept of evolutionary development antedated Darwin, whose achievement was to provide a convincing account of its mechanisms. At first, the evangelical movement was able to deal with the theory on its merits, but soon realized that it was the vehicle of substantial challenges to the Christian worldview. The parallel growth of higher criticism led to theological liberalism in its modern form. Also, and far more fundamentally, evolutionary theory was seen to provide a scientific rather than a theological rationale for human improvement. The concept of progress as the dynamic of history replaced millennial expectation among the educated classes.

The evangelical movement responded negatively to these developments. The Prophetic and Bible conferences of the 1880s and 1890s were important in turning the movement away from the mainstream of theological debate toward what came to be known as fundamentalism. This latter development was characterized by pessimism, cultural separation, and a shift to a dramatic form of premillennialism. This meant a curtailment of broader forms of social action and an increased emphasis on missions and inner-city evangelism. (In part, of course, this was a reaction against the social gospel of the liberal churches). Dispensationalism produced a rigid schema of the end-times that gave shape and coherence to the whole movement and determined what its priorities were going to be. Integral to the whole development was a renewed emphasis on the doctrine of the inerrancy of scripture.

By the mid-twentieth century this consensus began to break down with the emergence of a newer generation of evangelicals nurtured in fundamentalism, but with a broader vision of the Christian faith. Fuller Theological Seminary, *Christianity Today*, and the Billy Graham Crusades each represent the emergence of part of the evangelical movement from a stricter fundamentalism into an engagement with the wider culture.[35] The movement has had its difficulties, but it has resulted in conservative evangelicalism becoming much more diverse and imaginative. Its politics is derived not so much from premillennial dispensationalism as from a cultural critique of contemporary American life. Evangelicals now find themselves part of a much broader association of conservative Catholics, Jews, and others whose religious convictions have led them to a similar position. They form one of the sides in the so-called culture wars.[36]

Evangelicals now find themselves part of a much broader association of conservative Catholics, Jews, and others whose religious convictions have led them to a similar position.

Associated with, but not identical to this movement is what is generally referred to as the religious right, a composite phenomenon which needs careful assessment. The religious right is a body of opinion that adopts conservative positions on matters like abortion, school prayer, and homosexuality, but in addition has much to say on the subjects of defense and foreign policy, often adopting militantly patriotic positions. These concerns usually indicate a dispensational outlook that leads to what others regard as bizarre conclusions. Many members of this school of thought see the United States as God's chosen instrument in world politics. They interpreted the Cold War (1947-1989) as a major sign of the end-times and were indifferent to the possibility of nuclear exchange in view of the imminence of the tribulation and the rapture. How well this ideology will survive in the twenty-first century and the electronic age is another question.

Recent American history suggests that premillennial and postmillennial ideas are largely dependent on external circumstances for their acceptability. They are attractive in times of major cultural change, when questions of identity and purpose are answered with reference to spiritual rather than material realities. But they do not exhaust the possibilities before us. Amillennialism also has a long historical and theological pedigree and needs serious consideration. Its greatest immediate merit is that is that it avoids the trap premillennialism and postmillennialism fall into. One of the clearest teachings of scripture is that we should not speculate about when the second coming will be.

In Mark 13 the disciples ask Jesus directly when the end will come. After a harrowing description of the tribulation, Jesus eventually says, "No one knows about that day or hour, not even the angels in heaven, nor the Son, but only the Father. Be on guard! Be alert! You do not know when that time will come."[37] They put the same question to him at the Ascension, and receive, if anything, an even blunter reply, "It is not for you to know the times or dates the Father has set by his own authority." The proper attitude for the Christian, as the early Friends grasped so clearly, is vigilance. "So you also must be ready, because the Son of Man will come at an hour when you do not expect him."[38]

Perhaps the reason for these warnings is that the Church is not the only instrument of God's activity in the world, hard though it might be to say so. A wider view might see the process of history itself as a divine instrument, so that to study history is to engage the mind with the purposes of God. This is surely a sound, biblically based conclusion. One might say that without this broader understanding of what was happening in the world, there could have been no prophetic tradition. Not only did the prophets speak the word of God, but they also saw deeply into the mind of God and the manner of his dealings with those who were not of the chosen people. We must remember finally that those who were judged fit to enter the messianic kingdom included folk who did not understand how they came to be in that company.[39]

> *A wider view might see the process of history itself as a divine instrument, so that to study history is to engage the mind with the purposes of God.*

Waiting for the End

We live in the end-times, at an historical juncture at which the Church is active in the world and there is nevertheless widespread resistance to God's will. To understand our own position we need a broader perspective than just our immediate concerns and interests; movements influence us, and we measure trends of thought against more than one lifetime. Martin Niemoeller said, "When the Nazis came for the Communists, I said nothing because I was not a Communist. When they came for the trade unionists, I said nothing because I was not a trade unionist. When they came for the Jews, I was not involved because I was not a Jew. Then they came for me." Niemoeller was a pastor, and he knew the parable of the last judgment.

This famous statement illustrates clearly the principle that decisions about political matters and the social order cannot be left to immediate response to circumstances. History flows; it does not stop and start. If we keep our eyes on the judgment we will have a sure sense of where history comes from and where it is going; we will understand how we are part of the process. But if we close our eyes to history, it is likely to visit us with some very unpleasant surprises. The social conditions that bred Nazism were the outcome of defeat in war, impoverishment, personal insecurity, and a very deep tradition of European anti-Semitism. Christianity was as much part of the causes of these things as the solution because its adherents would not accept continuing responsibility for social and political activity.

Contemporary politics, then, is the raw material of history, which is a longer-term process and which Christians see as having a momentum, a meaning, and a purpose. It is not the product of chance or impersonal forces, but is under the control of Almighty God who is working out his purposes for us through time. So we are faced with the question of how the course of history, as we commonly understand it, can be linked with the ultimate realities of the millennium and the judgment. Our attitude to politics, if we take our Christianity seriously, will depend on how we see this connection. God desires justice here and now, as scripture teaches quite plainly.[40] This is one of the purposes of history. The struggle for justice will end in victory when God intervenes decisively at the last judgment. The very reason for the tribulation is that Satan can be expected to throw all he has into one last struggle to pervert the course of divine justice.

We have already noted that there have been premillennial movements that have calculated the date of the Second Coming and prepared for it by political insurrection. None, of course, has survived, and we have suggested on both historical and theological grounds that there are reasons to doubt that this is how the millennium will come. Similar considerations apply to the idea that the millennium will precede the return of Christ. Those who want to know the time of the Second Coming often move imperceptibly from preparing for it to procuring it, designing whole states in which there is government by the saints, as Calvin and Cromwell both sought to do. Historically, these régimes have been both religious and repressive. They fail because their theology is defective.

The following text, read in its entirety, shows why. "For it is by grace you have been saved, through faith—and this not from yourselves, it is the gift of God—not by works, so that no one can boast. For we are God's workmanship, created in Christ Jesus to do good works, which God prepared in advance for us to do."[41] In this passage, works are the logical consequence of justification by faith, but they are the works *God* has prepared for us to do. We therefore need to exercise close discernment to understand what these tasks are. We know that they will be part of God's intentions for the world, but it is not our business to decide what they should be. Idealists as well as theocrats can end up thwarting God's will with the best of intentions. We have all paid the price of their mistakes.

> *Works are the logical consequence of justification by faith, but they are the works God has prepared for us to do.*

So to see the purpose of political action as the establishment of the millennium is attractive but mistaken. The error does not lie in the desire for peace or the hunger and thirst for righteousness, but the spirit in which they are pursued. The motivation for Christian social action should not be that it forms part of some grand cosmic scheme that we have been privileged to understand, but, much more simply, that God's desire for justice here and now requires that this is what we should do. God will take care of the millennium. As Christians and Friends, what we need to do is to ask what principles should guide us when we consider how to vote or what social movements and programs to support either with time or personal service. There are many places where we might begin this process, but for now, I will choose just three themes to illustrate what religion has to say about politics.

First there is the claim that wealth is dangerous. Every Christian knows that it is more difficult for a camel to go through the eye of a needle than for a rich man to enter the kingdom of heaven and that the love of money is the root of all evil.[42] These familiar observations are designed to reinforce the message that wealth has a tendency to corrupt. If it is serious about the dangers of wealth, therefore, the Church will be unable to avoid the hard questions of economic justice. The prophets knew this well. "The Lord enters into judgment against the elders and leaders of his people... 'It is you who have ruined my vineyard; the plunder from the poor is in your houses. What do you mean by crushing my people and grinding the faces of the poor?' declares the Lord, the Lord Almighty."[43] This is not just a question of justice toward those to whom it is denied. Indifference toward the poor, together with such offences as idolatry, adultery, and theft, is one of the marks of the sinful, according to Ezekiel. The Old Testament is of no use to us unless we recognize the realities with which it deals in our own days. It is infallible. It warns us that we ignore the poor at our peril.

Then there is patriotism. It would be unnatural not to love one's country and one's own kin dearly, but painful though it is, the gospel demands a different loyalty. Preaching to the Athenians, Paul deliberately emphasizes the unity of the human race, saying, "From one man he made every nation of men..." and draws the conclusion, among other things, that we are therefore God's offspring. Speaking specifically of Christians, he writes, "There is neither Jew nor Greek, slave nor free, male nor female, for you are all one in Christ Jesus. If you belong to Christ, then you are Abraham's seed, and heirs according to the promise."[44] Christian participation in warfare and oppression of all kinds has often made a mockery of these words, but the kingdom requires that Paul's words be practiced. Worldly distinctions will have no importance when Christ comes to judge us. Christians can never place national or political loyalties higher than that. We must measure the duties of secular citizenship by the standards of the kingdom and not the other way round.

Third, there is the case of those who are so convinced of the power and immediacy of the Holy Spirit that they have dispensed with the moral law as a guide to conduct and rely instead on direct inspiration. This religious antinomianism has now developed a secular form in the relativism and self-gratification of contemporary life, which is equally dangerous because it undervalues the public, normative, exemplary function of moral standards. Society is not, and is unlikely to be, composed of morally upright, spirit-filled individuals whose existence renders the laws superfluous. Christian morality may not coincide with that of society generally, but if churches have confidence in the truth of what they preach, they will have every right to enter the public arena with the intention of changing the prevailing climate of opinion wherever they think this challenge should be made.

These three examples illustrate the complex relationship between the ethics of the kingdom and the standards of the secular world. Because politics inevitably involves controversy and compromise, many Christians prefer to remain aloof from it. Individuals may have good reasons for this attitude, but for the Church collectively it is inadequate because it fails to look at the political process from a kingdom perspective and does not relate the pursuit of justice now with the judgment to come. Those with a lively belief in the imminent return of Christ and a sense of millennial urgency will not make this mistake.

If the churches have the courage to operate within a broader concept of morality, they may find common cause with non-Christians who nevertheless have the same concerns. It has been argued earlier that Friends distinctive doctrine of the light implies that universally recognizable moral standards exist and are discoverable. This being so, it is a dereliction of duty if the Church fails to engage in debates over public morals, the state of the family, the care of the elderly, the sanctity of human life, the nature and quality of public entertainment, the state of the arts, the news media, and the standards of intellectual and public life. That cannot be done from a Christian ghetto; cooperation with non-Christians of the same mind is essential and inevitable.

> *If the churches have the courage to operate within a broader concept of morality, they may find common cause with non-Christians who nevertheless have the same concerns.*

Political involvement is therefore not an option. It is one of the duties of a church that takes the doctrine of the Second Coming seriously. This is not to say that churches should become political parties, but it does imply that there is a Christian duty of citizenship and that churches, each in its own way, need to give leadership to and expression of the convictions of their congregations. This is in part a matter of vision, a proclamation and explanation of what the state and political institutions can and should be doing or not doing. It is in part a matter of practice, social service within society, and the informal relationships that sustain the state. It is not just to do the good but also to build up convictions and habits of mind by engaging in public debate that will serve to extend the kingdom until the return of the king.

NOTES

[1] Rev.1:8, 21:6, 2:13.
[2] See G.E.Ladd, *Jesus and the Kingdom* (London: SPCK, 1966) Ch.5.
[3] Luke 8:10.
[4] Luke 16:1-8, Matt. 14:45, Mark 12:41-43, Luke 14:28-30, Matt. 7:24-25, Luke 12:35-40, Matt. 25:1-13.
[5] Luke 14:16-2; *see also* Matt.3:10, 8:5-11, 22:1-4, Luke 22:24-30.
[6] Mark 9:1.
[7] Albert Schweitzer, *The Quest for the Historical Jesus* (London: A & C Black, 1911).
[8] Luke 17:21.
[9] C.H.Dodd, *The Parables of the Kingdom* (London: Nisbet & co. ltd., 1935), p.85.
[10] G.E.Ladd, *Crucial Questions about the Kingdom of God* (Grand Rapids, Mich.: Eerdmans, 1952), p.85.
[11] Matt.8:10-11, Mark 9:1, Mark 1:15.
[12] Six in Acts, four in First Corinthians, and once each in Romans, Galatians, Colossians and Second Thessalonians.
[13] Rev. 20:4-6.
[14] Louis Berkhof, *Systematic Theology*, Banner of Truth Trust, (1939), pp.705-7.
[15] Mark 13:9-22 (and parallels), 2 Thess.2:1, 2 Tim.3:1-5.
[16] Micah 4:1-6, Isa. 66:18-24.
[17] St. Augustine, *The City of God*, Book XX (Cambridge: Harvard University Press), Chapters 5-8.
[18] John 5:19-29, Matt.12:29.
[19] Donald Bloesch, *Essentials of Evangelical Theolog,y*, Vol. 2, (San Francisco: HarperCollins, 1978), pp. 189-194.
[20] Op cit. p. 419.
[21] This is called "realizing eschatology" in *Heaven on Earth: Quakers and the Second Coming*, by Ben Pink Dandelion, Douglas Gwyn and Timothy Peat (Kelso, Scotland: Curlew Productions; Birmingham, England: Woodbrooke College, 1998) p.149 *et seq.*
[22] George Fox, *Journal*, (Nickalls), pp. 419-420.
[23] George Fox, *Journal*, (Nickalls), p. 263.
[24] Matt.25:32.
[25] See Oscar Cullmann, *Christ and Time* (Philadelphia: Westminster Press, 1950).
[26] Rev. 17:12-14.

[27] The first four dispensations are recorded in the early chapters of Genesis. The dispensation of the Mosaic law begins at Sinai and lasts until the dispensation of grace begins with Pentecost. The dispensation of the millennium will begin at the second coming. See the chart in Charles C. Ryrie, *Dispensationalism Today* (Chicago: Moody Press, 1965), p.84.

[28] See Daniel P. Fuller, *Gospel and Law, Contrast or Continuum?* (Grand Rapids, Mich.: Eerdmans, 1980), Ch. 2.

[29] See Ian Bradley, *The Call to Seriousness* (New York: Macmillan Publishing House, 1976).

[30] See John L. Hammond, *The Politics of Benevolence* (Norwood, N.J.: Ablex Publishing Corp., 1979).

[31] See Donald W. Dayton, *Discovering an Evangelical Heritage* (New York: Harper and Row, 1976).

[32] Timothy L. Smith, *Revivalism and Social Reform* (Baltimore, MD: Johns Hopkins University Press, 1980) p.167.

[33] Richard J. Carwardine, *Evangelicals and Politics in Antebellum America* (New Haven, CT: Yale University Press, 1993) p. 320.

[34] Whether the revivals contributed in any way to the wider formation of the American character has been argued and questioned. See Hammond, pp. 200-201.

[35] See, e.g., Joel A. Carpenter, *Revive Us Again*, Oxford, (1997).

[36] See James Davison Hunter, *The Culture Wars* (New York: Doubleday & Co., 1993).

[37] Mark 13:32-3, Acts 1:7.

[38] Matt. 24:44, Luke 12:40.

[39] Matt. 25:34.

[40] Jer. 21:12, Amos 5:15, 2 Cor. 7:11.

[41] Eph. 2:8-10.

[42] Matt.19:24, 1 Tim. 6:10.

[43] Isaiah 3:14-15, Ezek. 18:12.

[44] Eph.3:14-16, Acts 17: 26 and 29, Gal. 3:28-29.

10

The Friends Church
and Its Future

10

The Friends Church and Its Future

Mark Twain is supposed to have said, "Reports of my death are somewhat exaggerated." This is a clever remark for a variety of reasons. The wit signals the identity of America's foremost humorist, and the idea that news of a death can be exaggerated is ridiculous. What nobody else would have done is to insert the sly word "somewhat" into the remark in such a way as to make us involuntarily think of an exaggerated death and not an exaggerated report. We realize we have been tricked, and laugh. At least, this writer does. The death of Christianity, likewise, has been somewhat exaggerated over the years. Nietzsche has his fable of the man with a lantern standing in the square at midday crying, 'God is dead! We have killed him!'

Nietzsche was making a cultural rather than a religious point, but what he says is challenging nonetheless. Regardless of the existence or non-existence of God in a religious, or absolute sense, the *belief* in God that was once a common motivating force in western culture, both in individuals and institutions, has lost its power. It was always open to us to maintain this belief, but for whatever reason, we chose not to do so, and the result is a secular society. In what follows, readers are invited to keep this distinction very clear in their minds. Religious belief is a sociological fact regardless of the existence or non-existence of the object of that belief. Similarly, sociological realities can both encourage and hinder the formulation and development of religious belief.

In what follows, we shall be move back and forth between these two ways of looking at religion. Sometimes we shall look at matters of substantive faith, at other times we will consider social realities relevant to the practice of religion. My purpose is to rebut the argument that the power of religious belief is in terminal decline. I will argue, to the contrary, that religion in the United States (in spite, or perhaps *because of,* the separation of church and state) is flourishing and can be expected to continue in this happy state. It is essential to make this case because the Friends Church needs these conditions in order to prosper. But it is not enough to show that the churches in general are in a satisfactory condition we must also be able to show how the Friends Church can benefit from that state of affairs.

This chapter begins with an examination of the place of religious belief in the wider culture to which we belong. It is essential to do this because this is the arena where the gospel is to be preached and also because many religious people have yet to come to terms with the possibility that the last forty years may have seen a radical and fundamental change in the way our culture and our society thinks about its place in the world. Most of us have a range of assumptions and attitudes that can loosely be called "modern," But we are now beginning to encounter people who describe themselves as "postmodern." If there has been a general shift in intellectual assumptions from modern to postmodern, then we will need to understand what has been going on and at least to understand the mind-set of those to whom we wish to bring the word of life.

The Consequences of the Enlightenment

The foundations of the modern world were laid toward the end of the seventeenth century in the intellectual movement known as the Enlightenment, now commonly called modernism. Perhaps its most significant feature was the development of scientific method, which we can define as the abstraction of general principles from observed phenomena in order to make accurate predictions. Scientific method, in order to discover the truth, requires an open mind willing to relinquish as far as possible any presuppositions the observer brings to the experimental process. The ideal scientist is an unbiased observer who uncovers the laws that constitute the universe while releasing any personal biases that might affect the results of an enquiry.

The rise of modern science required a redefinition of nature. Nature was no longer a capricious external reality populated by hostile forces that had to be avoided or placated. There was no longer any justification for superstitions like the belief in witchcraft, sea monsters, fairies, or sacred and therapeutic wells and streams. Plainly, accounts of these things were mistaken or had some other, scientifically ascertainable explanation if they did not arise simply from deluded imagination. This redefinition had unfortunate consequences for Christianity, because miracles could easily be seen as scientifically impossible interruptions in the processes of nature.

The scientific revolution associated with the Enlightenment emphasized the importance of reason and sought to base all aspects of human life on a rational footing. If the world of our experience follows principles of order, regularity, and predictability, it is therefore rational. Because we are able to recognize this rationality, we must ourselves also be rational. So we are primarily mental beings observing a material world and our relationship with it is that of observer and observed. It is reason and scientific observation that provide the truth about the world and form the basis for any certainty we might come to. It can therefore be claimed that the truths of reason are indubitable, open to all, and provide the basis for human solidarity. If this is the case, these principles of reason can be applied to politics and seen to provide sound reasons for resisting the claims of arbitrary and unrepresentative government. A quick glance at the Declaration of Independence, to say nothing of the character and background of the Framers, will amply illustrate this.

Historically, these developments have been accompanied by a radical change in the place of religion in society. In the Middle Ages, the faith of the Catholic Church was the faith of individual people, society, and all its institutions. The institutional church was dovetailed into the social order in a way that is quite foreign to modern understanding. None of this has survived. *Secularization* is the term applied to the process whereby western society took leave of its religious past and developed into what it is today. In modern western societies, we are free to believe or disbelieve as we wish. Heresy and schism are no longer public offences, because religious offences only have political consequences when there is a state-sanctioned religion and the security of the state depends on its preservation

Public attitudes toward religion, and those of governmental and quasi-governmental agencies, vary from the indifferent to the hostile. Often churches themselves are not agreed on the moral and spiritual advice they should give. In societies where religious commitment is weak, like those of Western Europe, there is little support and reinforcement for the views of people of faith. Instead, there is diversity. As the common culture of religious observance has slowly weakened, the idea has grown that the state should be neutral in the ideological conflicts in society and that it is not the business of the state to enforce moral standards beyond the maintenance of law and order.

A number of factors created this process of secularization, not least the loss of property, jurisdiction, powers of taxation, and political influence that the churches in Western Europe once enjoyed. As these privileges were abolished, secular influences began to outweigh spiritual ones. The rise of modern science accelerated the process by providing rational explanations for a wide range of phenomena, like disease, previously accounted for by religion. The area of mystery in ordinary human life was radically reduced. Instead, routine, experimentation, calculation, and the fruits of pragmatism characterized life for many people. The result was what Max Weber called the "disenchantment of the world."

So it appears that the development of modern society has been inimical to religion, both in institutional terms and in the matter of personal conviction. If this is the case, it will be increasingly difficult for churches to maintain their membership, let alone attract new members in significant numbers. It is not that society is for some reason hostile to religion; it is simply that the construction of meaning in the modern world takes place elsewhere than in the church and comes through intellectual means and materials that do not require the supernatural. Although the churches can be expected to survive for the purposes of those who require them, they cannot look forward to a future as a cultural force, because they represent an outdated worldview that cannot command majority, or even relatively widespread, support.

But is religion, in fact, in such a perilous condition? It is certainly true that religion is now a private pursuit rather than a public standard of meaning and morality. But there is reason to believe that in the United States, whatever may be the case in Europe, religious belief has been on a steadily rising trend since the seventeenth century. It can be debated whether this trend has leveled off or whether religion, in this case organized Christianity, has reached what we might call maximum market penetration. Whatever the case, church membership in the United States seems to be both high and constant in the long run.[1] In other parts of the world, where a weakening of religious commitment might have been expected as the influence of modernity has spread, we can see a similar pattern. There is no doubt that religion has been significantly influenced by the process of secularization, but not quite in the way some of the opponents of religious belief might have expected.

> *It is not that society is for some reason hostile to religion; it is simply that the construction of meaning in the modern world takes place elsewhere than in the church and comes through intellectual means and materials that do not require the supernatural.*

The Challenge of Postmodernism

What we have described as modernism certainly looks like common sense. The last few decades, however, have seen the rise of an influential new interpretation of human experience that raises serious questions about the worldview we have just described. We have to be cautious as soon as we use the word "postmodernism," because it is new, controversial, capable of arousing violent reactions, and extremely hard to define. It is perhaps best to follow one of its originators, who used the term, "the postmodern condition."[2] We are not dealing with a consistent school of thought here, but with a broad, contemporary, intellectual movement with its own particular doctrines and controversies, about which all generalizations must be qualified. Originating, possibly, in French literary theory, postmodernism is now an attitude to knowledge that influences all of the humanities, including theology. There are places where it is a new academic orthodoxy.

One only has to live for a time in a large American city to understand the nature of this challenge and the nature of postmodern society. There are now few common standards by which to evaluate questions of faith and morals, and there is no generally accepted narrative, or explanation, for our place in this society. Society no longer endorses and validates religious belief. It must be sustained solely by individual choice and commitment. Although the culture may still be informed by religious principles, society is not. One cannot look beyond oneself or one's own small group for any broader religious encouragement. Postmodern society values diversity over unity, relativism over absolutism, and individual choice over the prescriptions of the group. Those who do not accept this scheme become outsiders.

> *Postmodern society values diversity over unity, relativism over absolutism, and individual choice over the prescriptions of the group. Those who do not accept this scheme become outsiders.*

Basic to the postmodern outlook is the conviction that language is the means whereby human beings construct reality. Language is not just a tool; it is the medium through which we reach understanding. Although we may think that we have access to reality through our senses, we actually learn to deal with the world by means of speech. As children, we learn what words signify through the conventions of the society we live in and thus come to see the reality language constitutes for us. One of the sources of this idea is not in fact French, but comes from the philosopher Wittgenstein. It is the claim that language is self-referent, because we have no independent means of talking about it. Words do not, therefore have meanings, they have uses.

The various schools of postmodernism have extended this idea so that hermeneutics, the study of meaning, assumes a central place in intellectual life. What we might have thought of previously as a technique for understanding written texts now becomes our central tool for living, and the concept of text is extended to cover the whole range of signs, linguistic and non-linguistic, to which we are exposed in the course of an ordinary day—whether they be books, advertisements, TV talk shows, or anything else that has a message. Hermeneutics then becomes the critique of signs and their significance. This can be a fairly complicated matter, because language can be differentiated into different forms of discourse, ways of speaking appropriate to different social tasks and the interests of particular communities.

Postmodernism therefore concludes that if we have no access to reality beyond linguistic convention, we are unable to talk about truth as an abstract and independent reality. The use of the word may indicate what is generally acceptable to a given group, but it is philosophically impossible to postulate truth as an independent standard by which disputes between different viewpoints can be arbitrated. The word "truth" expresses the generally accepted standards of what Stanley Fish calls "interpretive communities," but in a postmodern world we have to learn how to live without reference to some ideal standard beyond that. This is directly contrary to the principles of modernism and represents a fundamental change of outlook.

Certain consequences flow from this understanding of the world. If we have access to reality through language, critical questions arise about how language is used and who decides what standards are to be observed. As soon as we ask these questions, we have moved beyond the quest for meaning as the interpretation of texts to a critique of how the social reality constituted by texts is established. History and contemporary politics both suggest that those who possess power establish dominant meanings. It is necessary to bring to the interpretation of texts different kinds of hermeneutic principle designed to bring out matters inadvertently or deliberately neglected. The hidden message must be brought out into the open.

One final consequence needs to be discussed, because it is important in itself and it indicates that not all postmodernists think alike. This is the distinction between what may be called skeptical and affirmative postmodernism[3] and what adherents of these two positions have to say about the individual. If we follow the logic of postmodernism to a certain point, we find ourselves in a position of fairly extreme skepticism. If language constitutes our understanding of the world and our place in it, and if reality is socially constructed, there is no real reason to assert an irreducible core of individuality in the human being. From the rejection of truth, we have moved to a rejection of the soul and become less a person than a succession of roles. We must be clear that not all postmodernists go that far. In making a critique of the position, we should not define it from the extremes.

People who encounter these ideas for the first time tend to be shocked. Most of us take it for granted that truth exists and that there are standards of reason and morality to which we can confidently appeal in preaching the gospel. The notion that there is no reason beyond preference for the adoption of any belief and moral code is contrary to everything we have been brought up to believe. Even more offensive is the idea that there is no irreducible core of human personality beyond the conditioning of our cultural environment. These concepts are now seriously debated in many circles, and they are not going away. So where does that leave the religious community? Are we faced with a new barbarism that is destructive of everything we value? Well, hardly.

Evangelicalism and Postmodernism

So what should the evangelical response to these challenges be? We might endeavor to maintain our appeal in terms of the modernist worldview and make a rejection of postmodernism as one of the intellectual characteristics of the evangelical faith. On the other hand, we might conclude that because we are in a postmodern world and because there are no principles of reason to which both sides in an argument may appeal, we should use postmodern strategies and present the faith in postmodern terms. It is crucially important that we have this debate, because the outcome will vitally affect our ability to carry out the great commission.[4] Perhaps we should remember that when Paul preached the gospel at Athens, he did not approach pagans through Jewish presuppositions but by means of their own literature and mythology.[5] There is a real possibility that we may now, for the first time in a thousand years, be in that position ourselves.

What Paul did was not to relinquish his belief in the truth, but to make his appeal on the basis of where people already were.

"Though I am free and belong to no man, I make myself a slave to everyone, to win as many as possible. To the Jews I became like a Jew, to win the Jews. To those under the law I became like one under the law (though I myself am not under the law), so as to win those under the law. To those not having the law I became like one not having the law (though I am not free from God's law but am under Christ's law), so as to win those not having the law. To the weak I became weak, to win the weak. I have become all things to all men so that by all possible means I might save some. I do all this for the sake of the gospel, that I may share in its blessings."[6] All the elements of an evangelical approach to postmodernism can be found in these words. To follow in Paul's footsteps will be difficult, controversial, and troublesome—as it was in his own times—but this is the task we have to undertake. There are two directions in which, without accepting its basic principles, evangelicals can benefit greatly from postmodernism.

> *Perhaps we should remember that when Paul preached the gospel at Athens, he did not approach pagans through Jewish presuppositions but by means of their own literature and mythology. There is a real possibility that we may now, for the first time in a thousand years, be in that position ourselves.*

An Assessment of Postmodernism

First, it needs to be said that hermeneutics, one of the major tools of postmodernism, was a theological preoccupation long before literary theorists caught up with it. However, in the last few decades, postmodern hermeneutical principles have immeasurably increased our ability to draw meaning out of all kinds of texts, including scripture itself. In essence, these principles are no more inimical to religion than science is. It is the uses they are put to that can create intellectual difficulty. Perhaps the most significant lesson evangelicals can draw from these principles is that there may be meanings in texts that the authors themselves did not grasp. Though some might find this surprising, we saw earlier that this is exactly the principle in use when the canon of the New Testament was settled. So the Church is already well aware of this postmodern principle.

> *Perhaps the most significant lesson evangelicals can draw from these principles is that there may be meanings in texts that the authors themselves did not grasp.*

Then there is the case of the objective observer. Postmodernism claims that it is impossible to obtain the data on which we would be justified in making generalizations about great matters of human destiny. It follows that if the truth as historically understood is unknowable, we cannot meet the condition of objectivity that alone guarantees accuracy. All judgments are therefore partial and necessarily biased. Taken to an extreme, this principle is a barrier to any kind of communication, but it has considerable utility in a modified form. It is perfectly consistent to say that there are sound reasons for believing that truth exists and is accessible to us, but that our understanding of truth is qualified rather than absolute and comes to us from a variety of sources. The fact that people do not perceive things directly or completely is not in itself a sufficient reason to deny their existence.[7] But it *is* a reason not to be dogmatic and serves as a standing reminder to Christian thinkers not to go beyond what the evidence warrants.

Nor is postmodernism without its own inconsistencies. The problem with the claim that there is no absolute truth is that people persist in behaving as if there were. There is also the very serious practical question of whether a society can function adequately without the cohesiveness that comes from a common outlook on matters of particular importance. Politics commonly rests on ethics, and ethics commonly rests on a worldview of some sort. The reason for pressing this point is that societies must have some generally accepted standard whereby disputes are settled. This presupposes a basic loyalty or sense of obligation to the state whereby it acquires legitimacy. The drawback of the postmodern vision of society is that it contains no hint that there may be serious conflict between the values of its numerous and diverse cultural communities. Without some court of appeal, disputes will be decided by who can shout loudest, not who is the most persuasive.

> *The problem with the claim that there is no absolute truth is that people persist in behaving as if there were.*

Lastly, postmodernism is open to objection at what its advocates probably see as its strongest point: that words are our only means of access to reality and we cannot transcend the linguistic universe in which we live. It seems to follow from this that the evidence of our senses is meaningless without some form of linguistic identification and that we need vocabulary to function successfully. However, if we *do* encounter the world directly, the monopoly of the word is broken. It may still be a very significant part of our experience, but that is not enough to sustain its exclusive claims. Indeed, one way of verifying postmodernism would be to establish that in the developing child the acquisition of vocabulary precedes concept formation. So far as we know, that is not the case. In fact, we manipulate the world quite successfully without words. We can do so because the phenomenal world does display order and regularity, and we can make accurate predictions about how it will behave. Engineers, navigators, surgeons, pharmacists, and architects do not deal in philosophical niceties. Consequently, one can take issue with the claim that there can be no general truths transcending culture because all claims to truth are culture specific and independent of any external reality.

The Possibility of a Postmodern Church

These matters suggest that the parochial debates we have been having with ourselves over evangelicalism and the Quaker tradition now have to be seen in a vastly different context if we, as evangelicals and Friends, are to preach the gospel plausibly and convincingly to our contemporaries. The main historical consequence of modernism was to make scientific knowledge and in particular mathematical knowledge the paradigm of what all knowledge should be. What was true was what could be measured. By definition, ethical and religious convictions that are concerned with value are not quantifiable and were, therefore, relegated to the margins of both society and intellectual life. This placed Christianity in a bind. If it accepted the premises of modernity, it had to relinquish its supernatural claims. If it rejected modernity, it rejected the terms and the logic in which it was obliged to make its case.

But if, as postmodernists claim, we are living through the collapse of grand schemes of meaning such as modernism provided, this is no longer the situation. There are equally compelling and authoritative ways of encountering the truth that do not depend on an appeal to some absolute external standard, and they are once more available. The number of people who are converted just by reading the Bible in the privacy of a previously atheistical bedroom is minimal. It does not happen like that. The Church is an interpretive community *par excellence,* and its witness to the truth is to be found in its common life. The Church makes transcendent claims to be sure, but it comes to these claims as the apostles came to them—by a process of gradual realization. A postmodern Church will not relinquish its claim to the truth, but it will be able to lead its members to it by means of experience and tradition rather than argument. It may well have more in common with the early Church than it has with the Church of more recent times.[8] In fact, most of us encounter Christ not in the study, but through symbolism and imagery, through the worship service and prayer, through personal devotion and above all in the company of his friends; that is, the Church.

> *A postmodern Church will not relinquish its claim to the truth, but it will be able to lead its members to it by means of experience and tradition rather than argument.*

In these circumstances, it appears that a wholehearted endorsement of either modernism or postmodernism would be a mistake. When the evangelical movement reached its accommodation with modernism, it chose too narrow a standpoint and neglected a wider range of arguments than it could have used to make its case. Faced with postmodernism, evangelicalism is in a quandary again. Although modernism was not generally hospitable to religion, common-sense realism found an acceptable niche within it. [9] Postmodernism, though, may better be able to make a place for religion. Though postmodernism denies the possibility of the transcendent truth on which Christianity is based, it values diversity, has no place for margins, and accepts the validity of interpretive communities—including the churches. With modernism, the problem is survival, but postmodernism provides a place to stand.

These, then, are the circumstances of the times. Evangelical Friends who are concerned for the future will have ultimately to come to terms with them, not specifically but as part of the wider evangelical movement to which they belong. Behind any assessment of American church life today lies this debate. It is very unlikely Friends will have anything original to say, but their future depends on its outcome. In many ways this book represents a postmodern sensibility. I have emphasized the importance of small groups able to meet specific needs, cellular rather than hierarchical structures, the experience of truth in community and in experience, and the importance of tradition and custom in forming identity. My argument does depart from postmodern thought in my presentation of Quakerism as a narrative—an interpretation of reality that gives shape and meaning to a community that is based upon it, and which is true.

The Persistence of Religion

Historically, Christianity has been one of the major forces defining the character of western culture, and nobody who is unacquainted with the main outlines of its history and doctrines can be considered educated. This is not just the influence of a specifically religious tradition but the historical events and philosophical controversies that have been shaped by the faith. One might claim with reasonable accuracy that until almost within living memory, the élites of western society, including the United States, operated on Christian assumptions with the Christian worldview. This is no longer the case, however. Although Christianity is significant as a cultural fact, it is no longer the dominant worldview. One might expect the consequence to be a weakening of religious faith and commitment and a declining church, but, apart from the nations of Western Europe, this does not appear to be the case. Christianity is alive and well in most parts of the world.

So what might explain the resilience of religious faith? Perhaps modernist thought concentrated too closely on the effects of technology, as postmodern thought might have predicted it would. It is quite possible that there are other influences at work that have the effect of enhancing rather than discouraging religious belief. If our worldview is influenced by our increasing command over the natural world, it also might be influenced by more mundane matters. Anybody who has ever lived in an inner-city housing project or encountered an automated phone answering system, for example, will know how malign technology can be. It is, quite literally, dehumanizing. Perhaps modernism underestimated the degree to which our worldviews are influenced by experiences like this.

Modernism underestimated what Peter Berger calls the "displacements and discontents of modernization." Although modernization doubtless has a secularizing effect in some ways, there are also other ways in which it might encourage the continuation of religious commitment. Freedom and rapid change are not unmixed blessings. Together with economic progress come uncertainty, insecurity, and the seemingly gratuitous devaluation of tried and trusted ways of doing things. In this light, religious belief looks like a rational response by self-aware beings to the undesirable aspects of changing circumstances. We have a plausible, but quite unforeseen, consequence of modernism: that the churches satisfy a demand for meaning and social cohesion that the wider society is no longer able to provide because of its exclusive preoccupation with novelty and change.[10] Morality is a good test of this.

> We have a plausible, but quite unforeseen, consequence of modernism: that the churches satisfy a demand for meaning and social cohesion that the wider society is no longer able to provide....

Moral behavior is fundamentally a public activity and societies customarily endorse some kinds of behavior and not others. Individuals who exercise moral choices need reinforcement for what they do, and traditional societies generally provide such an endorsement by means of the worldview on which they are based. Within these worldviews individuals can find an explanation of their personal status and destiny, and thereby a plausible reason for their choices. One can read such diverse works as *Beowulf*, the *Iliad,* or the *Bhagavad-Gita* and see clearly how moral visions are derived from a clear understanding of the nature of reality and the moral roles it defines for us. Societies offer "plausibility structures" in which to live.[11]

The Effects of Pluralism

What is new about our situation is that modern society provides a much wider range of roles than traditional societies and a much wider range of choice. It is correspondingly more difficult to provide one single worldview or one consistent moral code based on anything more than pragmatism or convenience. The breakdown of Christianity as a unifying worldview in western society means that the Church is no longer the sole provider of a plausibility structure. A range of possible plausibility structures has emerged. This inevitably alters the position of the churches. Instead of facing the challenge of secularism, the real challenge churches face is pluralism—the diversity of plausibility structures. This is a significant distinction, because it materially alters the position the church is in, the nature of its task, and the priorities under which it ought to be operating. A renewed Friends Church will need to understand this situation.

Christianity responded to the pluralizing trend of modernism during the twentieth century in several ways.[12] The first, and perhaps boldest, move was that of liberal theology that sought to preserve as much of the Christian message as possible by trading away elements it considered inessential. Indeed, some it its earlier advocates strongly supported the secular culture as leading logically to the principles of liberal religion. Some schools of thought in this tradition effectively capitulated to secular culture. The death of God school proved short-lived, but the movement associated with Don Cupitt[13] continues to assert Christian symbolism and spirituality, but to deny the reality of God in any objective sense. Many liberal Quakers take or took one or other of these positions.

Evangelical Friends, however, just like liberal Friends, followed the larger group with which they were identified. Evangelical Christianity responded to the challenge of modernity in two principal ways that continue to be debated. One was to sever any link with the culture at large and to offer one worldview, which was by definition separate and independent and inaccessible unless one was willing to commit oneself totally to it. This was the fundamentalist option. Out of this grew what Harold Ockenga called the "new evangelicalism," a conservative evangelical attempt to re-engage the secular culture and transform it rather than simply taking up an isolated defensive position. Berger calls these the "ghetto" and the "crusading" responses. It is significant that "crusade" was the word chosen for the Billy Graham campaigns, the paradigm of the new evangelicalism in the second half of the twentieth century.[14] The word conveys a sense of conviction, confidence, and purpose.

Setting the Course for the Friends Church

This sets the scene for a re-appraisal of the direction the Friends Church is taking. We are at a time when modernity seems to have the capacity to create the desire for religious answers to life's questions, but postmodernism is saying that we must expect a variety of answers. Society at large is no longer characterized by one contest between the plausibility structures of religion and secularism. Instead we find competition between many self-generated plausibility structures, of which the Christian Church is simply one—albeit a very large one possessed of a long and distinguished historical pedigree. Modernity produced a neutral observer of the world making rational choices, but in the condition of postmodernity, we think in terms of models instead. A plausibility structure, says Berger, is simply a conception of the possible. The Friends Church, therefore, must present itself as a conception of the possible and, in the marketplace of ideas, provide good reasons for why it should be adopted.

What I have just argued brings us to the point at which we can place the Friends Church within the wider evangelical community and claim that the problems and opportunities facing this community give form and shape to the particular problems facing Friends. As an evangelical church first, Friends will have to make decisions about evolution and science and how to cope with a postmodern world. These are not matters that call for minutes at yearly meetings, but they figure in the work done in our seminaries across a range of disciplines. They will need to be considered at length in the church at large. We therefore face a leadership question and need to seek out those who are able to offer us informed and committed advice as time passes and the intellectual perspective shifts.

> *The Friends Church, therefore, must present itself as a conception of the possible and, in the marketplace of ideas, provide good reasons for why it should be adopted.*

The Distinctives and the Future of Friends

Friends' future as a separate entity probably depends on how we negotiate these difficulties. If we are not to turn our backs on the world and return to fundamentalism, we shall have to find a way to live in it. If we are going to give up our distinctive characteristics, we had better do it quickly. This would involve a re-evaluation of our faith and practice and might have serious results. There would be yearly meetings who would wish to remain Quaker. Other yearly meetings might opt for complete independence, and the possibility always exists of amalgamation, affiliation, or absorption by another church. If we are going to think of a Quaker-less future for the Friends Church, we need to start considering these options forthwith.

> *If we are not to turn our backs on the world and return to fundamentalism, we shall have to find a way to live in it. If we are going to give up our distinctive characteristics, we had better do it quickly.*

The central argument of this book is a denial of these possibilities in favor of the following thesis: (a) The Friends Church is an integral part of evangelical Christianity, and an historic denomination in its own right; (b) evangelical Christianity is a loose association of churches and traditions with strong internal similarities and differences so that there is no specific and generic evangelicalism; (c) the evangelical churches in the United States occupy unique theological and sociological niches, and this is where they gain their strength and capacity to grow; (d) the declining numbers of the Friends Church can be explained by its failure to find and occupy a distinct niche; (e) a powerful and accessible niche is waiting to be found in the historic character and practices that make Friends distinctive.

To sustain this argument I shall rely on two main generalizations about American religion. Certainly they are debatable, but that is the nature of suggestions of this kind. I begin with the claim that the United States is a country in which there is a high level of religious commitment expressed in terms of church membership and attendance. Figures are released periodically from religious, academic, market research, and various other kinds of organizations. These need to be approached with caution, because such surveys are always a methodological minefield. The Gallup organization asks people whether they are members of a church or synagogue and whether they have attended in the past six months on other occasions than weddings, funerals, or special holidays. On this definition of religious adherence, the population divides into 56 per cent churched and 44 per cent who are not.[15]

Although this proportion seems to fluctuate year on year, Gallup claims that is fairly constant over the last two decades. Bearing in mind possible regional variations and the tendency for respondents to give the answers they think interviewers are looking for, it might be cautious to accept a lower figure as more likely. Nevertheless, compared with the United Kingdom, where total church attendance is usually put at about 5 percent of the population, the American figure is impressively high. That may not, however, be the most important feature of the situation. The claim has been advanced that church attendance and membership have shown an increasing trend since colonial times and has now reached a high and apparently stable plateau.[16]

The consequences of this are both challenging and reassuring. The churches will continue to preach the gospel and hope for conversions, but the prospects of major expansion seem limited. At the same time it should be noted that the high level of religious adherence that has occurred may be due to the wall of separation and the absence of a state church in the United States on the European pattern. Without the gravitational pull of a state church with an over-whelming formal membership and a historic connection with sources of finance and institutions of learning, it is far easier for new and independent churches to develop and flourish. This may be the rea-son for the high level of church membership and adherence noted, whatever the exact proportion of church members in the popula-tion at large.

The Growth of the Evangelical Churches

Something else should be noticed. In recent decades the evan-gelical churches have increased in numbers, and the liberal denomi-nations have suffered a considerable loss in membership. The South-ern Baptist Convention, for example, gained five million members between 1958 and 1993. Over the same period, the United Method-ist churches declined by just under two million members, and other mainline denominations exhibit the same pattern with similar ag-gregate losses. What seems to have happened is a distinct realign-ment of religious affiliation in a conservative direction. This is not what one would have expected if one opted for the liberal response to modernism as an accommodation with the secular world. Liberal church leaders chose a disastrous strategy, and the present state of their denominations is the result.[17] This appears to be where the new evangelicals have come from.

But is it the appeal of conservative religion that helps conserva-tive (that is, evangelical) churches to grow? This seems to be the most obvious conclusion, but conceivably it is it is not so much the content of doctrine that is attractive in a given church, but the pre-cision and conviction with which doctrine is presented. In other words, what people require is a church that can give definite answers to definite questions. One could say that this is precisely what distinguishes conservative from liberal religion and that the belief produces the certainty. However that may be, these developments are significant for the Friends Church. It has the declining membership of the liberal churches and an unclear self-identity. Its slow decline is therefore what one might expect. The way out of this impasse is to present a much clearer visage to the world and more demanding membership requirements.

> *What people require is a church that can give*
> *definite answers to definite questions.*

A number of theories have been advanced as to why the evangelical churches appear to be flourishing, when many people expected the challenges of modernity and postmodernity to weaken them considerably, if not fatally. It is possible to argue that churches flourish when they are in competition with one another. Alternatively, they may be attractive because they are willing to make demands on people, thereby indicating the seriousness with which they take themselves. Suggestions have also been made that churches represent refuges for people who desire more order and purpose than the secular world can provide, or that they are the base camps of those who feel threatened by the perceived decline in the status of Christianity and Christians.[18]

What concerns us here is the light these theories may be able to shed on the condition of the Friends Church. Friends are something of an anomaly because they fit the general theory by virtue of their evangelical belief, but they fail to fit the theory in that (with some exceptions) they do not enjoy a high level of vitality measured by such criteria as self-confidence and a pattern of continuous expansion. It would be a fair to say that as far as Friends are concerned, each theory seems to be operative to some degree in the case of some yearly and monthly meetings. It would be mistaken to conclude, however, that to get back in the game Friends need to become more discontented, more sheltered from society, more strictly disciplined, and devoted to aggressive growth.

Building Strength in Changing Times

What we see here are the long-term effects of the general movements of thought we have discussed as modernism and postmodernism, secularization and pluralism. They form the framework within which contemporary church life is lived. Questions of survival, growth, and change have to be approached theoretically as well as practically, because the short-term questions reflect the long-term trends. Thus, to assert simply that a renewed emphasis on evangelism, a stricter discipline, or some other strategy is what we need, without understanding the context in which that solution makes sense, is to deprive ourselves of understanding. Without such understanding we will not have the ability to change as circumstances change, to fine-tune our efforts, or to be in command of our own destiny.

Central to the situation we are now in is the postmodern critique of modernism, which is reflected accurately in so many features of contemporary society. It is significant because it generates the social conditions in which people live and in which the gospel has to be preached. It also seems to be objectionable to evangelical principle and inimical to evangelical concerns. If we simply content ourselves with the immediate judgment that society is abandoning its previous general moral and social principles in favor of individualism and relativism, we will find ourselves feeling threatened and pessimistic. We will be back in the defensive posture so many evangelicals adopted a hundred years ago. Such fears are understandable, but they are misplaced. They are no basis for the strategy of either the evangelical movement at large or the Friends Church in particular.

History will tell us, if we listen to it, that evangelicals see clearly, but sometimes too simply. Clarity has its advantages, as the great movements of social reform inspired by evangelicalism show, but the problem with simplicity is that it can misread the signs of the times. Faced with modernism, the evangelical movement was not entirely comfortable and adopted modernist principles reluctantly. Though times have changed, it retains a modernist mindset in its understanding of authority, biblical exegesis, and the nature of human knowledge. Now it is faced with postmodernism and a similar challenge to adaptation. On the surface, the principles of postmodernism seem unattractive and dangerous, leading to the kind of society against which scripture issues stern warnings.[19] We might find on analysis, however, that these principles are surprisingly hospitable and may even encourage evangelicalism. If there is a free-for-all, evangelicals need to remember they are part of the all.

The Advantages of an Open Society

In a postmodern society there is no generally accepted system of belief, though there may well be very powerful ideologies that enjoy widespread support. At the same time there is a variety of different and competing groups, some religious and some not, each with its own understanding and message, but none in a position to enforce its outlook on anybody else, either by official or unofficial means. The Friends Church takes its place as one of these competing groups. It has explicit and implicit allies and opponents in the competition for members and the propagation of ideas. Although the Friends Church may regret the passing of a Christian culture in the United States, this may, ironically, turn out to be its salvation.

> *Although the Friends Church may regret the passing of a Christian culture in the United States, this may, ironically, turn out to be its salvation.*

To understand how this might be the case, we must first get rid of nostalgia and anxiety. Deep in the collective memory of the Protestant evangelical churches is the time when American society was deeply imbued with religious values, and it made some sense to regard the United States as a Christian society. Perhaps school prayer is a symbol of those times, and that is why so many evangelicals loudly call for its restoration. But the society school prayer symbolized is no more, and it is unlikely to return. Naturally, this can be interpreted as a victory for secularism and a setback to the position of religion and the churches in society. In some minds it creates an anxiety that the diversity that is now symbolized by the absence of school prayer is a sign of increasing national apostasy and leads to reactionary social attitudes of all kinds.

This is not the only way of looking at the question, however. Someone without this particular cultural memory—a recent newcomer to the United States, for example—will see a different picture. To begin with, a European visitor will be highly impressed with the visibility and vitality of American church life of whatever denomination. Whether or not the Supreme Court has pursued an anti-religion policy in recent years, the churches do not appear to have been materially affected. To come from the United Kingdom to the United States is to enter a different religious world, one in which broad masses of the people take the Church seriously and in which there is an unmistakable air of Christian optimism.

One of the reasons for this is doubtless the habit of self-reliance. Evangelicals have always been both quarrelsome and cooperative. They have argued loudly with one another and also networked through a broad system of alliances. Denominationalism, which allows for common and diverse interests at the same time, seems very well adapted to the evangelical mind. This situation produces a number of very clear evangelical identities, which the different churches represent. Each, within its own theological and historical experience, can offer a distinctive identity that provides moral and spiritual guidance and a sense of where the believer fits into the greater scheme of Christian and human experience. The supporting community of the individual church provides the very plausibility structure for religious faith that the breakdown of a larger societal vision was thought to have made more difficult.

What I have characterized as a postmodern society may actually not be as recent a development as we might think. In Europe there was a struggle to establish the principle of religious freedom, and that struggle inevitably involved the principle of diversity defeating the principle of uniformity. Dissenting churches at different periods from the Reformation onward had to establish themselves against the greater economic and social power of state-backed churches. But in the United States this was never the situation. Protected by the Constitution from state interference, the American churches flourished and competed because they were often strongly opposed to one another on significant matters of doctrine.

It seems then, that religious commitment is not necessarily weakened when a society loses a single, commonly held worldview. In Europe, there was an attempt to maintain the religious monopoly of the state churches, but it failed. In the United States, on the other hand, religious freedom allowed all kinds of churches to flourish without restriction. The Americans are now a deeply religious people and the Europeans are not. Therefore, the validation of religion by society at large is not necessary to preserve faith. If society places the responsibility of choice above the responsibility of conformity to a publicly endorsed religious position, the imperative of choice may replace the imperative of conformity. An imperative it remains, however, and the need to obey it will ensure that diversity will encourage, not discourage, a wide range of religious commitment.

Our commitments, and those of the communities or ideas that we devote ourselves to, are generally the outcome of controversy and confrontation. History reveals an apparently unlimited capacity in human beings both to suffer and to persecute for the sake of their convictions. This is because, though they disagree as to its nature and requirements, people are united in the belief that the truth matters and devotion to it is one of the highest virtues. In postmodern society, contrary to the theory, religious groups will continue to provide meaning in their members' lives, and they will continue to define themselves against other groups that are dissimilar or antagonistic, particularly when there is something important at stake. In religion as in politics, it seems, the antagonism between small parties and churches seems more intense the closer they appear to outsiders to be.

This is because every positive implies a negative. The convictions we adopt necessarily involve the rejection of those we do not. One does not become a Catholic in order to live as a Protestant, nor does one join the Orthodox to avoid ritual. If one believes that one of the marks of the true church is healing and speaking in tongues, one will hardly be content with sacramental signs. This is not a matter of personal taste but what one believes to be true and what one wishes to reject as false. Inevitably, there will be conflicts between the theological positions taken by competing churches, and churches will define themselves by differentiating themselves from their competitors.

As Christian Smith puts it: "…evangelicalism maintains its religious strength in modern America precisely because of the pluralism and diversity it confronts. American evangelicalism, we contend, is strong not because it is shielded against, but because it is— or at least perceives itself to be—embattled with forces that seem to oppose or threaten it. Indeed, evangelicalism, we suggest, thrives on distinction, engagement, tension, conflict, and threat. Without these, evangelicalism would lose its identity and purpose and grow languid and aimless. Thus…the evangelical movement's vitality is not a product of its protected isolation from, but its vigorous engagement with pluralistic modernity."[20] This analysis supports the claim that, as one of the evangelical subcultures, Friends will flourish only if they are distinctive and if they vigorously promote their distinctiveness.

It is not enough for the Friends Church to rest on its laurels as part of the broader evangelical movement. To flourish, more is necessary. We have portrayed the Friends Church as a small but significant section of the evangelical movement. We have asked why it does not seem to be living up to its potential and what can be done about it. Confessional and theological arguments aside, we should be able to see that the conclusion Smith comes to *vis-à-vis* evangelicalism in general, will serve as a model for the situation of the Friends Church in particular. To survive is to differentiate and have confidence in oneself. The siren voices are wrong. We need Friends distinctives now as we have never needed them before.

Epilogue

This chapter began with the suggestion that we are going through times of far-reaching intellectual and social change, which are bound to have significant repercussions on the content and practice of religion. Contemplating the world around us, it is possible to come to the conclusion that as the technology and other changes of the twentieth century work themselves out, many of the old religious and intellectual landmarks with which we are familiar may be swept away. The idea of the Flood is almost irresistible. There is a new world coming, but to get there we have to survive the waters.

I have tried to suggest that with a suitable ark, there is no reason why the Friends Church should not survive substantially intact. Unlike the *Titanic*, the ark Friends need for modern times is an intellectual and spiritual one and is equipped with three protective hulls. The first is the enduring power of religion despite the processes of modernization and secularization. The second is the development of a proactive evangelicalism, itself partly the product of modernity. Third, is the covenantal theology of Quakerism, which provides the distinctiveness that is the precondition for survival in a pluralistic age.

The image of survival throughout a disastrous flood has its limits, though. We live in challenging times, but whether we choose to consider them as hostile and potentially destructive is another matter. These changing times are hospitable and not inimical to faith and the imagery of arks and deluges is inappropriate. To be sure, nobody is going to look out for the well being of the Church except the Church herself, but in modern society there is every possibility of receiving a fair hearing if we wish to avail of ourselves of it. There is no earthly reason for Christians to be pessimistic. There is a fair wind behind us and only our own hesitations will prevent us taking advantage of it.

As we enter a new millennium, the most significant feature of the religious scene in the United States and most other countries in the world is that the plausibility of the religious view of life remains unimpaired to any significant degree. Certainly there are places where religious confession and observance have declined, sometimes steeply. But these are few. In Asia, Africa, and North and South America, religion in general and Christianity in particular are in excellent health. The possibility (and for some, the hope) that the modernity would result in the end of faith has not been realized. The consequence is that religious ideas—Hindu, Muslim, or Christian—preserve their intellectual, spiritual, and moral vitality against all expectations.

It appears, though, that there are certain preconditions for the continuance of this state of affairs. The United States, and any other society that tries to live by democratic principles, will almost inevitably have to come to terms with the lack of one overriding set of cultural assumptions. In these societies, almost by definition, the boundaries between social groups will be porous. Unless any particular group wishes to lose its identity, it will have to be clear about its reason for existence and what it stands for. The continuing strength of the evangelical churches is probably due to their precise doctrine, recognizable boundaries, clarity of purpose, engagement with society, and their willingness to constantly define and redefine where they stand. There is not the slightest reason why the evangelical movement should slacken in its endeavors, or why the Friends Church should surrender to pessimism and identity confusion at a time when the signs point to the opportunity for major renewal.

This is not so much a reflection on the truth of evangelical claims as a conclusion about the position of any historically grounded and culturally significant body of opinion in the contemporary world. What is significant about the evangelical faith is that it is essentially adventurous and expansionary, and it lives by proclamation and controversy. One of the main points I have tried to show is that this necessitates an engagement with society, not a withdrawal from it. When evangelical theology and practice have coincided in this respect, the movement has been at its best. I have expressed reservations about Fundamentalism for exactly this reason. I prefer to see a longer and wider evangelical tradition, which is more complex and internally diverse and which is alive to the whole range of cultural challenges in the modern world.

As the Friends Church contemplates the future, then, what will it see as the way forward? Its most important task is a spiritual rather than a theological one: to realize that it is faced with an opportunity, possibly as challenging as the holiness revival. There is a real possibility of growth because the evangelical movement is not struggling against adversity, but enjoying a stiff following wind. If the analysis I have given is anywhere near correct, it is the clear self-image evangelicals possess that is responsible for the advantageous position they enjoy against other churches who are more ready to go along with the spirit of the times. Friends are well positioned to take advantage of this if they can think through the nature of their opportunity.

We serve Christ best by giving him of our best. This is true of both personal discipleship and the devotion of the Church. In the parable of the talents,[21] each of the servants was given a portion of the master's money to deal with and multiply during his absence. We usually concentrate on the fate of the unprofitable servant who buried his talent in the ground, and we forget that the Lord did not appoint a committee to manage his affairs. Instead, he gave responsibility to a number of very different people, each of whom carried out his duties in a particular and acceptable way. So it is with the churches, including the Friends Church. Our individual traditions are our talents, and when we use them to the full we are likely to hear the Lord say, "Well done, thou good and faithful servant..." But if we take our Quaker heritage and bury it in the sand, a very different destiny awaits us. This is the choice that lies before us. Renewing the Quaker vision is not a strategy for survival; it is to safeguard that portion of his wealth entrusted to us by the Lord himself. We had better make sure we know what we are supposed to do with it.

NOTES

[1] Roger Finke and Rodney Stark, *The Churching of America 1776-1990* (Piscataway, NJ: Rutgers University Press, 1992).

[2] Jean-François Lyotard, *The Postmodern Condition: A Report on Knowledge,* tr. Bennington and Massumi (Minneapolis: University of Minnesota Press, 1984).

[3] See Pauline Marie Rosenau, *Postmodernism and the Social Sciences* (Princeton, N.J.: Princeton University Press, 1992).

[4] See Millard J. Erickson, *Postmodernizing the Faith* (Ada, Mich.: Baker Books, 1998).

[5] Acts 22:17-32.

[6] 1 Cor. 9:19-23.

[7] Eccles. 8:17.

[8] See Robert E. Webber, *Ancient-Future Faith* (Ada, Mich.: Baker Books, 1999), pp.25-38.

[9] See Mark A. Noll, *The Scandal of the Evangelical Mind* (Grand Rapids, Mich.: William B. Eerdmans Publishers, 1994), pp. 83-107.

[10] Peter L. Berger, *A Far Glory – the Quest for Faith in an Age of Credulity* (New York: Free Press, 1992), p.33.

[11] See Peter L. Berger, *The Sacred Canopy* (New York: Doubleday & Co., 1967); Free Press , (1992).

[12] Berger, *A Far Glory,* p.41-5.

[13] Dean of Emanuel College, Cambridge, England, *alma mater* of John Harvard.

[14] Berger, p.43.

[15] George H. Gallup, Jr., and D. Michael Lindsay, *Surveying the Religious Landscape* (Harrisburg, Pa: Morehouse, (1999).

[16] Finke and Stark, Chapter 1.

[17] For a full discussion see Dean M. Kelley, *Why Conservative Churches Are Growing* (Macon, Ga.: Mercer University Press,1986).

[18] See the discussion in Christian Smith, *American Evangelicalism— Embattled and Thriving* (Chicago: University of Chicago Press, 1998), Ch. 3.

[19] See Judg. 21:25.

[20] Smith, p. 89.

[21] Matt. 25:14-30.

Glossary

These notes are intended as a traveling companion. They include explanations of theological terms, short accounts of personalities, institutions and historical events mentioned in the text.

Altar call—An invitation issued at the end of a sermon inviting people to come to the front of the Church. It may be to confess Christ and be converted, to rededicate oneself after a relapse, or to accept the offer of spiritual comfort and counseling.

Anabaptism—Sixteenth-century movement for the reform of the Church, particularly in Switzerland, Germany, and the Netherlands. The Anabaptists believed that the Church should be a visible fellowship of committed believers separated from the world and characterized by love. Their central principles included adult baptism, the authority of the scriptures, pacifism, and the separation of church and state. They were severely persecuted. Modern Hutterites, Mennonites, and Brethren come from this tradition.

Apocalyptic—Strictly speaking, secrets specially revealed to an author, which is why Revelation is sometimes called *The Apocalypse*. Also understood to mean having to do with the end of the world. The word carries overtones of a cosmic drama.

Apotheosis—Raising something or somebody to the status of a God, hence, the ultimate development of anything.

Canon—The list of books regarded as scripture and included in the Bible. There are differences between the churches as to what is included. The Catholic and Orthodox churches accept the books of the Apocrypha as binding. Protestants generally do not, though in some circumstances may accept them as having persuasive force.

Conservative Friends—Not all evangelical Friends welcomed the innovations of the nineteenth century. Before 1861, when all Quaker worship was carried on in silence, meetings that followed the teaching of John Wilbur, a theological opponent of Joseph John Gurney, separated and formed their own yearly meetings, notably in New England and Ohio. Ohio Yearly Meeting survives, combining silent worship and devotion to the scriptures. After the Civil War there were other separations due to a widespread suspicion of where the revivals were leading. Iowa and North Carolina conservative yearly meetings are the result of these separations, but are much less traditional than Ohio.

Deism—Rationalistic form of Christianity that maintains a belief in God as first cause but denies the possibility of miracles, providence, or answers to prayer—preferring to find evidence of God's nature in the rational character of the creation.

Discipline—Also called 'Faith and Practice.' A book that operates as the constitution of a yearly meeting, setting out its principles, structure, and procedures. Disciplines commonly contain a statement of faith and criteria for membership.

Enlightenment—An eighteenth-century intellectual movement that rejected traditional forms of political and religious authority and believed in the power of reason to ameliorate the human condition.

Episcopacy—Government of the church by bishops, normally deriving their authority by their place in direct line of succession to the apostles. Some churches do not appoint bishops and instead govern themselves by synods—general assemblies that include both clerical and lay people.

Epistle—A formal letter written in annual session by a yearly meeting. Historically, these were addressed to both members and other yearly meetings and often contained doctrinal and moral guidance, exhortation, and encouragement. Between the separations in the nineteenth century and the modern period of reconciliation, circulation was limited to those yearly meetings of similar theological outlook. This was called being "in correspondence" with another yearly meeting.

Eschatology—Branch of theology dealing with the last things—death, resurrection, judgment, heaven, and hell.

Evangelical Friends International (EFI)—An association of Friends churches that developed throughout the twentieth century as several yearly meetings left Friends United Meeting and eventually set up their own organization, augmented by many yearly meetings previously their mission fields in Latin America, Africa, and Asia.

Fast meeting—Nineteenth-century term for a silent meeting in which the ministry begins before an adequate time has passed to enable Friends to center and the meeting to gather.

Friends United Meeting (FUM)—Successor body to the Five Years Meeting. An association of yearly meetings from North America, the Caribbean, and Africa, having in addition, representatives from the yearly meetings in Canada and the eastern United States where previously separated yearly meetings reunited during the second half of the twentieth century but wished to retain some of their previous affiliations.

Fundamentalism—Movement within conservative evangelicalism beginning in the early years of the twentieth century, usually associated with the five points—the inerrancy of scripture, the deity of Christ, the substitutionary atonement, the bodily resurrection, and the second coming. These doctrines were believed to be the fundamentals of Christianity that were under attack from the forces of secularism within the churches. Fundamentalism preached a strict personal morality and disengagement from a fallen world. Today premillennial dispensationalism is usually regarded as one of the main features of fundamentalism. The word is generally, and quite falsely, used as a synonym for conservative evangelicalism.

Gathered Churches—Reformation tradition believing that churches are gathered by Christ and are responsible to him rather than to ecclesiastical authorities. The gathered church principle is essentially congregational but is not confined to specifically Congregational churches.

Great Awakening—The evangelical revival of the early eighteenth century associated with such figures as Jonathan Edwards, John Wesley, George Whitefield, and others. The term is extended. The revivals of the early nineteenth century become the Second Great Awakening, and the holiness revival later in the century is sometimes called the Third Great Awakening. Visionaries look for a Fourth.

Gnosticism—First-century mystical and philosophical movement that taught that the worlds of matter and spirit are in irreconcilable conflict as a consequence of which the soul is entombed in the body. Against a complex mythological background including the perversion of the creation and the captivity of the spirit, Christ is presented as a cosmic redeemer bringing the secret spiritual lore by which release may be obtained.

Hedge—Name given to the practices by which the Society of Friends preserved its distinctiveness. These included the rule against marrying out, plain dress and speech, the institution of disownment, and a guarded education in Friends schools.

Hermeneutics—The study of interpretation. To ask the meaning of a book or a passage is not just to comprehend what is written. Attention needs to be given to the presuppositions one brings to the act of reading and the conscious and unconscious assumptions of the writer. The meaning of the text arises out of the interaction of these things, and this is the subject matter of hermeneutics, originally a technique for studying scripture, but now of much wider application.

Historical-Critical Method—General name for an approach to the study of the Bible that emphasizes sources, context, and historical origins in order to establish meaning rather than the requirements of doctrine or the experience of the Church.

Imputed righteousness—In Christian theology one can be saved without being perfect. This raises the problem of how someone who is not good can be acceptable to God. A simple solution to the problem is to say that the goodness of Christ is "imputed" to us as a consequence of the atonement and our acceptance of it. Short of the state of perfection, Christ makes up the deficit between what we are and what we ought to be.

Justification—In theology, God's action in forgiving us, remitting the consequences of our sins and regarding us as righteous, even though we might not be.

Liberation theology—Movement of thought originating in the Catholic Church in Latin America during the 1960s, but spreading rapidly elsewhere. It questioned the morality of a gospel that claims to bring good news to the poor but does nothing to relieve them of their burdens, finding in scripture the principles of radical political action to bring justice to those who are without it.

Metaphysics—Philosophical term for the study of ultimate reality, arising out of various aspects of human experience, like the existence of illusion, the relation between the general and the particular, and justifications for the conviction that there are realities which are not accessible to the senses.

Millennium—The thousand-year period during which, according to Revelation 20:4-6, Christ will reign on earth with the saints. Premillennialism is the belief that the second coming will precede the rule of the saints; postmillennialism, that it will follow; amillennialism, the doctrine that we are already living in the millennium.

Minute—Record of a decision made in a Friends meeting to transact church business. Because there is no voting, the minute reflects the sense of the meeting as discerned and expressed by the clerk and confirmed by the agreement of the meeting as something those present can unite in.

Modernism—A word used in two senses, (a) the intellectual system which replaced medieval habits of thought, notably scientific enquiry based on observation and mathematical regularity, and (b) nineteenth and twentieth-century movement which attempted to bring traditional doctrines and concepts into harmony with contemporary thought.

Montanism—Prophetic movement in the second-century church that did not so much propound new doctrines as provide an unwelcome challenge to accepted institutions and relatively settled ways.

Monthly Meeting—The basic unit of the Society of Friends. A local worshipping community that meets monthly for the transaction of business, and is affiliated to a yearly meeting. In some places there are quarterly meetings, but they are often moribund.

New paradigm churches—Churches that make their appeal by appearing as untraditional as possible. The décor and layout of these churches often resemble an auditorium or a concert hall more than a traditional church building, and there is a studied informality about their music and vocabulary. They range from the mega-church to the house church.

Nicene Creed—Though called by this name, the most familiar of the Christian creeds was given its present form some time later than the Council of Nicea in 325 AD. It reflects and adjudicates on the theological controversies of the day and has been accepted as authoritative for most of Christian history. The Western version states that the Holy Spirit "proceeds from the Father and the Son." The Orthodox Church does not recognize the "filioque" clause, the Latin word for "and the Son."

Old and New School—Terms indicating divisions of opinion over doctrinal and organizational matters in the U.S. Presbyterian and Congregational churches during the early nineteenth century.

Ordinances—Protestant term for the ceremonies of baptism and the Lord's Supper. The emphasis here is that they are to be observed because they are the commands of Christ not because they take their place in a wider system for the transmission of grace by outward observance.

Orthodox—The word can be used in two senses: (a) the body of evangelical Friends prior to the revivals, (b) the Eastern Orthodox Church.

Parousia—Greek word for the second coming of Christ

Pelagianism—The doctrine that human beings are able of their own volition to take the first steps towards salvation without the assistance of divine grace. First preached by the British monk Pelagius in the fourth century.

Pentecostalism—Arising out of the holiness movement at the beginning of the twentieth century, Pentecostalism is the fastest growing and possibly the largest form of Protestant Christianity in the modern world. Its distinctive feature is the claim that truly converted Christians will receive the spirit in the same way as those who entered the Church at Pentecost and that, therefore, speaking in tongues is a sign of genuine conversion, and healing one of the signs of the true Church.

Pietism—Seventeenth-century movement for the reform of the Lutheran church from within. It emphasized personal conversion, discipleship, prayer, Bible study, and good works in small groups able to act as a leaven to the larger body. Through the Moravian movement, pietism entered England and was one of the major influences in the development of Methodism.

Postmodernism—Contemporary movement of thought that believes that language is our only means of access to the world and that all our ideas about reality are merely constructions of language and doubts the possibility of absolute truth or any general understanding of the significance of human life.

Premillennial dispensationalism—Interpretation of the Bible in terms of a succession of "dispensations" whereby God establishes relationships with successive groups of people and in which the promises made in one dispensation are carried over for fulfillment later. Hence, prophecy is an important feature of dispensationalism, which has a developed theory of the millennium and last judgment and looks for signs of the end in current affairs now.

Predestination—There are several forms of this doctrine, and it is hard to define. Broadly it implies that God has destined some to salvation, and because not all will be saved, others are destined to be lost. This is not seen as unjust because all deserve to be lost, and it is a gracious act of God to save any.

Prevenient grace—The grace by which God moves the sinner to repentance.

Process theology—Modern school of thought that seeks to use the philosophical system of Alfred North Whitehead (1861-1947) in theology, seeing events as the basic elements of the cosmos. The process conception of God allows a more intimate relationship between God and the creation than traditional theologies and conceives of God as developing in some way as the cosmos develops.

Puritanism—Sixteenth and seventeenth-century movement to "purify" the English church. Doctrinally it sought to move the church in a Reformed direction. Organizationally it included both presbyterian and congregational beliefs about church government. Puritanism was one of the driving forces in the outbreak of the English Civil War (1642-46) and in the settlements in New England. Puritan worship, church buildings, and lifestyles were plain. Many Quaker practices originated in Puritanism.

Rapture, The—The first event of the end-times, in which the saints will be gathered up to meet Christ in the clouds. (Matt.24:30, 1Thess.4:15-17)

Richmond Declaration of Faith—Statement of faith issued by a conference of evangelical yearly meetings at Richmond, Indiana in 1887. The Declaration has had a chequered career, though appearing in most of the Disciplines of the evangelical yearly meetings in the United States.

Reformed Tradition—The thought of the Reformation churches that followed Calvin rather than Luther. While it is often called "Calvinism" this term is probably too restrictive, in view of the diversity of the tradition, and the breadth of Calvin's thought. It is notable for the doctrine of predestination in various forms and its exalted conception of the majesty and power of God.

Regeneration—Another name for the rebirth of the soul consequent upon conversion.

Routinization of charisma—Term from the sociology of religion to mark the process whereby the founders of new religious movements impress their followers by the power of their personalities, but when they die, the groups they leave behind attempt to embody these informal personal qualities in formal institutional expectations and leadership roles.

Secularization—In the sociology of religion, the process whereby, over some centuries, the institutions of society have gradually ceased to enshrine religious values.

Social Gospel—Nineteenth and early twentieth-century movement of thought that sought to find solutions to the problems of industrial change in Christian religious principles. It represents a dissatisfaction with those critiques of society that fail to give proper weight to the social causes of moral failure and expands the concept of moral failure to the conduct of business, government, and other institutions that have the power to promote beneficial social change but decline to do so,

Synod of Dort (Dordrecht)—Conference of the Dutch Reformed Church 1618 to 1619 which repudiated the moderate Calvinistic views of James Arminius (d.1609) and the Remonstrant party.

Testimonies—General name for the ethical and spiritual aspects of the Quaker faith, like simplicity, equality, truth-telling, and pacifism. The moral principles in accordance with which Friends try to live.

The Thirty-nine Articles—The historical statement of faith of the Anglican communion showing both Lutheran and Calvinistic influences and illustrating the desire of Queen Elizabeth I that her Church should follow a middle way in the controversies of the Reformation.

Tribulation, The—A period of increasing distress that will indicate the imminence of Christ's return.

Unitarianism—Rejection of the doctrine of the Trinity usually because of misgivings over certain features of the doctrine of the incarnation. Unitarianism usually leads to skepticism over the divinity of Christ.

Westminster Confession of Faith—Classical statement of the Reformed faith commissioned by the English Parliament in 1643, having profound influence in all parts of the world influenced by Puritanism, notably the British Isles and North America.

Yearly Meeting—The Friends Church and the wider Society of Friends is organized into autonomous bodies called yearly meetings, which are made up of affiliated monthly meetings. Yearly meetings usually cover a fairly definite area, but there can be yearly meetings of more than one persuasion in a particular place. In the state of Ohio there are meetings belonging to Wilmington, Lake Erie, Indiana, Ohio Valley, and Ohio yearly meetings, and Evangelical Friends Church Eastern Region. They reflect almost every kind of Quakerism in North America. The yearly meeting meets annually, as its name implies, and is responsible for the Discipline and seeing that its provisions are carried out.

Bibliography

The following is a list of many of the works consulted during the writing of this book.

Abraham, William J. *The Divine Inspiration of Holy Scripture*. New York: Oxford University Press, 1981.

Ausmus, Harry J. *The Polite Escape—On the Myth of Secularization*. Athens: Ohio University Press, (1982)

Bales, Dorlan. "Barclay's Apology in Context." Ph.D. diss., University of Chicago, 1980.

Balmer, Randall. *Blessed Assurance, A History of Evangelicalism in America*. Boston: Beacon Press, (1999)

Barbour, Hugh, and Arthur Roberts. *Early Quaker Writings, 1650-1700*. Grand Rapids, Mich.: Eerdmans, 1973.

Barclay, Robert. *Barclay's Apology in Modern English*. Edited by Dean Freiday. Newberg, Ore.: Barclay Press, 1967.

Barker, Lawrence E. "Development of the Pastoral Pattern in Indiana Yearly Meeting of the Religious Society of Friends." Earlham School of Religion M.A. Thesis, 1963.

Bass, Clarence B. *Backgrounds to Dispensationalism*. Ada, Mich.: Baker Book House, 1960.

Beach, W., and H.R. Niebuhr, eds. *Christian Ethics*. N.p.: Ronald Press, 1955.

Berger, Peter L. *A Far Glory—The Quest for Faith in an Age of Credulity*. New York: Free Press, 1992.

_____. *The Sacred Canopy*. New York: Doubleday, 1967; New York: Free Press, 1992.

Berkhof, Louis. *Systematic Theology*. N.p.: Banner of Truth Trust, 1939.

Bloesch, D.G. *Essentials of Evangelical Theology*. San Francisco: HarperCollins, 1978.

Bradley, Ian. *The Call to Seriousness*. New York: Macmillan, 1976.

Brown, Raymond E. *The Churches the Apostles Left Behind*. Mahwah, N.J.: Paulist Press, 1984.

Bruce, F.F. (Frederick Fyvie). *The Canon of Scripture*. Downers Grove, Ill.: Inter-Varsity Press, 1988.

Caffrey, Augustine. *The Affirmation Mysticism of Rufus Matthew Jones*. Ann Arbor, Mich.: University of Michigan Microfilms Inc., 1967.

Caldwell, Patricia. *The Puritan Conversion Narrative*. New York: Cambridge University Press, 1983.

Carpenter, Joel A. *Revive Us Again*. New York: Oxford University Press, 1997.

Carson, D.A., and J.D.Woodbridge, eds. *Hermeneutics, Authority and Canon*. Grand Rapids, Mich.: Zondervan, 1986.

Carwardine, Richard J. *Evangelicals and Politics in Antebellum America*. New Haven, Conn.: Yale University Press, 1993.

Cassirer, Ernst. *The Philosophy of the Enlightenment*. Princeton, N.J.: Princeton University Press, 1951.

Childs Brevard S. *Biblical Theology in Crisis*. Philadelphia: Westminster Press, 1970.

Chilton, Bruce and J.I.H. McDonald. *Jesus and the Ethics of the Kingdom*. Eerdmans ,1997.

Clark, D., and J. H. Smith. *David B. Updegraff and his Work*. N.p.: Privately published, 1895.

Cohen, Charles Lloyd. *God's Caress—The Psychology of Puritan Religious Experience*. New York: Oxford University Press, 1986.

Cooper, Wilmer A. "Rufus M. Jones and the Contemporary Quaker View of Man." Ph.D. diss., Vanderbilt University, 1956.

_____. *A Living Faith*. Richmond, Ind.: Friends United Press, 1990.

Cullman, Oscar. *Christ and Time*. Philadelphia: Westminster Press, 1950.

Dandelion, Ben Pink, Doug Gwyn, and Timothy Peat. *Heaven on Earth: Quakers and the Second Coming*. Kelso, Scotland: Curlew Productions; Birmingham, England: Woodbrooke College, 1998.

Dayton, Donald W. *Discovering and Evangelical Heritage*, New York: Harper and Row, 1976.

_____. *Theological Roots of Pentecostalism*. Grand Rapids, Mich.: Zondervan, Asbury Press, 1987.

Dieter, Melvin E. *The Holiness Revival of the Nineteenth Century*. Lanham, M.D.: Scarecrow Press, 1980.

Dodd, C. H. *The Parables of the Kingdom*. London: Nisbet & co. ltd., 1935.

Dulles, Avery. *Models of Revelation*. New York: Doubleday & Co., 1983.

Eeg-Olofsson, E. *The Conception of the Inner Light in Robert Barclay's Theology*. (Lund, Sweden: CWK Gleerup, 1954).

Erickson, Millard J. *Christian Theology*. 3 vols. Ada, Mich.: Baker Book House, 1985.

_____. *Postmodernizing the Faith*. Ada, Mich.: Baker Book House, 1998.

Ferguson, Duncan S. *Biblical Hermeneutics, An Introduction*. London: SCM Press, 1985.

Finke Roger, and Rodney Stark. *The Churching of America 1776-1990*. Piscataway, N.J.: Rutgers University Press, 1992.

Finney, Charles. *Lectures on Systematic Theology*. London: William Tegg, 1851.

_____. *Lectures on Revival*, (1845). Minneapolis, Minn.: Bethany House, undated.

Fisher, B. Eugene. "A Study of Toleration among Midwest Quakers 1850-1900." Master's thesis, Earlham School of Religion, 1972.

Fodor, James. *Christian Hermeneutics*. Oxford: Clarendon Press, 1995.

Freiday, Dean, ed. *The Day of the Lord: Eschatology in Quaker Perspective*. Newberg, Ore.: Barclay Press, 1981.

Fuller, Daniel P. *Gospel and Law—Contrast or Continuum?* Grand Rapids, Mich.: Eerdmans, 1980.

Gallup, George H. Jr., and D. Michael Lindsay. *Surveying the Religious Landscape*. Harrisburg, Pa.: Morehouse, 1999.

Garman, Mary, Judith Applegate, Margaret Benefiel, and Dortha Meredith, eds. *Hidden in Plain Sight*. Wallingford, Pa.: Pendle Hill Publications, 1996.

Gerstner, John H. *A Primer on Dispensationalism*, Phillipsburg, N.J.: Presbyterian Reformed Publishing Co., 1982.

Good, Donald Graham. "Elisha Bates, American Quaker Evangelical in the Early Nineteenth Century." Ph.D. diss., University of Iowa, 1967. Ann Arbor, Mich.: University Microfilms International, 1980.

Green, Michael. *I Believe in the Holy Spirit*. Grand Rapids, Mich.: Eerdmans, 1980.

Grider, Kenneth J. *Entire Sanctification: The Distinctive Doctrine of Wesleyanism*. Kansas City, Mo.: Beacon Hill Press, 1985.

_____. *A Wesleyan-Holiness Theology*. Kansas City, Mo.: Beacon Hill Press, 1994.

Gurney, Joseph John. *Observations on the Religious Peculiarities of the Society of Friends*. London: N. pub., 1827.

Gwyn, Douglas. *The Covenant Crucified*. Wallingford, Pa.: Pendle Hill Publications, 1995.

Hamm, Thomas. *The Transformation of American Quakerism*. Bloomington: Indiana University Press, (1988)

Hammond, John L. *The Politics of Benevolence*. Norwood, N.J.: Ablex Publishing Corp., 1979.

Hart, D.G. *Defending the Faith—J. Gresham Machen and the Crisis of Conservative Protestantism in Modern America*. Baltimore, Md.: Johns Hopkins University Press, 1994.

Harvey, David. *The Condition of Post-Modernism.* Malden, Pa.: Blackwell, 1989.

Hekman, Susan J. *Hermeneutics and the Sociology of Knowledge.* Notre Dame, Ind.: University of Notre Dame Press, 1986.

Heppe, Heinrich. *Reformed Dogmatics.* Ada, Mich.: Baker Book House, 1978.

Hobbs, Barnabas C. *Earlham Lectures.* Richmond, Ind.: Nicholson & Bro., 1885.

Hodge, Charles. *Systematic Theology.* New York: Scribner's & Sons, 1871.

Hunter, James Davison. *Evangelicalism—The Coming Generation.* Chicago: Chicago University Press, 1987.

_____. *The Culture Wars.* New York: Doubleday & Co., 1993.

Hylson-Smith, Kenneth. *Evangelicals in the Church of England 1734-1987.* Edinburgh: T&T Clark, 1989.

Johnson, Charles A. *The Frontier Camp Meeting.* Dallas: Southern Methodist University Press, 1955.

Jones, Charles E. *Perfectionist Persuasion: The Holiness Movement and American Methodism 1867-1936.* Lanham, Md.: Scarecrow Press, 1974.

Kelley, Dean M. *Why Conservative Churches Are Growing.* Macon, Ga.: Mercer University Press, 1986.

Kelsey, David H. *The Uses of Bible in Recent Theology.* Minneapolis, Minn.: Fortress Press, 1975.

King, Rachel Hadley. *George Fox and the Light Within.* Philadelphia: Friends Book Store, 1940.

Klemm, David E. *The Hermeneutical Theory of Paul Ricoeur.* London: Associated University Presses, 1983.

Knight Henry H., III. *A Future for Truth.* Nashville: Abingdon Press, 1997.

Ladd, G.E. *Crucial Questions about the Kingdom of God.* Grand Rapids, Mich.: Eerdmans, 1952.

_____. *The Presence of the Future.* Grand Rapids, Mich.: Eerdmans, 1974.

_____. *Jesus and the Kingdom.* London: SPCK, 1966.

Laird, Rebecca. *Ordained Women in the Church of the Nazarene.* Kansas City, Mo.: Nazarene Publishing House, 1993.

LaRondelle, H.K. *Perfection and Perfectionism.* Berrien Springs, Mich.: Andrews University Press, 1971.

Littell, Franklin H. *The Origins of Sectarian Protestantism.* New York: Macmillan, 1964.

McDonald, L.M. *The Formation of the Christian Biblical Canon.* Nashville: Abingdon Press, 1988.

McKnight, Edgar V. *Meaning in Texts.* Minneapolis, Minn.: Fortress Press, 1978.

Meier, Gerhard. *The End of the Historical-Critical Method.* Concordia, 1974.

Metzger, B. *The Canon of the New Testament.* Oxford: Clarendon Press, 1987.

Nichols, J., and W.R. Bagnall, trans. *The Writings of James Arminius.* Ada, Mich.: Baker Book House, 1977.

Opie, John, ed. *Jonathan Edwards and the Enlightenment.* Lexington, Mass.: D.C. Heath, 1969.

Outler A.C. *John Wesley.* New York: Oxford University Press, 1964.

Palmer, Richard E. *Hermeneutics.* Evanston, Ill.: Northwestern University Press, 1969.

Peters, John L. *Christian Perfection and American Methodism.* Nashville: Abingdon Press, 1964.

Peterson, David. *Possessed by God—A New Testament Theology of Sanctification and Holiness.* Grand Rapids, Mich.: Eerdmans, 1995.

Pettit, Norman. *The Heart Prepared: Grace and Conversion in Puritan Spiritual Life.* New Haven, Conn.: Yale University Press, 1966.

Pinnock, Clark. *The Scripture Principle.* New York: Harper & Row, 1984.

Reeves. Thomas C. *The Empty Church.* New York: Free Press, 1996.

Roberts, Arthur. "Concepts of Perfection." B.D. diss., Nazarene Theological Seminary, 1951.

Rogers, J.B., and D.K. McKim. *The Authority and Interpretation of the Bible.* New York: Harper & Row, 1979.

von Rohr, John. *The Covenant of Grace in Puritan Thought.* Atlanta, Ga.: Scholars Press, 1986.

Rosenau, Pauline Marie. *Postmodernism in the Social Sciences.* Princeton, N.J.: Princeton University Press, 1992.

Ryrie, Charles C. *Dispensationalism Today.* Chicago: Moody Press, 1965.

Sandeen, Ernest E. *The Roots of Fundamentalism.* Chicago: Chicago University Press, 1970.

Saucy, Robert L. *The Case for Progressive Dispensationalism.* Grand Rapids, Mich.: Zondervan, 1993.

Smith, Christian. *American Evangelicalism—Embattled and Thriving.* Chicago: Chicago University Press, 1998.

Smith, Timothy L. *Revivalism and Social Reform.* Baltimore, Md.: Johns Hopkins University Press, 1980.

Stoever, William K.B. *'A Faire and Easie Way to Heaven.'* Indianapolis: Wesleyan Publishing House, 1978.

Sowell, Thomas. *A Conflict of Visions.* New York: William Morrow, 1987.

Swinburne, Richard. *Revelation.* Oxford: Clarendon Press, 1992.

Synan, Vinson. *The Holiness-Pentecostal Movement in the United States.* Grand Rapids, Mich.: Eerdmans, 1971.

Terrell, John Timothy. "The Movement from Sect to Denomination in Nineteenth-Century Gurneyite Quakerism." Master's thesis, Earlham School of Religion, 1985.

TeSelle, Eugene. *Augustine the Theologian.* London: Burns and Oates, 1970.

Toon, Peter, ed.. *Puritans, the Millennium and the Future of Israel*. Cambridge: James Clarke, 1970.

Torrance, T.F. *Reality and Evangelical Theology*. Philadelphia: Westminster Press, 1982.

Tuke, Henry. *The Principles of Religion*. London: Phillips & Fardon, 1801.

Webber, Robert E. *Ancient-Future Faith*. Ada, Mich.: Baker Book House, 1999.

Wesley, John. *Works*. Edited by A.C. Outler. Nashville: Abingdon Press, 1984.

White, R.E.O. *Christian Ethics*. Louisville, Ky.: John Knox Press, 1981.

Williamson, G.H., ed. *Foxe's Book of Martyrs*. Pomfret, Vt.: Little, Brown & Co., 1965.

Woodbridge, J.D. *Biblical Authority—A Critique of the Rogers/McKim Proposal*. Grand Rapids, Mich.: Zondervan, 1982.

Wynkoop, Mildred Bangs. *Foundations of Wesleyan-Arminian Theology*. Kansas City, Mo.: Beacon Hill Press, 1967.

Youngblood, Ronald, ed. *Evangelicals and Inerrancy*. Nashville: Thomas Nelson, 1984.

Index